Core Principles of Accounting

Mr Brian Ngiba (General Editor)
Dr Anrusha Bhana
Mr Makofe Lepheana CA(SA)
Ms Lonah Mbhalati CA(SA)
Prof Tankiso Moloi
Mr Kabelo Morake
Mr Nhlanhla Ngcobo
Ms Thembi Rafube

juta

Core Principles of Accounting

First published 2021

Juta and Company (Pty) Ltd
First floor, Sunclare building, 21 Dreyer street, Claremont 7708
PO Box 14373, Lansdowne 7779, Cape Town, South Africa
www.juta.co.za

ISBN: 978 148513 159 5 (Print)
ISBN: 978 148513 160 1 (Web Pdf)

Project specialist: Samantha Simmons
Editor: Lee-Anne Ashcroft
Proofreader: Language Mechanics
Cover designer: Drag and Drop
Typesetter: Wouter Reinders

Typeset in 10 on 13 pt Cambria

Acknowledgements
The authors would like to thank all who have contributed to the development of this publication. Families who sacrificed time away from their loved ones, colleagues and mentors who provided helpful insights. A special thanks to:
- Faith Ngwenya, Technical Executive: South African Institute of Professional Accountants Johannesburg
- Prof Olu Olugbara, Executive Dean: Faculty of Accounting and Informatics, Durban University of Technology

CONTENTS

PREFACE.. vii

ABOUT THE AUTHORS.. ix

CHAPTER 1 BRIEF HISTORY OF ACCOUNTING, RAPID TECHNOLOGICAL ADVANCES AND A BRIEF OUTLINE OF PROFESSIONAL ACCOUNTING BODIES IN SOUTH AFRICA............................ 1
1.1 EARLY TRADE AND ACCOUNTING: A BRIEF OVERVIEW.. 1
1.2 DOUBLE ENTRY BOOKKEEPING... 3
1.3 MORDERN ACCOUNTING AND REPORTING 4
1.4 THE FUTURE OF ACCOUNTING AND REPORTING 6
1.5 PROFESSIONAL ACCOUNTING ORGANISATIONS IN SOUTH AFRICA...................... 8
1.6 SUMMARY... 8

CHAPTER 2 THE REVISED CONCEPTUAL FRAMEWORK AND THE PRESENTATION OF FINANCIAL STATEMENTS.. 11
2.1 INTRODUCTION.. 11
2.2 SCOPE AND REVISION OF THE FRAMEWORK 12
2.3 OBJECTIVES OF FINANCIAL REPORTING.. 12
2.4 FUNDAMENTAL AND ENHANCING QUALITATIVE CHARACTERISTICS OF USEFUL FINANCIAL INFORMATION... 12
2.5 FINANCIAL STATEMENTS AND THE REPORTING ENTITY....................................... 13
2.6 ELEMENTS OF FINANCIAL STATEMENTS.. 13
2.7 RECOGNITION AND DERECOGNITION CRITERIA 14
2.8 MEASUREMENTS.. 15
2.9 OBJECTIVES AND SCOPE OF IAS 1 (PRESENTATION OF FINANCIAL STATEMENTS) 15
2.10 PRESENTATION AND DISCLOSURE 18
2.11 ANNUAL FINANCIAL STATEMENT PRESENTATION FORMATS............................... 18
2.12 SUMMARY... 25

CHAPTER 3 INVENTORIES (IAS 2) 32
3.1 INTRODUCTION.. 32
3.2 DEFINITION OF INVENTORY (as per IAS 2, par 6) 32
3.3 INVENTORY MOVEMENT.. 34
3.4 COST FORMULAS FOR THE TRANSFER OF INVENTORY 37
3.5 DISCOUNTS 37
3.6 COST OF INVENTORY 39
3.7 COST OF A MANUFACTURED PRODUCT (cost per unit) 41
3.8 VALUATION OF INVENTORY AT YEAR END 46
3.9 SUMMARY.. 50

CHAPTER 4 FINANCIAL INSTRUMENTS: SHARE CAPITAL... 56
4.1 INTRODUCTION.. 56
4.2 DEFINITIONS (IAS 32, par 11).. 57
4.3 DIFFERENT TYPES OF SHARES 58
4.4 DISTRIBUTIONS TO EQUITY HOLDERS.. 59
4.5 CHANGES TO SHARE CAPITAL 60
4.6 SUMMARY.. 68

CHAPTER 5 REVENUE FROM CONTRACTS WITH CUSTOMERS (IFRS 15) 74
5.1 INTRODUCTION.. 74
5.2 OBJECTIVE OF IFRS 15.. 74
5.3 APPLICATION OF THE STANDARD 74
5.4 DEFINITIONS.. 75
5.5 FIVE STEPS FOR REVENUE RECOGNITION 75
5.6 CONTRACT COSTS.. 87
5.7 AMORTISATION 87

5.8 IMPAIRMENT 88
5.9 PRESENTATION 88
5.10 SUMMARY 90

CHAPTER 6 PROVISIONS AND CONTINGENCIES (IAS 37) **93**
6.1 INTRODUCTION 93
6.2 DEFINITION AND RECOGNITION OF A PROVISION.. 93
6.3 DEFINITION AND RECOGNITION OF A CONTINGENT LIABILITY...................................... 93
6.4 DEFINITION AND RECOGNITION OF A CONTINGENT ASSET 94
6.5 ONEROUS CONTRACTS 95
6.6 SUMMARY 96

CHAPTER 7 INTANGIBLE ASSETS (IAS 38 and IFRS 3) **98**
7.1 INTRODUCTION 98
7.2 OBJECTIVE OF THE STANDARD 99
7.3 SCOPE 99
7.4 DEFINITIONS.. 99
7.5 DEFINITION OF INTANGIBLE ASSET 100
7.6 RECOGNITION AND INITIAL MEASUREMENT OF AN INTANGIBLE ASSET 100
7.7 COST OF AN INTERNALLY GENERATED INTANGIBLE ASSET 102
7.8 SUBSEQUENT MEASUREMENT 106
7.9 USEFUL LIFE, AMORTISATION AND IMPAIRMENT.. 109
7.10 INTANGIBLE ASSETS WITH INDEFINITE USEFUL LIVES 111
7.11 GOODWILL... 112
7.12 DISCLOSURE 113
7.13 SUMMARY 114

CHAPTER 8 STATEMENT OF CASH FLOWS (IAS 7) **119**
8.1 INTRODUCTION 119
8.2 PURPOSE 119
8.3 SECTIONS OF THE STATEMENT OF CASH FLOWS.. 120
8.4 CALCULATION OF CASH FLOWS 120
8.5 SUMMARY 127

CHAPTER 9 THE EFFECTS OF CHANGES IN FOREIGN EXCHANGE RATES (IAS 21) **136**
9.1 INTRODUCTION 136
9.2 DEFINITIONS.. 137
9.3 UPFRONT GUIDELINES FOR CONVERTING CURRENCIES 137
9.4 FOREIGN CURRENCY TRANSACTIONS 137
9.5 INITIAL MEASUREMENT 138
9.6 SUBSEQUENT MEASUREMENT 138
9.7 SALES TO FOREIGN ENTITIES.. 141
9.8 SUMMARY 142

CHAPTER 10 PROPERTY, PLANT AND EQUIPMENT (IAS 16) **144**
10.1 INTRODUCTION 144
10.2 DEFINITIONS.. 144
10.3 INITIAL MEASUREMENT.. 144
10.4 SUBSEQUENT MEASUREMENT 145
10.5 SUMMARY 148

CHAPTER 11 GOVERNMENT GRANTS (IAS 20)... **151**
11.1 INTRODUCTION 151
11.2 DEFINITIONS.. 151
11.3 EXCLUSIONS FROM DEFINITIONS 152
11.4 IMPORTANCE OF GOVERNMENT GRANTS TO USERS OF FINANCIAL STATEMENTS 152
11.5 RECOGNITION 152
11.6 DIFFERING SCHOOLS OF THOUGHT 154

11.7 ACCOUNTING FOR TRANSACTIONS THAT WILL NOT TOUCH PROFIT OR LOSS IN FUTURE 155
11.8 SUMMARY 157

CHAPTER 12 IMPAIRMENT OF ASSETS (IAS 36) **159**
12.1 INTRODUCTION 159
12.2 DEFINITIONS 159
12.3 OBJECTIVE OF IMPAIRMENT TESTING 160
12.4 IDENTIFYING IMPAIRMENT 160
12.5 MEASUREMENT OF THE RECOVERABLE AMOUNT 161
12.6 REVERSAL OF AN IMPAIRMENT LOSS PREVIOUSLY WRITTEN OFF 162
12.7 CASH GENERATING UNITS 164
12.8 COST MODEL AND REVALUATION MODEL 164
12.9 SUBSEQUENT REVALUATIONS OR DEVALUATIONS 167
12.10 REALISATION OF REVALUATION RESERVE 168
12.11 SUMMARY 174

CHAPTER 13 ANALYSIS AND INTERPRETATION OF FINANCIAL STATEMENTS **177**
13.1 INTRODUCTION 177
13.2 PROFITABILITY RATIOS 178
13.3 LIQUIDITY RATIOS 179
13.4 SOLVENCY RATIOS 181
13.5 LIMITATIONS OF FINANCIAL STATEMENT ANALYSIS 181
13.6 SUMMARY 192

CHAPTER 14 INCOME TAXES (IAS 12) **195**
14.1 INTRODUCTION 195
14.2 DEFINITIONS 195
14.3 EXPLANATION OF DEFINITIONS 196
14.4 CURRENT TAX 198
14.5 DEFERRED TAX 200
14.6 TAX EXPENSE 201
14.7 PRESENTATION AND DISCLOSURE 201
14.8 SUMMARY 204

CHAPTER 15 EVENTS AFTER REPORTING PERIOD (IAS 10) **208**
15.1 INTRODUCTION 209
15.2 DEFINITIONS 209
15.3 RECOGNITION AND MEASUREMENT 209
15.4 RECOGNITION AND MEASUREMENT 210
15.5 EXCEPTION 210
15.6 SUMMARY 210

PREFACE

This book, written by eight prolific authors who have cumulative industry and university teaching experience spanning several decades, is about the 'core principles of accounting' that form the foundation on which complicated and legalistic accounting rules and concepts solidly stand.

The book features 15 comprehensive chapters: Chapter 1 documents the barter system of trade and reflects on the system of account in African communities. Chapter 2 introduces important changes in the revised framework of financial statements. Chapter 3 discusses the principles of conversion costs, allocation of fixed costs and valuation of inventory at year end. Chapter 4 provides a simplified explanation of financial instruments and share capital. Chapter 5 is concerned with International Financial Reporting Standard (IFRS) 15. Chapter 6 delineates important definitions, recognition criteria and disclosure of provisions, contingent liabilities and contingent assets. Chapter 7 deals with International Accounting Standard (IAS) 38 on intangible assets. Chapter 8 discusses the use of the statement of cash flows. Chapter 9 expounds the definitions of relevant terms in accounting for foreign transactions. Chapter 10 gives with exemplars the definitions of property, plant and equipment in accordance with IAS 16. Chapter 11 explains accounting treatment of government grants and how accounting policy makes a difference. Chapter 12 deals with IAS 36, a standard governing measurement and disclosure of impairment of assets. Chapter 13 describes the process of critical evaluation of financial information contained in financial statements. Chapter 14 enunciates the concepts of transactions and accounting treatment of taxes according to IAS 12. Chapter 15 explicates the underlying principles of IAS 10, the standard on events after reporting period.

This book provides a valuable window on core principles of accounting with many practical examples. It also gives a timely glimpse into the future of accounting. It exposes a glaring oversight of accounting that has plagued the industry and business world for decades.

Effective communication of accounting principles and the demonstration of their practical application to students are simultaneously challenging and stimulating. Students should learn the principles with great enthusiasm, tenacity and dedication in order to apply their acquired knowledge and skills. In the burgeoning context of global hyperconnectivity, interdependence, knowledge economy and the fourth industrial revolution, it is essential to provide accounting practitioners, both professionals and students, with the tools to survive and thrive on the ever-widening frontiers of the accounting discipline. This book is a good step in that direction. It is equally a direct response to a clarion call by South African students to decolonise the curriculum.

Professor Olu Olugbara
Executive Dean, Faculty of Accounting and Informatics
Durban University of Technology

ABOUT THE AUTHORS

Brian Ngiba (professional accountant (SA))
Brian is currently enrolled for a PhD in public sector accounting with the University of South Africa (UNISA). With 20 years' academic experience in higher education, he is a lecturer and former acting head of the Department of Financial Accounting at the Durban University of Technology (DUT). He is also a former financial accounting subject leader of the Southern African Accounting Association (SAAA) and has served as a board member for a number of companies. His academic qualifications include an MBA (UKZN), a BTech (Taxation) (DUT), an ND (Accounting) (DUT), a diploma in project management (BSU) and an MDP (B-BBEE) (WITS).

Dr Anrusha Bhana (PhD, SAIPA)
Anrusha is currently a lecturer and acting head of the Department of Financial Accounting at DUT. She has 19 years' academic experience. Her academic qualifications include a PhD (Management Sciences) (DUT), an MBA (UKZN), a BTech (Financial Information Systems) and an ND (Financial Information Systems) (DUT).

Makofe M Lepheana (CA(SA))
Makofe is a senior lecturer at the University of Limpopo, specialising in taxation. He has previously trained with one of the Big 4 audit firms, in external auditing. He is a qualified Chartered Accountant and has recently completed his Master's Degree in Taxation.

Lonah Mbhalati (CA(SA))
Lonah is a senior lecturer of accounting at the University of Johannesburg with experience in both industry and academia. She is currently completing her MCompt at the University of South Africa. She is also a board member at the Young African Entrepreneurs Institute (YAEI) and a member of the Endunamoo School of Accounting CTA & ITC Professional team.

Prof Tankiso Moloi (PhD, FCMA, CGMA)
Tankiso is currently a professor of accounting and ETDP SETA and UJ research chair in 4IR skills in the School of Accounting at the University of Johannesburg. He is a board and governance leader and finance executive with 16 years' experience in leading strategic business units in the higher education, mining and national statistical services sectors. His academic qualifications include a PhD (Finance), an MCom (Accounting), an MSc (Financial Management), an MA (International Relations), a BCom Hons (Accounting) and a BCom. He is a fellow of the Chartered Institute of Management Accountants (CIMA, AICPA). He has completed the Executive Program in Artificial Intelligence and the Executive Program in Block Chain Technologies at MIT.

Kabelo M Morake
Kabelo is a lecturer in the Department of Commercial Accounting at the University of Johannesburg. He has extensive financial accounting and financial management experience after spending more than a decade in the corporate world. He holds a Master's degree in international accounting and is pursuing his studies with a PhD (Financial Management).

Raphael Nhlanhla Ngcobo (MCom (Accounting))
Raphael is currently a senior lecturer in the Department of Financial Accounting at UNISA. He has co-authored three textbooks that are prescribed in a number of universities in South Africa. His qualifications include an MCom (Accounting) (UP), a BCom Hons (Accounting) and a BCom (Accounting and Auditing) (UNISA).

Thembekile Rafube (MAcc)

Thembekile has 22 years' experience in higher education and is currently a lecturer of accounting technology in the Department of Accountancy at the Vaal University of Technology. Her academic qualifications include a Master's in accountancy, which she obtained through a two-year Mandela Australian scholarship at Curtin University of Technology, Perth (Western Australia), as well as a B Tech and an ND in cost and management accounting (VUT).

Michael Colin Greenham (CA(SA))

The late Michael Colin Greenham qualified as a chartered accountant in 1974. He worked for Deloitte and later as a director at Mica Hardware for 20 years, where he took the franchise from South Africa into the UK. Proudly South African, he returned to share his knowledge of practice and industry as a senior lecturer at the Durban University of Technology. Michael contributed passionately to the high standards of the financial accounting programmes until he was laid to rest in 2019.

CHAPTER 1

BRIEF HISTORY OF ACCOUNTING, RAPID TECHNOLOGICAL ADVANCES AND A BRIEF OUTLINE OF PROFESSIONAL ACCOUNTING BODIES IN SOUTH AFRICA

LEARNING OUTCOMES

After studying this chapter, you should be able to:
- Understand the history of bookkeeping and accounting.
- Understand current practices in accounting and reporting in general.
- Understand the future of accounting.
- Understand accounting bodies in South Africa.

PREAMBLE

The word 'accounting' appears to have been derived from the verb 'account'. Different forms of companies will use the system of accounting in order to account for their activities during a certain time frame, known as the financial year. In its basic form, accounting could be seen as a system that gives effect to the recording of transactions; classification and summarisation of information; and eventually, the publication and dissemination of this information in a form of an integrated report (in some countries, financial statements or annual reports), which is later used by economic agents to make certai n decisions about the organisation.

Historical records show that the system of accounting began years ago, with clay tokens being used as a measure to keep track of goods and animals (Kinding, 2019). This simple form of accounting has since evolved into a complex system that stores and organises a wealth of information. Rather than being performed manually, accounting is now executed by computer software, making the work of a professional accountant far easier when it comes to coping with the magnitude of transactions.

As an agent in the bigger scheme of accounting, Mr Mhlongo (known as Njomane) would do well to understand why accounting for transactions is important. This includes:
- understanding why he has to adopt a system of accounting
- knowing why transactions that have taken place in the business would have to be structured, analysed and reported
- knowing why there is a need for financial statements and accompanying information
- knowing why economic agents place such great importance on historical data.

1.1 EARLY TRADE AND ACCOUNTING: A BRIEF OVERVIEW

Bartering (or the barter system) typically includes the exchange of goods for other goods. My grandmother would tell stories of her upbringing in the small town of Nquthu in KwaZulu-Natal. We would be sitting outside in a ring, encircling her, as she explained how their household grew maize and vegetables in the fields. At the same time, their neighbours nurtured and grew livestock, particularly chickens.

In order to feed their chickens as well as fulfil their own need for carbohydrates (usually in the form of pap), these neighbours required maize. At the same time, to balance their meal with protein, my grandmother's family required eggs and meat. Therefore, in order for each family to satisfy their needs, they had to trade with each other. (In this kind of a setting, it is not clear how settlement and values were determined and how this would have been recorded. In today's system of accounting, which relies on recorded transactions, this would pose a challenge.)

Goods would also be exchanged for services. As a boy, my grandfather became a shepherd, working for a rich owner of goats, sheep and cattle. He was employed to herd the animals for a particular period, typically a year. At the end of each year, he was compensated with some form of livestock.

Across the globe, Kinding (2019) reports that trade and agriculture have always been the anchor of the economy, even during medieval times. To explain the unit of account, Kinding (2019) uses the example of the Mesopotamians, who used different clay tokens as a representation of different goods (as mentioned above). Clay tokens were either added or subtracted when the good was traded or consumed. This kept the accounting system simple, as it was not necessary to recalculate the livestock or their harvest each time there was trade or consumption. In essence, clay tokens accounted for value.

The assumption is that Mesopotamians would have used different shapes of clay tokens, which may well have looked as shown in Figure 1.1.

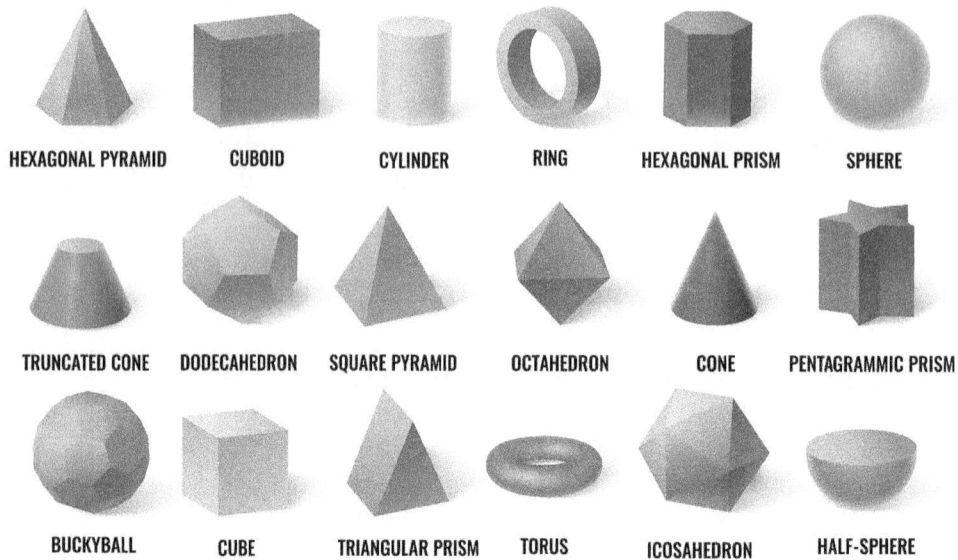

Figure 1.1: Imagining different shapes that might have been used by Mesopotamians in their clay tokens
Source: YouTube pictures

Dontigney (2017) posits that Greeks, Romans and Egyptians enhanced the token system. Instead of using differently shaped clay tokens as a representation of different goods, they began to draw symbols (eg sheep, goats, cattle, chickens, fish, camels, horses, donkeys and agricultural products) onto the clay tokens. A clay token with a cattle drawing would probably have been more valuable than one with a chicken.

Figure 1.2: Imagining different drawings that might have been used by Phoenicians on their tokens
Source: https://i.ebayimg.com/images/g/MzQAAOSwI8laPF9Q/s-l300.jpg

The way in which Mesopotamian, Greek, Roman and Egyptian agents would add or subtract clay tokens during transactions (Kinding, 2019; Dontigney, 2017) is considered the beginning of primitive accounting (Dontigney, 2017).

Furthermore, in the Far East, Kinding (2019) and Tien, Duyen, Nhung, Loan and Chinh (2014) indicate that around 3000 BC, the Chinese began to develop a tool, the abacus, that was helpful for counting and calculating. According to Zhou (2018), a Chinese abacus is 'a calculating and numerical recording tool that shop-keepers used to tally figures'.

Figure 1.3: An abacus
Source: http://3.bp.blogspot.com/-I-8D1q03fqA/T87Jo7qHBVI/AAAAAAAACHE/R666fURodig/s1600/Abacus.png

1.2 DOUBLE ENTRY BOOKKEEPING

In the middle ages, coinage (the use of coin) was adopted. Accounting changed from being concerned with goods (ie a system for recording transactions in order to monitor their stocks) to dealing with money-backed transactions (Kinding, 2019).

During the crusades (1094–1291), international trade boomed. European trade markets opened routes and linked up with Middle Eastern markets. Trade between the Europeans and the Middle Easterners, especially in Genoa and Venice, resulted in some European merchants becoming extremely wealthy (Tien et al, 2014).

However, even though money-backed transactions had been adopted, single entry bookkeeping was still the order of the day (Kinding, 2019). Single entry bookkeeping was concerned with three things:

1. Keeping track of money exchanged
2. The destination of the money (where the money went)
3. The players in the transaction (who owed what).

As international trade increased, the single entry bookkeeping system struggled to keep up with the ever-increasing volume of transactions. A new system was needed.

In 1493 AD, a book titled *Summa de Arithmetica, Geometria, Proportioni, et Proportionalita* [Summary of arithmetic, geometry, proportions, and proportionality] by Luca Pacioli was published. This mathematical treatise (known as the 'Venetian model') provided a description of double entry bookkeeping as we understand it today. The double entry bookkeeping system allowed more detailed information and recorded each transaction twice – once as credit and once as debit (Baskett, 2011; Tien et al, 2014; Kinding, 2019).

According to Boxwell (2018/19), Pacioli's system accounted for much broader activities such as assets, liabilities, income and expenses. It introduced the terms 'debito' (leftness) and 'credito' (rightness) (Baskett, 2011). However, Pacioli did not provide a realistic interpretation of debit and credit as they were used in Venice at the time (Baskett, 2011).

Table 1.1: Leftness and rightness

Item	Debito (leftness)	Credito (rightness)
Assets	X	
Liabilities		X
Expenses	X	
Income		X

Source: Author's illustration

Pacioli's system of double entry bookkeeping was based on the premise that if anything of value had been taken by a merchant or a banker, something had to be given back in its place. It is the reason why still today we use offsetting entries to balance values (ie a debit is matched with a credit and an asset is matched with a liability) (Casey & Vigna, 2018).

Summa de Arithmetica, Geometria, Proportioni, et Proportionalita is an essential document in accounting history (Boxwell, 2018/19). It introduced a better way to keep track of large amounts of money and complex transactions, providing a description of how journals and ledgers were to be used. Furthermore, it warned that 'merchants were not to rest until debits were equal to credits' (Boxwell, 2018/19).

While Pacioli has been given the credit for it, his may not necessarily have been the first treatise to propose the double entry bookkeeping. There is evidence to support that it had already been evolving in other Italian cities. According to Campbell (2017), it may have been Benedetto Cotrugli who invented the double entry bookkeeping system in his treatise entitled '*Of Trading and the Perfect Trader*', although Pacioli must still be given credit for codifying and writing a book on the accounting process.

1.3 MORDERN ACCOUNTING AND REPORTING

Accounting has evolved over time. Technology, globalisation, the rise of non-state actors demanding accountability, the emergence of the concept of stakeholders, legislation, financial crises and corporate failure, among others, have all had a role to play.

With this evolution, the manner in which reporting is done has changed significantly. The rise of sustainability reporting, integrated reporting, the Codes of Good Governance alongside the related legislation, International Accounting Standards and International Financial Reporting Standards have enhanced the content and format of accounting and corporate reports.

Historically, the focus of reporting was on financial information. Over the years, this has expanded to include a significant amount of non-financial (environmental, social and governance (ESG)) information to form what is known as the integrated report. In countries that have not adopted integrated reporting, these fall under annual or sustainability reports.

Figures 1.4 to 1.6 illustrate the changes in Old Mutual's reporting from 1999 to 2018. One can see how the length of the reports as well as the number of items have risen drastically. It is reasonable to expect that the manner in which the information is mined, packaged and disseminated to interest groups will also shift as technology advances.

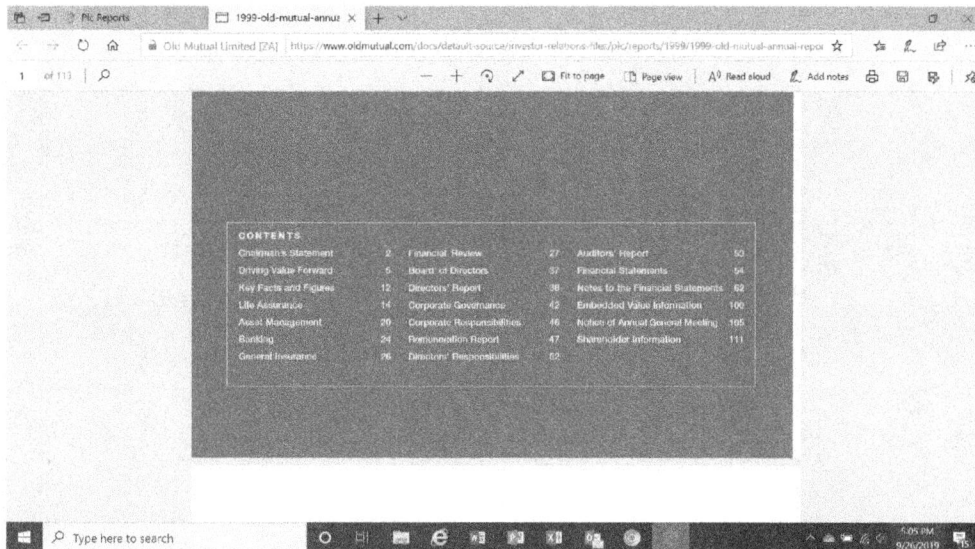

Figure 1.4: Old Mutual's 1999 annual report

Source: Old Mutual (1999)

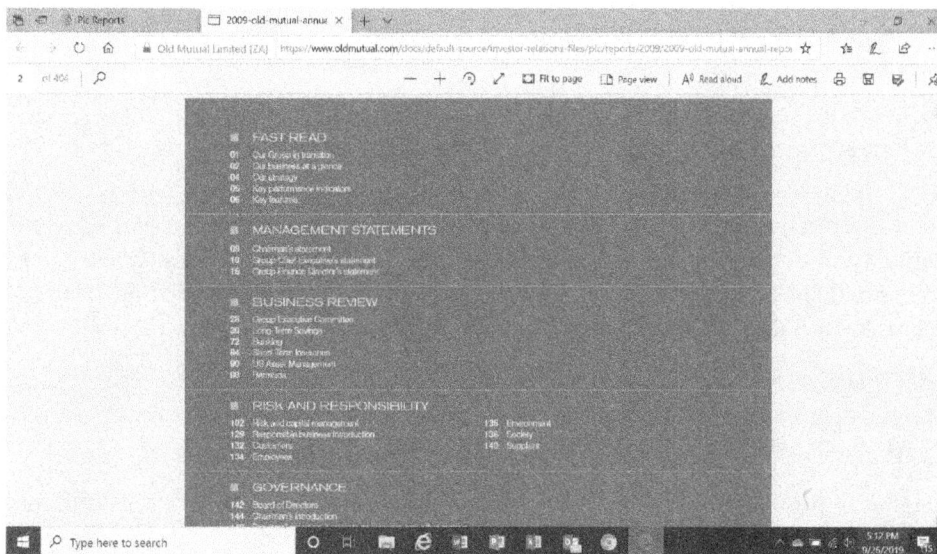

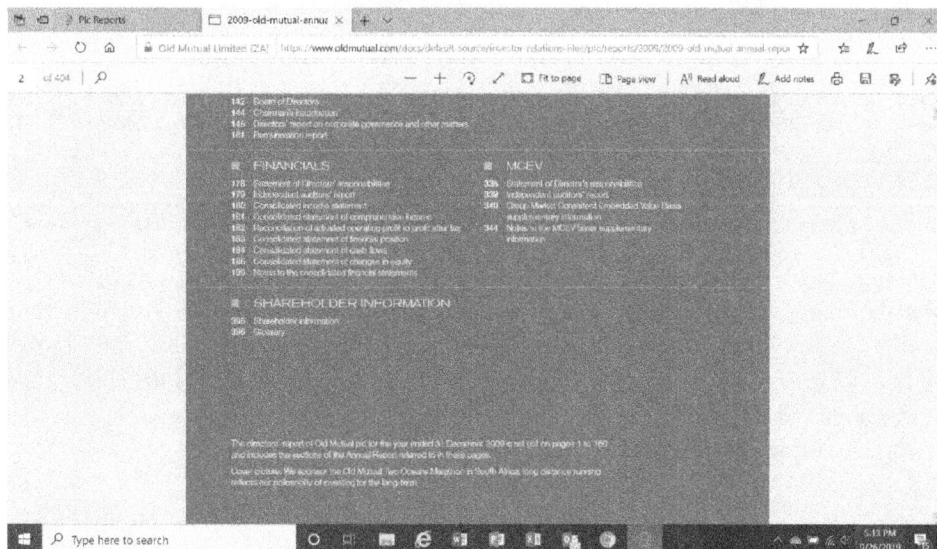

Figure 1.5: Old Mutual's 2009 annual report

Source: Old Mutual (2009)

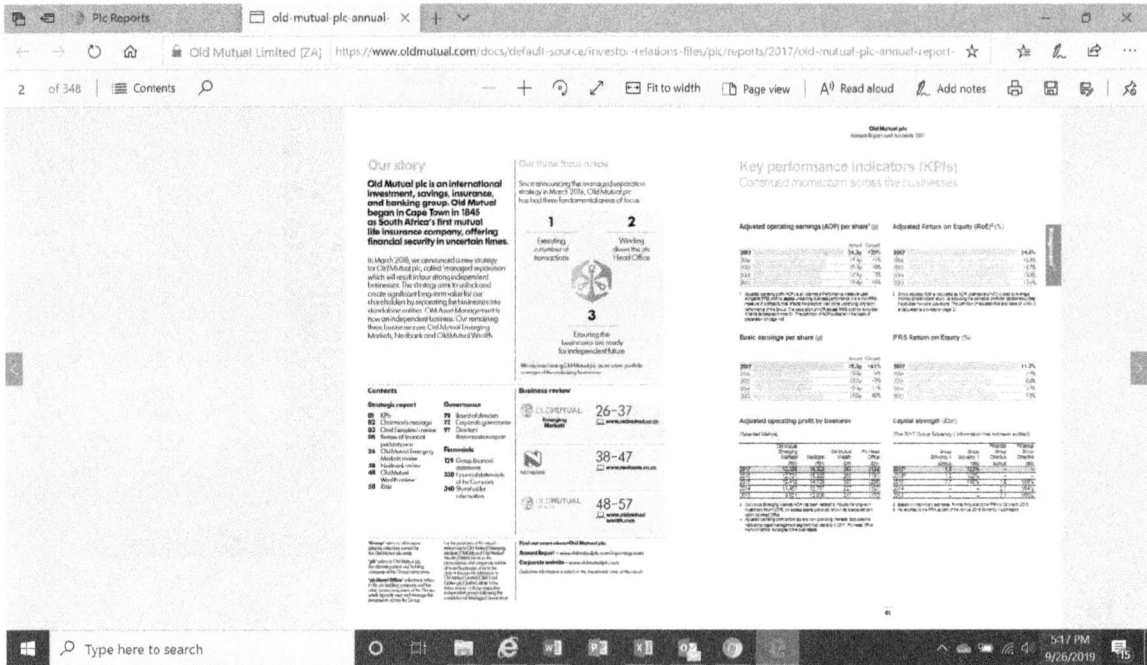

Figure1.6: Old Mutual's 2018 annual report (latest available)

Source: Old Mutual (2018)

1.4 THE FUTURE OF ACCOUNTING AND REPORTING

With the advent of the double entry accounting system came the need for a third party to verify (audit) books in order to ensure that what was being reported represented the true state of affairs. A lot of power shifted to accountants, auditors and bankers. According to Casey and Vigna (2018), audited/clean books came to be regarded as a sign of fairness and honesty. Bankers became an engine for financial intermediation (Moloi, 2014). Further, they became crucial for speeding up the circulation of money (Casey & Vigna, 2018).

However, even with these checks and balances in place (ie the verification of books to ensure that what was being reported represented the true state of affairs), failures such as those that happened at Enron in the US and recently Venda Mutual Bank (VBS) and Steinhoff in South Africa are still being reported.

Casey and Vigna (2018) place the blame on society for not properly holding financial institutions such as banks and stock exchanges accountable. Financial institutions have been made indispensable by society. This has allowed them to become gatekeepers, essentially deciding who plays a role in the economy and the extent of that role. They restrict access to finances, charge exhobitant fees and curtail innovation through their monopolistic behaviour.

The world is changing rapidly. Technology is advancing at an incredible rate. Human life, economics and politics have all been affected by the constant new developments in information technology (Moloi & Marwala, 2020). Casey and Vigna (2018) have pinned their hope on the emergence of new technologies as part of the solution to the misbehaviours of the financial sector. Blockchain technology, for example, holds a promise of rebooting the relationship between financial institutions and society, and the manner in which reporting is done.

Blockchain technology has a decentralised approach to accounting. It is not managed by one institution (ie a government agency or the bank) (Casey & Vigna, 2018), but rather transactions are 'stored in multiple copies on multiple independent computers within a decentralized network'. No single entity has sole control of the ledger. Any of the computers on the network may effect changes, however these must follow the rules that are dictated by a 'consensus protocol'. Essentially, a concensus protocol is an algorithm which tracks whether the majority of the users in the network agree before any changes are made.

CORE PRINCIPLES OF ACCOUNTING

According to Catalini (2017), the key principles underlying the blockchain technology are as follows:

- **Distributed database:** Parties in the blockchain have access to the entire database and its history. Each party can verify the transactions of the transacting partner without the central authority or the intermediary.
- **Peer to peer transmission:** Because there is no central node in the blockchain technology, communication occurs between users (peers). As the node stores each information item, it will also forward it to others.
- **Transparency with pseudonymity:** Every member of the network has visibility to transactions. In order to ensure that users/nodes belong to the network, each has a unique character, an alphanumerical address which is its identifier. Users can decide to remain anonymous or provide proof of identity to others.
- **Irreversibility of records:** The chain means that every transactional record is linked to the records that came before it. Records cannot be altered. A variety of algorithms and approaches are deployed to ensure that the information that is on the database is permanent. In addition to this, these algorithms and approaches ensure that the information on the databases is available to all other members in the network. This ensures that no one can secretly alter records.
- **Computational logic:** The digital nature of the ledger means that blockchain transactions can be tied into computational logic (and the program). This gives access to algorithms and rules that automatically trigger transactions between nodes.

The steam engine epitomised the first industrial revolution; electrification epitomised the second industrial revolution, making mass production possible; the third industrial revolution was characterised by the advent of mainframe computing. We have now entered the fourth industrial revolution (4IR): technological advancements are fusing physical, digital and biological spheres. Disruptive technologies (innovations which significantly alter the way that consumers/businesses/industries operate) such as the Internet of Things (IoT); robotics and robotic process automation (RPA); augmented reality (AR) and virtual reality (VR); and artificial intelligence (AI) are changing the nature of the world as we have known it (Moloi & Marwala, 2020; Harari, 2018; Agrawal, Gans & Goldfarb, 2018). According to Moloi and Marwala (2020), the 4IR holds the promise of leveraging the cumulative effect of these technologies to improve lives, business efficiencies and productivity.

According to Marwala and Hurwitz (2017), the 4IR is characterised by AI. Simply speaking, AI is a branch of computer science concerned with making machines smart. The measure of AI is human intelligence, hence AI refers to the abililty of machines to mimic the actions of human beings.

As technology evolves, accounting and reporting will have to evolve with it. Professional accounting organisations (PAOs) are expected to play an important role in this because while technology, driven by AI, will transform the finance and accounting industries, it is unlikely to replace the need for expert knowledge and decision making (ICAEW, 2018). Robotic processes will slowly be deployed to eliminate some tedious and repetitive tasks, allowing financial staff to prioritise higher-impact responsibilities (Vordenbaeumen, 2019).

1.5 PROFESSIONAL ACCOUNTING ORGANISATIONS IN SOUTH AFRICA

South Africa has 12 PAOs. These are presented in Table 1.2.

Table 1.2: Professional accounting bodies in South Africa

Name	Acronym	Website
Association of Chartered Certified Accountants	ACCA South Africa	https://www.accaglobal.com/
Chartered Institute of Business Management	CIBM	https://www.chartsec.co.za/
Institute of Management Accountants—South Africa	CIMA-South Africa	https://www.cimaglobal.com/Our-locations/Africa/South-Africa/
Institute of Accounting and Commerce	IAC	https://www.iacsa.co.za/
South African Institute of Business Accountants	SAIBA	https://www.saiba.org.za/
South African Institute of Chartered Accountants	SAICA	https://www.saica.co.za/
Southern African Institute of Government Auditors	SAIGA	https://www.saiga.co.za/saiga/
South African Institute of Professional Accountants	SAIPA	https://www.saipa.co.za/
The Southern African Institute of Chartered Secretaries and Administrators	CSSA	https://www.chartsec.co.za/
Association of Accounting Technicians	AAT-South Africa	http://www.accountingtechniciansouthafrica.co.za/
Institute of Certified Bookkeepers	ICB	https://www.icb.org.za/
Institute of Internal Auditors	IIA-South Africa	https://www.iiasa.org.za/

Source: Author's illustration; information on PAOs extracted from IFAC

1.6 SUMMARY

This chapter began with a brief history of accounting and bookkeeping, discussing early trade and how it was accounted for, particularly in African communities where history is not well recorded. The chapter later introduced modern accounting and reporting. The fourth industrial revolution, and the general changing nature of the world, necessitates that the accounting profession position itself to remain relevant in an era that is characterised by technology. This chapter discussed the manner in which the accounting profession is to be impacted, given the rapid changes in technological developments. Finally, in order to prepare students for their potential future professional certifications, various professional accounting bodies were outlined.

EXERCISES

Exercise 1.1
1. By using an example, explain what the barter system is.
2. In your view, is the barter system a fair way of transacting? Discuss.

Exercise 1.2
1. How did transacting work during the Mesopotamian era?

2. How was the system used by Greeks, Romans and Egyptians different to that of the Mesopotamians?
4. Explain what an abacus is. What relatively recent invention replaced it?

Exercise 1.3
1. Evaluate the difference between single entry bookkeeping and double entry bookkeeping.
2. What was the main driver that led to a move to a double entry bookkeeping system?

Exercise 1.4
1. What are the main drivers of modern accounting?
2. Why are verification costs expected to decline with the adoption of blockchain technology?
3. Explain the term 'disruptive technologies'.
4. Define the term 'artificial intelligence'.
5. How do you think disruptive technologies will affect the accounting profession?

Exercise 1.5
Given the number of existing accounting bodies in South Africa, which one is best suitable for you? And why?

REFERENCES

Agrawal, A., Gans, J. & Goldfarb, A. 2018. *Prediction machines: The simple economics of artificial intelligence.* Boston, MA: Harvard Business Review Press.

Baskett, J.H. 2011. A revisionist history of accounting: from the origins of private property to Venice in the Pacioli era. *International Business and Economic Research Journal*, 1(12): 1–13.

Boxwell, A. 2018/19. *Accounting history.* Available at: https://www.businessaccountingbasics.co.uk/accounting-history/ (accessed on 20 June 2019).

Campbell, R. 2017. *History of bookkeeping.* Available at: https://ww.bizfluent.com/about-4740424-history-of-bookkeeping.html (accessed on 20 June 2019).

Casey, M.J. & Vigna, P. 2018. In blockchain we trust. *MIT Technology Review.* Available at: https://www.technologyreview.com/s/610781/in-blockchain-we-trust/ (accessed 26 September 2019).

Catalini, C. 2017. How blockchain application will move beyond finance. *Harvard Business Review.* Available at: https://www.services.hbsp.harvard.edu/api/courses/662598/items/H03HRT-PDF-ENG/sclinks/cf807bda be63dd4b0dec039fa31ddb6a (accessed 26 September 2019).

Dontigney, E. 2017. *What is primitive accounting?* Available at: https://www.bizfluent.com/info-12041628-primitive-accounting.html (accessed 20 September 2019).

Harari, Y.N. 2018. *21 Lessons for the 21st century.* London: Jonathan Cape.

ICAEW. 2018. *Artificial intelligence and the future of accountancy.* Available at: https://www.icaew.com/-/media/corporate/files/technical/information-technology/thought-leadership/artificial-intelligence-report.ashx (accessed 19 November 2020).

IFAC 2019. *Professional accountancy organisations.* Available at: https://www.ifac.org/about-ifac/membership/country/south-africa (accessed 10 October 2019).

Kinding, A. 2019. *Historical development of accounting.* Available at: https://www.bizfluent.com/about-4731157-historical-development-accounting.html (accessed on 10 August 2019).

Marwala, T. & Xing, B. 2018. Blockchain and artificial intelligence. Available at: https://arxiv.org/ftp/arxiv/papers/1802/1802.04451.pdf (accessed 19 November 2020).

Marwala, T. & Hurwitz, E. 2017. *Artificial intelligence and economic theory: Skynet in the market.* Heildelberg: Springer.

Moloi, T. & Marwala, T. 2020. *Artificial intelligence in economics and finance theories.* Heildelberg: Springer.

Moloi, T. 2009. Assessment of corporate governance reporting in the annual report of South African listed companies. Masters dissertation, University of South Africa.

Moloi, T. 2014. Leading external and internal indicators of credit risk in the top South African banks. Doctoral thesis, Universidad Central de Nicaragua.

Moloi, T. 2014. Leading internal and external sources of credit risk in the top South African banks. *Risk Governance and Control: Financial Markets & Institutions*, 4(3): 51–65.

Old Mutual. 1999. *Annual report – 1999.* Available at: https://www.annualreports.com/Company/old-mutual-plc (accessed 19 November 2020).

Old Mutual. 2009. *Annual report – 2009.* Available at: https://www.annualreports.com/Company/old-mutual-plc (accessed 19 November 2020).

Old Mutual. 2018. *Annual report – 2018*. Available at: https://www.annualreports.com/Company/old-mutual-plc (accessed 19 November 2020).

Tien, D., Thi Ha Duyen, C., Thi Thuy Nhung, P., Thi Phuong Loan, B. & Nhu Chinh, D. 2014. *What is the historical development of accounting?* Available at: https://www.slideshare.net/choig3/historical-and-development-of-accounting (accessed 10 August 2019).

Vordenbaeumen, H. 2019. Voices 3 ways accountants can implement AI today. *Accounting Today*. Available at: https://www.accountingtoday.com/opinion/3-ways-accountants-can-implement-ai-today (accessed 10 August 2019).

Zhou, R. 2018. The Chinese abacus. Available at: https://www.chinahighlights.com/travelguide/culture/the-chinese-abacus.htm (accessed 26 September 2019).

CHAPTER 2

THE REVISED CONCEPTUAL FRAMEWORK AND THE PRESENTATION OF FINANCIAL STATEMENTS

LEARNING OUTCOMES

After studying this chapter, you should be able to:

- Understand the background around the conceptual framework.
- Understand the need for the conceptual framework.
- Explain the objective of financial reporting.
- Understand and be in a position to explain the qualitative characteristics of useful financial information.
- Understand and be in a position to discuss financial statements and the reporting entity.
- Discuss the criteria for including assets and liabilities in financial statements (recognition); as well as understanding guidelines on when to remove assets and liabilities in financial statements (de-recognition).
- Discuss various measurement bases. Further, be in a position to discuss factors to be considered when selecting a measurement basis.
- Understand concepts on presentation and disclosure in the annual financial statements. Further, understand guidelines on including income and expenses in the statement of profit or loss and other comprehensive income.

PREAMBLE

As an agent in the bigger scheme of accounting, Mr Mhlongo (known as Njomane) would like to understand the revised conceptual framework and the guidelines governing the presentation of financial statements (IAS 1). It is particularly important for Njomane, as a business owner, to be familiar with the major changes from the previous conceptual framework, which include guidance on measurement, presentation and disclosure, the reporting entity as well as recognition and de-recognition criteria.

Since the definition of assets and liabilities, including the guidance on recognition as well as the clarification of concepts on measurement of uncertainty, prudence, stewardship and substance over form, have all been updated, Njomane has some studying to do to ensure he stays abreast of the developments in this space.

The international accounting standard-setting body, known as the International Accounting Standard Board (IASB), is an independent standard-setting body of the International Financial Reporting Standards (IFRS) Foundation. Recently, the IASB published the revised conceptual framework. According to the IASB, the conceptual framework sets out to describe the objectives as well as the concepts for the general purpose of financial reporting and has the following three purposes:

1. To assist the IASB in developing the IFRS standards that are based on the consistent concepts

2. To assist preparers in developing accounting policies for transactions or events to which no standard applies or when standards allow a choice of accounting policy

3. To help all other stakeholders to understand and interpret the standards.

2.1 INTRODUCTION

The original conceptual framework for financial reporting was published in 1989. Somewhere around 2004, the IASB together with the Financial Accounting Standard Board (FASB), which is a US standard-setting body, initiated a joint project to revise their individual conceptual frameworks (IFRS, 2018a; IFRS 2018b).

The project between the IASB and FASB led to the publication of the revised chapters on the objectives of financial reporting and the qualitative characteristics of useful information in 2010. However, this joint initiative was suspended due to each body needing to focus on other 'pressing' projects (IFRS, 2018a).

In view of the work that had been conducted, the IASB constituencies, during the public consultations that took place in 2011, requested the IASB to proceed and finalise the revision of the conceptual framework project (IFRS, 2018a). The IASB therefore reactivated the project in 2012, without the participation of the FASB.

The reactivation process yielded the first discussion paper in 2013. This discussion paper was made available to all the IASB constituencies in order for them to study the document in detail and offer their input. It did not cover all aspects intended to be part of the revised framework because chapters such as 'the objective and the qualitative characteristics of useful information', for example, had just been published in 2010. The intention was to ensure that the chapters which had been part of the joint project with FASB did not change, save for some minor adjustments (IFRS, 2018a).

In 2015, the exposure draft (ED) was issued by the IASB. It contained all envisaged chapters that would be part of the revised framework.

2.2 SCOPE AND REVISION OF THE FRAMEWORK

The old conceptual framework which had been issued in 1989 and partly revised in 2010 had to be revisited yet again. The IASB (2018b) indicated that even though the old framework was still useful, it was incomplete and required serious improvements. Gaps in measurement, presentation and disclosure had been identified by the IASB constituencies during the 2011 agenda consultation. There was a need for updating definitions (eg of assets and liabilities) as well as to clarify certain aspects such as the role of the measurement of uncertainties (IASB, 2018b).

A balance had to be found between brevity and simplicity in defining high-level concepts, and providing sufficient detail for the revised conceptual framework to be deemed useful to both the IASB as well as the constituencies. According to the IASB (2018b), the revised conceptual framework would achieve what it was intended to be – a practical tool that would be useful in the development of accounting standards as well as making judgements when the application of a concept did not lead to a unified (single) answer.

The revised conceptual framework is seen as 'a tool to assist the IASB in developing and revising IFRS standards that are based on the consistent concepts' (IASB, 2018a). It will apply directly to the development of accounting policies in terms of paragraph 11(b) of IAS 8, which deals with accounting policies, changes in accounting estimates and errors. Some sections of the revised conceptual framework will be used by the board (ie IASB) only (IASB, 2018a).

2.3 OBJECTIVES OF FINANCIAL REPORTING

The main objective of financial reporting is to provide information that users will find useful in the process of decision making in terms of the provision of resources to the entity. They would ordinarily rely on financial reports for their financial information requirements.

Users of financial reports include the following (IASB, 2018a):
- **Existing and potential investors:** These would need to make decisions around purchasing, selling or holding equity or debt instruments.
- **Lenders and other creditors:** These would need to make decisions around providing or settling loans and other forms of credit.
- **Shareholders:** These would need to make decisions around voting or otherwise influencing management actions.

In order to make their decisions, users will need to assess the prospect for future net cash inflows to the entity as well as management's stewardship of the entity's economic resources. This can only be done when there is reliable information on the entity's economic resources, claims against the entity, changes in those resources and claims, and the overall efficiency and effectiveness of management.

2.4 FUNDAMENTAL AND ENHANCING QUALITATIVE CHARACTERISTICS OF USEFUL FINANCIAL INFORMATION

Section 2.3 dealt with the objectives of financial reporting, namely the provision of information that users will find to be useful in the process of decision making. For information to pass the usefulness test, it must have two characteristics: **relevance** and **faithful representation** of the underlying transaction or event (IASB, 2018b). Both relevance and faithful representation are guiding concepts that apply throughout the revised conceptual framework (IASB, 2018a):
- **When does financial information become relevant?** First, it must be capable of affecting the decision being taken, ie it must give insight into the entity's affairs. Second, it must have a predictive or confirmatory value.

- **When is financial information seen as faithfully representing the underlying transaction?** First, it must, to the maximum extent possible, be complete, neutral and free from errors. Neutrality is supported by the exercise of prudence, which is defined as the exercise of caution when making judgements in an environment that is uncertain. If caution is exercised, it will prevent the overstatement or understatement of the entity's economic resources, claims against the entity, expenses or income. Second, it must faithfully represent the substance of what it purports to represent. Financial information is by nature affected by a certain level of measurement uncertainty. However, this does not prevent it from being useful. In some cases, the most relevant information has high levels of measurement uncertainty, resulting in the most useful information being that which is slightly less relevant, but subject to lower measurement uncertainty.

There are four additional enhancing qualitative characteristics of financial information, namely **comparability**, **verifiability**, **timeliness** and **understandability**.

Cost remains a pervasive constraint on financial information that can be provided (IASB, 2018b). In this regard, a cost–benefit analysis can be a useful decision-making tool (IASB, 2018a) to ensure that the benefit of providing the financial information justifies the cost of providing it.

2.5 FINANCIAL STATEMENTS AND THE REPORTING ENTITY

The revised framework has brought with it a new chapter which deals with the financial statements and the reporting entity. The IASB (2018b: 5) defines the reporting entity as the entity 'that is required, or chooses, to prepare financial statements'. It states that:
- a reporting entity need not necessarily be a legal entity; and
- it can consist of a portion of an entity or more than one entity.

The boundary of a reporting entity, ie what needs to be included in its financial statements, is determined by the scope of its control. According to IASB (2018b, p5), 'when a reporting entity is not a legal entity or is not comprised of only legal entities connected by a parent–subsidiary relationship, the boundary is determined by information needs of the financial statements primary users'. According to the revised conceptual framework:
- the boundary of a reporting entity does not include arbitrary or incomplete information;
- the set of economic activities within the boundary of a reporting entity includes neutral information; and
- an explanation is provided as to how the boundary was determined and what constitutes the reporting entity (IASB, 2018b).

The concepts of consolidated and unconsolidated financial statements are also outlined in the new conceptual framework. The determining factor for preparing consolidated or non-consolidated financial information is control, ie whether one entity has control over the other entity (parent–subsidiary relationship). Should it happen that an entity consists of more than one entity, but these entities are not linked through a parent–subsidiary relationship, then its financial statements are combined financial statements. As the IFRS standards focus mainly on the consolidated financial statements, the revised conceptual framework requires more guidance as to how or when entities could prepare combined financial statements (IASB, 2018).

Financial information therefore could be presented in the form of a **consolidated financial statement**, **unconsolidated financial statements** or **combined financial statements**. The IASB (2018a) provides the following descriptions:
- **Consolidated financial statements** provide information about assets, equity, liabilities, income and expenses of both the parent and its subsidiary (or subsidiaries) as a single reporting entity.
- **Unconsolidated financial statements** provide information about assets, equity, liabilities, income and expenses of the parent only.
- **Combined financial statements** provide information about assets, equity, liabilities, income and expenses of two or more entities that are not all linked by a parent–subsidiary relationship.

2.6 ELEMENTS OF FINANCIAL STATEMENTS

There are five elements of financial statements: assets, liabilities, equity, income and expenses. As stated above, the revised conceptual framework has introduced changes to the definitions of assets and liabilities.

A comparison between previous definitions and the revised definitions is provided in Figure 2.1.

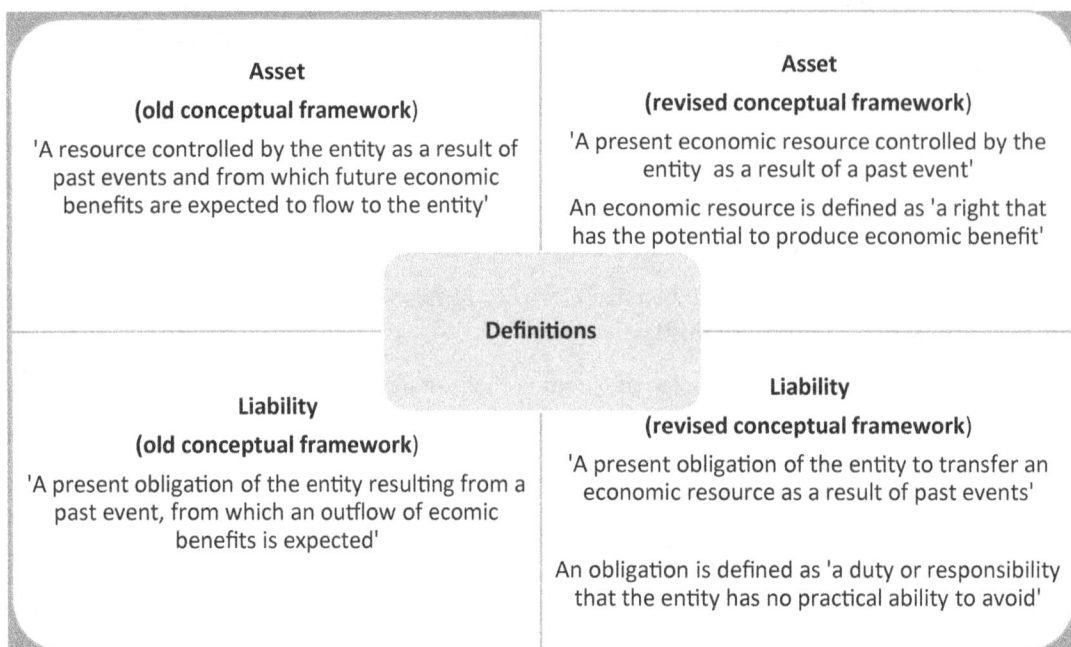

Asset (old conceptual framework)	Asset (revised conceptual framework)
'A resource controlled by the entity as a result of past events and from which future economic benefits are expected to flow to the entity'	'A present economic resource controlled by the entity as a result of a past event' An economic resource is defined as 'a right that has the potential to produce economic benefit'
Definitions	
Liability (old conceptual framework)	Liability (revised conceptual framework)
'A present obligation of the entity resulting from a past event, from which an outflow of ecomic benefits is expected'	'A present obligation of the entity to transfer an economic resource as a result of past events' An obligation is defined as 'a duty or responsibility that the entity has no practical ability to avoid'

Figure 2.1: Previous and the revised definitions
Source: IASB (2018b)

The main changes in the definition of an asset are (1) that it is now viewed as an economic resource and not the ultimate inflow of economic benefits, and (2) the term 'expected inflow' has been excluded, implying that there is no need for certainty or even likelihood that economic benefits will arise. The IASB (2018a) notes that a low probability of economic benefits might affect the recognition decisions, including the measurement of an asset.

The new definition of a liability clarifies that it is an entity's obligation to transfer an economic resource. Reference is no longer made to economic outflow, once again implying that there is no need for certainty or even a likelihood for an entity to transfer an economic resource.

According to the IASB (2018a: 8), 'if a duty or responsibility arises from the entity's customary practices, published policies or specific statements, the entity has an obligation if it has no practical ability to act in a manner consistent with those practices, policies or statement'. Further, 'if a duty or responsibility is conditional on a particular future action that the entity itself may take, then the entity has an obligation if it has no practical ability to avoid taking that action'.

The IASB (2018a: 6) defines equity as the 'residual after deducting an entity's liabilities from its assets'. In other words, equity is a residual interest after deducting claims against the entity from the entity's economic resources. There will be a need to revise this definition following the completion of a project on 'Financial instruments with characteristics of equity'.

The IASB (2018a) has defined income and expenses in terms of changes in assets and liabilities:
- Income is defined as an increase in assets or a decrease in liabilities that results in an increase in residual interest, other than those relating to the contribution from holders of equity claims.
- An **expense** is defined as a decrease in assets or an increase in liabilities that results in a decrease in residual interest, other than those relating to the contribution from holders of equity claims.
- As such, information about income and expenses will be as important as information about assets and liabilities.

2.7 RECOGNITION AND DERECOGNITION CRITERIA

Recognition is defined as the process of capturing for inclusion in the statement of financial position or the statement of financial performance an item that meets the definition of the elements of financial statements (IASB, 2018a). Recognition criteria are embedded in the qualitative characteristics of financial information, ie is the financial information useful to its users? This means that the item does not only have to meet the definition of the elements of financial statements but will also be appropriate if it results in the relevant and faithful representation of information on assets, liabilities, equity, income and expenses.

A new addition to the revised conceptual framework is derecognition, which previously was not covered. Derecognition refers to the removal of all parts of a recognised asset or liability from an entity's statement of financial position (IASB, 2018a). In the case of assets, derecognition will occur when the entity loses control of all or part of the recognised asset, whereas for a liability, derecognition will occur when the entity no longer has a present obligation for all or part of the recognised liability.

The most salient aspect of derecognition is that, according to the IASB (2018a), it aims to represent faithfully the remainder of assets and liabilities following derecognition, in part or full of a certain asset or liability. It further aims to faithfully represent the change in the reporting entity's assets and liabilities following the derecognition event.

2.8 MEASUREMENTS

According to the IASB (2018b), a measurement refers to a process of quantifying, in monetary terms, elements that are recognised in the financial statements. Essentially, there are two measurement bases, namely the **historical cost measurement base** and the **current value measurement base**. The revised conceptual framework does not favour one measurement base over any other (IASB, 2018b), however they differ in their approach and one may provide more useful information compared to the other, given certain sets of facts/situations.

According to the IASB (2018b), the **historical cost** measurement base would typically reflect the cost of acquiring or creating an asset. On the liabilities side, it would reflect a typical cost of taking on a liability. Historical costs are good for the purpose of providing relevant information about assets and liabilities as well as the price of the transaction that gave rise to each (IASB, 2018b).

The **current value** measurement base is a reflection of the value on the date of measurement. There are different characteristics of current value measurement, namely fair value, value in use (for an asset)/fulfilment value (for a liability) or current cost. According to the IASB (2018b), fair value refers to the price that would be received or paid to sell or transfer the asset or liability. Value in use or fulfilment value refers to the present value of cash flows and other economic benefits or obligations from the asset or liability (IASB, 2018b). Finally, the current cost refers to the cost of an equivalent asset or liability.

Qualitative characteristics of financial reporting have to be considered during the selection of a measurement base. As explained above, these two qualitative characteristics are relevance and faithful representation. The relevance of information provided by a measurement basis will be affected by two things: (1) the characteristics of the asset or liability, and (2) the contribution to the future cash flow (IASB, 2018a).

The characteristics of the asset or liability include the variability of cash flows and the sensitivity of the value to market factors or other risks (IASB, 2018a). The contribution to future cash flows is determined by whether cash flows are produced directly or indirectly in combination with other economic resources, and the nature of the entity's business activities (IASB, 2018a).

In terms of faithful presentation, a measurement basis would be affected by measurement inconsistency and measurement uncertainty. According to IASB (2018a), the financial statements containing measurement inconsistency (ie an accounting mismatch) may not faithfully represent some aspects of the entity's financial position and financial performance. While the measurement uncertainty will not prevent the use of a measurement base that provides relevant information, if the measurement uncertainty is too high, it might make it necessary to consider selecting a different measurement base (IASB, 2018b).

2.9 OBJECTIVES AND SCOPE OF IAS 1 (PRESENTATION OF FINANCIAL STATEMENTS)

IAS 1 aims to set out the structure and content of financial statements and the overall requirements for presentation. This includes the layout/format of financial statements, the considerations that should be taken into account and certain underlying assumptions when preparing content.

2.9.1 Objectives of IAS 1

The objective of IAS 1 is to prescribe how to present financial statements in order to achieve *comparability* with:
- an entity's own financial statements – from one financial period to another, and
- the financial statements of other entities.

This objective is achieved by setting out the following for financial statements:
- **Objective** (purpose)
- **Components** (statements that make up a complete set of financial statements)
- **General features** (overall considerations)
- **Structure and content** (covered under annual financial statements presentation formats below).

2.9.2 Scope of IAS 1

IAS 1 is applicable to all general purpose financial statements. General purpose financial statements attempt to satisfy the needs of that group of users who are not in a position to request financial statements that suit their specific needs. It applies to the financial statements of:
- single or individual entities, and
- a group of entities (combined and consolidated financial statements).

IAS 1 does not apply to the preparation of condensed interim financial statements.

It is the responsibility of the management of an enterprise to prepare and present the financial statements to the users thereof.

2.9.3 Components of financial statements

A complete set of financial statements comprises the following:
- Statement of profit or loss and other comprehensive income for the period (SoPL-OCI)
- Statement of financial position at the end of the reporting period (SoFP)
- Statement of changes in equity for the period (SoCE)
- Statement of cash flows for the period (SoCF)
- Notes, including accounting policy and explanations.

2.9.4 General features in the preparation of financial statements

When preparing annual financial statements, the following overall considerations must be considered.

Fair presentation and compliance with statements of IFRS

Financial statements should fairly present the following:
- Financial position (SOFP)
- Financial performance (SOPL-OCI)
- Cash flows (SOCF) of an enterprise.

The proper application of statements of IFRS and its interpretations will result in financial statements that achieve fair presentation.

Faithful representation

This is the fundamental qualitative characteristic according to the revised conceptual framework, which means that information in the financial reports must be complete, neutral and free from errors.

Fair presentation

Fair presentation is one of the general features listed in IAS 1 which is closely related to the fundamental characteristic, faithful representation, which means that financial statements are fairly presented when:
- there is faithful representation (complete, neutral and free from error),
- the definitions and recognition criteria of elements have been properly applied, and
- sufficient information is disclosed in such a way that the information is relevant, reliable, comparable and understandable.

However, where the management of an enterprise concludes that the application of a specific accounting statement would be misleading to the users of the financial statements and would thus not achieve fair presentation, management should then adopt the accounting treatment that would lead to fair presentation and provide the following additional disclosures required by IAS 1:

- The particular accounting statement that has not been complied with and has been departed from by management
- The accounting treatment that the particular accounting statement would have required in the circumstances
- The reason why that accounting treatment would be misleading
- The financial impact of the departure from the accounting treatment that is prescribed by that particular accounting statement.

It is only in extremely rare circumstances that such departures should be made.

Accrual basis
All financial statement components, except for statement of cash flows and entities where modified cash basis is prescribed, are prepared using the accrual basis of accounting. This means that transactions are recorded during the accounting period in which they occur, no matter whether cash is exchanged or not.

Materiality and aggregation
Items that are material should be presented separately in the financial statements. Items of a dissimilar nature and function should be presented separately unless they are immaterial. Where an item is not individually material, it should be aggregated with other similar items appearing in the financial statements. Item are considered material if they would influence the decision of the users. Companies have different materiality thresholds.

Going concern
An entity is assumed to continue to exist for the foreseeable future. Management is required to assess an entity's ability to continue as a going concern when preparing financial statements. In assessing the appropriateness of the going concern assumption, management should consider all relevant and available information about the future, which is at least 12 months from the reporting date.

Disclosure is required of any material uncertainties regarding events that may cast significant doubt on an entity's ability to continue as a going concern. Where the financial statements are not prepared on a going concern basis, the entity is required to disclose the following:

- The fact that the financial statements are not prepared on a going concern basis
- The basis upon which the financial statements are prepared (eg liquidation basis)
- The reasons for deviating from a going concern basis.

Offsetting
Offsetting is governed by the statement of IFRS, meaning that some items are permitted to be offset and some are not. Offsetting may affect the ability of users of financial statements to understand events or transactions, or conditions that have occurred. The concept of offsetting refers to the netting off of assets and liabilities or income and expenses. Offsetting may be applied to report gains and losses arising from similar transactions on a net basis, for example gains and losses that result from disposals of non-current assets, and gains and losses resulting from foreign exchange transactions. Where such gains and losses are material they should be reported separately.

Frequency of reporting
Entities are required to publish financial statements at least annually (preferably considered to be 52 weeks rather than 365 days). If the financial period is shorter or longer than a year, for example if the entity has changed its financial year end, then the entity must disclose:

- the reason why the reporting period is less than or more than a year, and
- the fact that the financial statements are not entirely comparable.

Comparative information

Numerical information in the financial statements should be disclosed with the comparative figures for the previous period. The disclosure of comparatives enhances the comparability of financial statements and assists the users in predicting trends in the financial information. Comparative information in respect of the previous reporting period should also be supplied for all narrative and descriptive information.

Where the presentation or classification of items in the financial statements is changed, the comparative amounts should also be reclassified unless the reclassification is impracticable. Additional information such as the nature of the reclassification, the amount of the affected items and the reason for the change should be provided.

Consistency of presentation

Consistency has to do with achieving the enhancing characteristic of comparability. It requires that similar principles or methods be applied when preparing financial statements. The presentation and classification of items in the financial statements should be retained within each accounting period and from one accounting period to the next, unless an accounting standard (statement of IFRS) requires such a change or a change would result in achieving fairer or more appropriate presentation.

2.10 PRESENTATION AND DISCLOSURE

According to IASB (2018a), the information on assets, liabilities, equity, income and expenses is communicated through the disclosures in the financial statements. Accordingly, it is the effective disclosure of this information that will promote relevance and faithful representation of the elements of financial statements. The IASB (2018b) notes that the revised conceptual framework does not specify whether the statement of financial performance should contain one statement with a separate section for profit or loss or contain two separate statements.

In its guidance, the IASB (2018a) indicates that the statement of profit or loss is the primary source of information about the entity's financial performance for the reporting period. Accordingly, the statement of financial performance includes the total for profit and loss with the principle being that all income and expenses for the reporting entity are classified and included in the statement of profit and loss.

The idea that all income and expenses for the reporting entity are classified and included in the statement of profit and loss means that income and expenses included in other comprehensive income will ordinarily be reclassified (recycled) to profit or loss in a future period. Where there is no clear basis for recycling, the IASB (2018b) indicates that the board (IASB) may decide that such income and expenses will not be reclassified to profit or loss. Accordingly, this could only be done if the IASB is of the view that such an exclusion may result in a statement of profit or loss providing more relevant information or a more faithful representation.

2.11 ANNUAL FINANCIAL STATEMENT PRESENTATION FORMATS

2.11.1 STATEMENT OF CHANGES IN EQUITY

Company name (Manzini Enterprises)

Name of statement (Statement of changes in equity for the year ended 31 December 2019)

Details	Share capital R	Other reserves R	Retained earnings R	Total R
Balance at 1 January 2019	xxx	xxx	xxx	xxx
Total comprehensive income	0	xxx	xxx	xxx
Profit for the year	0	0	xxx	xxx
Other comprehensive income	0	xxx	0	(xxx)
Dividends paid	0	0	(xxx)	(xxx)
Issue of share capital	xxx	0	0	xxx
Balance at 31 December 2019	**xxx**	**xxx**	**xxx**	**xxx**

2.11.2 STATEMENT OF FINANCIAL POSITION

Company name (Manzini Enterprises)
Name and date of statement (Statement of financial position for the year ended 31 December 2019)

	2019 R	2018 R
ASSETS		
Non-current assets	xxx	xxx
Property, plant and equipment	xxx	xxx
Intangible assets	xxx	xxx
Financial assets (non-current)	xxx	xxx
Current assets	xxx	xxx
Inventories	xxx	xxx
Trade and other receivables	xxx	xxx
Other current assets	xxx	xxx
Financial assets (current)	xxx	xxx
Cash and cash equivalents	xxx	xxx
TOTAL ASSETS	**xxx**	**xxx**
EQUITY AND LIABILITIES		
Total equity	xxx	xxx
Share capital	xxx	xxx
Retained earnings	xxx	xxx
Other components of equity	xxx	xxx
Total liabilities	xxx	xxx
Non-current liabilities	xxx	xxx
Long-term borrowings	xxx	xxx
Long-term provisions	xxx	xxx
Current liabilities	xxx	xxx
Trade and other payables	xxx	xxx
Short-term borrowings	xxx	xxx
Current portion of long-term borrowings	xxx	xxx
Current tax payable	xxx	xxx
Short-term provisions	xxx	xxx
Shareholders for dividend	xxx	xxx
TOTAL EQUITY AND LIABILITIES	**xxx**	**xxx**

2.11.3 STATEMENT OF PROFIT OR LOSS AND OTHER COMPREHENSIVE INCOME

Company name (Manzini Enterprises)

Statement of profit or loss and other comprehensive income for the year ended 31 December 2019

	2019	2018
	R	R
Revenue	xxx	xxx
Cost of sales	(xxx)	(xxx)
Gross profit	xxx	xxx
Other income	xxx	xxx
Distribution costs	(xxx)	(xxx)
Administrative expenses	(xxx)	(xxx)
Other expenses	(xxx)	(xxx)
Finance costs	(xxx)	(xxx)
Profit before tax	xxx	xxx
Income tax expense	(xxx)	(xxx)
Profit for the year	xxx	xxx
Other comprehensive income	xxx	xxx
Gains on property revaluations	xxx	xxx
Income tax relating to other comprehensive income	(xxx)	(xxx)
Total comprehensive income for the year	xxx	xxx

In the above statement, expenses have been grouped by function. This means the following:

1. Cost of sales includes all the costs related to acquiring the goods that have been sold where there is a trading organisation. In a manufacturing organisation, cost of sales consists of all the costs of manufacturing the goods that have been sold, such as raw and packing materials, depreciation on plant and machinery, rent for factory premises, wages paid to factory workers, insurance relating to plant and machinery, salaries relating to factory management, etc.

2. Distribution costs include any costs relating to moving goods out of the organisation. This will consist of product advertising costs, salaries for sales and marketing personnel, costs relating to running the motor vehicles of company representatives including depreciation on their vehicles, sales commissions, rent for sales office, etc.

3. Administrative expenses include all the costs of administering the entity. This will encompass the salaries of clerical staff, computer system costs relating to administration like a general ledger, the salary of the bookkeeper and the accountant, the depreciation on the accountant's company car if he has one, depreciation and insurance on accounting office equipment, etc.

4. Other expenses include all the expenses that do not fit into one of the categories above (ie if you cannot find a home for it anywhere else, put it into other expenses), such as the managing director's salary, credit losses, legal fees, etc.

EXAMPLE 2.1 Avionics Ltd

The following information pertains to Avionics Ltd for the year ended 31 December 2018:

	R
Sales (VAT inclusive)	4 900 000
Cost of sales	2 100 000
Interest income received	122 000
Interest expenses paid	18 000
Dividend income	344 000
Dividend declared and paid: ordinary shares	210 000
Directors' remuneration paid	200 000
Audit fee	112 000
Marketing costs	190 000
Delivery costs	298 000
Administrative costs	410 000
Plant and machinery at cost	620 000
Land and buildings at cost	1 300 000
Retained earnings as at 1 January 2018	366 000
Share capital: ordinary shares	1 500 000
Share capital: 8% preference shares as at 1 January 2018	400 000

Additional information:

1. The company was registered with 2 000 000 ordinary shares and 500 000 8% preference shares of no-par value. 600 000 ordinary shares were issued on 1 January 2018 for R1 per share. On 1 April 2018, 200 000 preference shares were issued for R1,50 each.

2. On 31 December 2017, 200 000 preference shares were in issue.

3. Preference dividends for the current year have not yet been provided for.

4. Land was revalued by a sworn appraiser in the current year to R1 500 000.

5. Old machinery was sold in the current year at a loss of R90 000 and old furniture was sold at a profit of R155 000; both transactions were not recorded.

6. Tax expense of R466 000 must still be provided for.

7. VAT is calculated at 15%.

REQUIRED:

1. Prepare the statement of profit and loss and other comprehensive income for the year ended 31 December 2018.

2. Prepare the statement of changes in equity for the year ended 31 December 2018.

3. Prepare the share capital note.

EXAMPLE 2.1 Solution – Avionics Ltd

1.

Statement of profit or loss and other comprehensive income for the year ended 31 December 2018

	R
Revenue [4 900 000 × (100/115)]	4 260 870
Cost of sales	(2 100 000)
Gross profit	2 160 870
Other income (122 000 + 344 000)	466 000
Distribution costs (190 000 + 298 000)	(488 000)
Administrative costs (200 000 + 112 000+ 410 000)	(722 000)
Finance costs	(18 000)
Profit before tax	1 398 870
Tax expense	(391 684)
Profit for the year	**1 007 186**
Other comprehensive income (1 500 000 – 1 300 000)	200 000
Total comprehensive income for the year	**1 207 186**

2.

Statement of changes in equity for the year ended 31 December 2018

Details	Ordinary share capital	Preference share capital	Retained earnings	Revaluation surplus	Total
Balances as at 1 Jan 2018	900 000	400 000	366 000	0	**1 666 000**
Other comprehensive income	0	0	1 007 186	200 000	**1 207 186**
New shares issued	600 000	300 000	0	0	**900 000**
Dividend declared/ paid (210 000 + 56 000)	0	0	(266 000)	0	**(266 000)**
Balances as at 31 Dec 2018	**1 500 000**	**700 000**	**1 107 186**	**200 000**	**3 507 186**

3.

Notes for the year ended 31 December 2018

Share capital

AUTHORISED	
2 000 000 ordinary shares	2 000 000
500 000 8% preference shares	500 000
ISSUED	R
1 500 000 ordinary shares	1 500 000
400 000 preference shares	700 000

EXAMPLE 12.2 Zonke Wonke Lounge and Shisanyama

An inexperienced accountant of Zonke Wonke Lounge and Shisanyama drafted the following financial statements for the year ended 31 December 2019:

Zonke Wonke Lounge and Shisanyama
Statement of comprehensive income for the year ended 31 December 2019

	R
Gross revenue	2 850 000
Cost of sales	1 643 000
GROSS PROFIT	1 207 000
Operating expenses	(939 000)
Investment income	6 000
NET OPERATING PROFIT	283 000
SA normal taxation	(132 875)
Increase in revaluation surplus on land	22 000
NET PROFIT FOR THE PERIOD	172 125
Ordinary share capital	200 000
Retained earnings at the beginning of the year	56 000
Revaluation surplus at the beginning of the year	48 000
NET COMPREHENSIVE INCOME	476 125

Operating expenses:

Directors remuneration	10 500
Insurance	90 000
Interest on overdraft	2 000
Interest on debentures	4 000
Administration and distribution costs	591 000
Loss on sale of assets	14 000
Sundry expenses	158 000
Leasing charges on plant	14 000
Depreciation on vehicles	32 000
Auditors remuneration	24 000
	939 500

Additional information:

1. On the 1 August 2019, 50 000 ordinary shares of R1 each were issued.

2. An ordinary dividend of 40 cents per share has been declared but not yet been paid.

3. Electricity of R9 500 is still payable at 31 December 2019.

REQUIRED:

1. Prepare the **statement of comprehensive income** and the **statement of changes in equity** for the year ended 31 December 2019.

2. Prepare the following notes to the financial statements of Zonke Wonke Lounge and Shisanyama for the year ended 31 December 2019:
   a) Profit before taxation note
   b) Finance costs
   c) Revenue

EXAMPLE 2.2 Solution – Zonke Wonke Lounge and Shisanyama

1.

Statement of comprehensive income for the year ended 31 December 2019

	R
Revenue (2 850 000 + 6 000)	**2 856 000**
Revenue from sales	2 850 000
Cost of sales	1 643 000
GROSS PROFIT	1 207 000
Other expenses (933 500 + 9 500)	(943 000)
Other income	6 000
Finance cost	(6 000)
PROFIT BEFORE TAXATION	264 000
Taxation	(132 875)
PROFIT FOR THE PERIOD	131 125
Other comprehensive income	
Revaluation surplus	22 000
TOTAL COMPREHENSIVE INCOME	153 125

Zonke Wonke Lounge and Shisanyama
Statement of changes in equity for the year ended 31 December 2019

Details	Ordinary share capital	Asset replacement reserve	Retained Earnings
Opening balance	**150 000	48 000	56 000
Total comprehensive income		22 000	131 125
New share issue	50 000		
Dividends paid (200 000 × 0,40)			(80 000)
Closing balance	**200 000**	**70 000**	**107 125**

2.

Notes to the financial statement on the 31 December 2019

a) **Profit before taxation**

   Expenses:

Directors' remuneration	10 500
Leasing charges on plant	14 000
Depreciation on vehicles	32 000
Auditors' remuneration	24 000
Loss on sales of assets	14 000

   Income:

Interest income	6 000

b) **Finance costs**

Interest on overdraft	2 000
Interest on debentures	4 000
	6 000

c) **Revenue**

   Revenue consists:

Revenue: sales	2 850 000
Interest income	6 000
	2 856 000

2.12 SUMMARY

This chapter introduces and discusses the most important changes in the conceptual framework. It provides the background and the thought patterns informing the changes in the newly revised conceptual framework. The presentation of financial statements (IAS 1) was also discussed, including its objectives, scope, contents and structure.

EXERCISES

Exercise 2.1
1. Who does the revised conceptual framework apply to?
2. How many chapters are in the revised conceptual framework?
3. In your view, why was the old conceptual framework reviewed? Discuss.

Exercise 2.2
1. Who are the users of financial reports?
2. For what do they use these financial reports?
3. Why do these users need the financial reports?

Exercise 2.3
1. Describe the concept of prudence.
2. Discuss the enhancing qualitative characteristics of financial information.
3. Discuss the fundamental qualitative characteristics of financial information.
4. Describe uncertainty.
5. Assess the concept of cost–benefit analysis in the usefulness of information.

Exercise 2.4
1. Discuss the difference between consolidated financial statements, unconsolidated financial statements and combined financial statements.
2. How can one determine the boundaries of a reporting entity?

Exercise 2.5
1. List and explain the five elements of financial statements.
2. What are the main changes in the definition of an asset?
3. What are the main changes in the definition of a liability?

Exercise 2.6
1. Describe recognition and de-recognition.
2. When will the asset or liability be recognised?
3. When will the asset or liability be derecognised?
4. Discuss the most salient aspect of de-recognition.

Exercise 2.7
1. Discuss various measurement bases.
2. Discuss factors to consider in selecting a measurement basis.
3. Relevance of information provided by a measurement basis is affected by characteristics of the asset or liability. Discuss.
4. Relevance of information provided by a measurement basis is affected by contribution to the future cash flows. Discuss.
5. The ability of a measurement basis to provide a faithful representation can be affected by measurement inconsistency. Discuss.
6. The ability of a measurement basis to provide a faithful representation can be affected by measurement uncertainty. Discuss.

Exercise 2.8 Umbono (Pty) Ltd
Umbono (Pty) Ltd declared a final dividend of 25 cents per ordinary share on 25 March 2019, in respect of financial year ended 28 February 2019. The junior accountant, Mr Molefe, has recorded the dividend as an expense in the statement of profit or loss and other comprehensive income, and as a liability in the statement of financial position for the year ended 28 February 2019.

The financial statements have not yet been finalised.

REQUIRED:
Discuss the recognition of the dividend by the junior accountant, with reference to the conceptual framework.

Exercise 2.9
Choose the most correct answer for each of the following multiple-choice questions.

Statement 1:
The qualitative characteristics that enhance usefulness of financial statements include the following:

A	Understandability, verifiability, timeliness, comparability
B	Assets, owner's equity, liabilities
C	Going concern and accrual basis
D	None of the above

Statement 2:
The following are the general features to consider when producing financial statements:

A	Going concern, accrual basis, offsetting, consistency of presentation
B	Going concern, accrual basis, offsetting, understandability
C	Going concern, accrual basis, assets, liabilities
D	None of the above

Statement 3:
Which of the following alternatives represent all the elements of the financial statements?

A	Assets, liabilities, income and expenses
B	Assets, owner's equity and liabilities
C	Statement of financial position, statement of comprehensive income, statement of changes in equity, notes
D	None of the above

Statement 4:
The following are examples of disclosure items in the notes to the statement of comprehensive income:

A	Increase in surplus of revaluation of land
B	Write-down of inventories, depreciation, impairment loss
C	Distribution costs, administration costs, other costs
D	None of the above

Statement 5:
The following are the two main components of a set of financial statements:

A	Statement of financial performance, statement of position
B	Going concern, accrual basis
C	Statement of financial position, statement of comprehensive income
D	None of the above

Statement 6:
Information is reliable under the following condition:

A	It is free from material error and bias
B	Its disclosure will affect the economic decision of users
C	It is capable of making a difference to a decision
D	None of the above

Statement 7:

Which of the following statements will be affected by the changes in revaluation surplus?

A	Statement of comprehensive income, statement of changes in equity
B	Notes to the financial statements, statement of financial position
C	Statement of changes in equity, statement of cash flow
D	None of the above

Exercise 2.10 Max (Pty) Ltd

The following is an extract of the trial balance of Max (Pty) Ltd at 31 December 2018:

	Dr	Cr
	R	R
Retained earnings (1 January 2018)		290 000
Non-current liabilities: loan from Ithala Bank		50 000
Share capital		480 000
Revenue		1 160 000
Interest from listed investments		25 000
Rent income		46 000
Cost of sales	600 000	
Interest expenses	19 000	
Other expenses	500 000	
Administration expenses	50 000	
Distribution expenses	50 000	
Investments	100 000	
Trade and other receivables	500 000	
Cash and cash equivalents		16 000
Current tax payable		25 600
Inventories	240 000	
Trade and other payables	450 000	
Taxation	3 600	
Land and buildings	400 000	
Vehicles – cost	200 000	
Vehicles – accumulated depreciation		80 000

Additional information:

1. Dividends of R30 000 were declared on the 31 December 2018. These had not been paid as at 31 December 2018.
2. Share capital constitutes 240 000 issued ordinary shares of no-par value, issued at R2,00 each.
   40 000 shares were issued on the first day of the year.
3. Accumulated depreciation on vehicles at 31 December 2017 was R50 000. There have been neither purchases nor sales of vehicles during the year.
4. Distribution expenses include depreciation on buildings of R9 000.
5. Administration expenses include audit fees of R10 000 and directors' fees of R14 000.
6. Interest expenses include interest on debentures of R8 000, and the balance towards interest on loan.
7. There are no components of other comprehensive income.

REQUIRED:

1. Draft the statement of comprehensive income and statement of changes in equity in the records of Max (Pty) Ltd for the financial year ended 31 December 2018 in accordance with IFRS.

2. Prepare only the following notes:
   a) Accounting policy:
      – Basis of preparation
      – Revenue
      – Inventory
   b) Profit before taxation
   c) Finance cost
   d) Taxation
   e) Dividends declared

Exercise 2.11 Beacon Ltd

The following information was extracted from the books of Beacon Ltd for the financial year ended 31 August 2019:

	R
16% R10 debentures	84 000
10% redeemable preference shares	138 000
Trade and other receivables	81 000
Revaluation surplus (1/9/2018)	75 000
Motor vehicles – at cost	108 750
– accumulated depreciation	5 250
Land and buildings at valuation (1/9/2018)	300 000
Trade and other payables	68 400
Cash and cash equivalents	68 920
Ordinary share capital (all issued at R1,00)	242 000
Provision for bad debts	7 200
Profit for the period	88 820

Additional information:

1. Land and buildings are to be re-valued by R75 000.
2. An amount of R5 000 is to be paid for share issue costs and preliminary expenses.
3. There was a new share issue of 42 000 ordinary shares at R1 each during the year.
4. The debentures are secured by a first mortgage bond over land and buildings. The first of three equal instalments of R28 000 is due for payment on 28 February 2026.
5. Provision for preference dividends is still to be made.
6. A dividend of 3 cents per ordinary share has been recommended for the year.
7. The preference shares are redeemable at the option of the company at a premium of 20 cents per share as from 1 September 2024.
8. Motor vehicles are depreciated at 20% per annum on the reducing balance method. Depreciation for the year has already been provided.
9. Inventories on hand at year end that was written down in 2009 to a net realisable value of R195 000 (its original cost was R225 000).
10. The company was incorporated with a share capital of 300 000 ordinary shares of no-par value and 120 000 redeemable preference shares of no-par value.
11. Retained earnings on the 31 August 2019 amounted to R80 080.

REQUIRED:

1. Prepare the statement of changes in equity for the year ended 31 August 2019, in compliance with IFRS.

2. Prepare **the 'asset and liabilities' section only** of the statement of financial position of Beacon Ltd at 31 August 2019.

3. Prepare the following notes to the financial statements in accordance with IFRS:
   a) Accounting policies:
      – Basis of preparation
      – Inventory
   b) Share capital
   c) Long-term loan

Exercise 2.12 Edifice Ltd

The following information has been extracted from the accounting records of Edifice Ltd for the financial year ended 28 February 2020:

	Dr	Cr
	R	R
Ordinary share capital		900 000
9% preference share capital		300 000
General expenses	75 000	
Directors' remuneration	120 000	
Dividends received from an unlisted company		18 000
Receivables	225 000	
Retained earnings – 1 March 2019		84 000
Accumulated depreciation: motor vehicles – 1 March 2019		81 000
Auditors' remuneration	18 000	
Interest on bank overdraft	11 400	
Interest received from an unlisted company		12 600
Interest received on receivables		2 250
Salaries and wages	180 000	
900 12% R100 mortgage debentures		90 000
Provisional tax payments	54 000	
Motor vehicles	360 000	
Cost of sales	656 250	
Payables		211 800
	1 699 650	1 699 650

Additional information:

1. Ordinary shares are valued at R1,00 each.
2. Preference shares are valued at R0,50 each.
3. The directors declared a dividend of 12 cents per ordinary share on 20 February 2017, payable to shareholders registered on 15 March 2017.
4. Depreciation on motor vehicles is provided for at 20% per annum using the reducing balance method.
5. Provision must still be made for:
   a) interest on the mortgage debentures for the whole year
   b) normal SA taxation, R68 550.
6. Auditors' remuneration includes an amount of R4 500 for other services rendered.
7. The turnover for the year amounted to R2 701 800.
8. A transfer of R54 000 must be made to the asset replacement reserve.
9. There is no other comprehensive income.

REQUIRED:

1. Prepare the statement of comprehensive income of Edifice Ltd for the financial year ended 28 February 2020, in accordance with IAS 1 and the Companies Act. Classify all expenses under the line item 'Other expenses'.

2. Prepare the statement of changes in equity of Edifice Ltd for the year ended 28 February 2020.

3. Prepare the following notes to the annual financial statements of Edifice Ltd for the financial year ended 28 February 2020, in accordance with IAS 1 and the Companies Act:
   a) Profit before tax
   b) Finance costs

Exercise 2.13 Zinga Ltd

The statement of financial position of Zinga Ltd at 31 December 2019 is as follows:

	R
ASSETS	
Non-current assets (carrying value)	648 000
Inventories	64 000
Receivables	44 000
Cash and cash equivalents	36 000
	792 000
LIABILITIES	
Share capital	440 000
Payables	46 000
Reserves	146 000
Debentures	160 000
	792 000

Use the following information to prepare an amended statement of financial position for Zinga Ltd:

1. The non-current assets have already been in use for a considerable time, and comprise the following:

	R
An administrative building on Lot 999, Umhlanga, at cost	400 000
Machinery (cost price R240 000)	180 000
Motor vehicles (cost price R100 000)	68 000
	648 000

The cost model is used to measure the property, plant and equipment. Machinery is depreciated on a straight line basis at 25% per annum. Motor vehicles are depreciated at 16% per annum. Depreciation has already been recorded for the current year. There is no depreciation on land and buildings.

2. The issued share capital comprises 320 000 8% redeemable preference shares @ R1,00 each and 120 000 ordinary shares @ R1,00 each. The company still has 80 000 unissued ordinary shares.

3. Payables comprise amounts owing in respect of goods purchased on 31 December 2019 totalling R25 600, as well as dividends owing to ordinary shareholders, R10 400 and to preference shareholders, R10 000.

4. Reserves consists of retained earnings amounting to R86 000, and an asset replacement reserve amounting to R60 000.

5. The debentures were secured by a first bond over Lot 999, Umhlanga, and comprise 10% R400 debentures.

REQUIRED:

1. Prepare an amended statement of financial position for Zinga Ltd at 31 December 2019 to comply with IAS 1 and IFRS.

2. Prepare the following notes in the financial statements:
   a) Accounting policies:
      - Basis of preparation
      - Property, plant and equipment
      - Inventories
   b) Share capital
   c) Interest bearing borrowing/debentures

REFERENCES

International Financial Reporting Standards (IFRS). 2018a. *Conceptual framework for financial reporting. IFRS conceptual framework project summary, March 2018*. London: United Kingdom.

International Financial Reporting Standards (IFRS). 2018b. A revised conceptual framework for financial reporting. *IFRS News*, special edition, June 2018. Publication Department, London: United Kingdom.

CHAPTER 3

INVENTORIES (IAS 2)

LEARNING OUTCOMES

After studying this chapter, you should be able to:

- Define inventories as per IAS 2.
- Perform the necessary calculation for mark-up percentages and VAT which must be charged to the perpetual or periodic system.
- Calculate inventories using the different cost formulas.
- Identify the different types of inventory:
  - In a service business: inventory will be called cost of service provided.
  - In a retail business: inventory will be called merchandise.
  - In a manufacturing business: inventory will be called raw materials, work in progress and finished goods.
- Identify the categories of inventories and their effects on the cost of conversion.
- Calculate and record the necessary entries for the cost of conversion.
- Determine the cost of inventories and its subsequent recognition, including any write-downs to net realisable value at year end.
- Determine the reversal of previous write-downs.
- Present and disclose the following in the financial statements:
  - Accounting policy note in respect of measurement of inventories, including the most used formula (IAS 2, par 36)
  - Inventories to be shown on a separate line on the face of the statement of financial position (IAS 1)
  - Notes supporting the inventories amount in the statement of financial position
  - Inventory write-downs
  - Reversal of any write-down of inventories.

PREAMBLE

Mr Mhlongo (known as Njomane) has been concerned about the large items of inventory not sold for the past year due to the high levels of competition in the market and the volatile economic climate. After several meetings with his business friend regarding the value of inventory and decrease in revenue, he recognises his need to obtain professional accounting advice and arrives in your office. Mr Mhlongo is of the opinion that the value of his inventory may be incorrect and he is unsure about what to do as this might have an impact on his profits in the future. He wants you to explain the best way to account for the cost or value of inventory, linked to checking inventory on a regular basis or annually, which will help him better manage the business.

3.1 INTRODUCTION

Inventory is an important asset of any organisation as it is the driving force of revenue production, which is the main aim of all profit organisations. As much as many non-profit organisations are not geared to produce revenue, keeping proper records and control of their inventory still play an important role for their survival. Therefore, correct measurement of inventory is important for all kinds of entities. This chapter seeks to discuss the accounting aspect of inventory records at initial and subsequent measurement, and to discuss the presentation of inventory in financial statements.

3.2 DEFINITION OF INVENTORY (as per IAS 2, par 6)

IAS 02 defines inventory as a tangible asset which is:

- in the form of materials or supplies to be consumed in the production or rendering of goods or services for sale, for example raw materials (wood to make furniture);
- held for sale in the ordinary course of business, for example finished goods (such as canned food at a grocery store) which are bought in their complete form or manufactured by the enterprise for the purpose of sale; OR
- in the process of production for sale, for example work in progress (such as semi-completed parts for the manufacturing of vehicles).

3.2.1 Different classifications of inventory

There are many classifications of inventory, which are dependent on the type of the entity concerned, however the three main elementary classifications are as follows:

- **IAS 2:** A property developer is an example of a person/persons or entity involved in the building and construction of properties with the purpose of selling these properties (eg flats, complexes, duplexes, townhouses, houses) as part of their ordinary course of business, so these properties would be classified as inventory (IAS 2).
- **IAS 40:** Property owner/owners is an example of a person/persons or entity that purchases property not for re-sale but for investment purposes, ie for capital appreciation or investment, so this would be classified as investment property (IAS 40).
- **IAS 16:** Property owner/owners is an example of a person/persons or entity that purchases a property for the purpose of doing business (eg a factory) which is called a non-current asset so this would be classified as property, plant and equipment (IAS 16).

3.2.2 Different categories of inventory

It should be noted that entities may own different classes of inventory or possibly one type of inventory. There are different classes of inventory relative to the type of business, as follows:

- Manufacturing entities
- Retailers
- Service entities.

Table 3.1 illustrates the three categories of inventory with generic examples and the types of organisation where these inventories would customarily be found.

Table 3.1: Three categories of inventories

Categories	Business	Types
Service	Consumable material	Stationery, cleaning material, electrical fittings, fuel
	Working in progress	Incomplete service contracts
Trading or retailer	Consumable material	Stationery, cleaning material, etc
	Merchandise	Trading goods, biscuits, cool drinks, clothing, etc
Manufacturing	Consumable material	Cleaning material, sandpaper, varnish, etc
	Raw material	Wood for furniture, leather for shoes, flour for bread
	Working in progress	Bread, shoes, furniture, etc, that is not completed
	Finished goods	Fully manufactured bread, shoes, furniture, etc

There are other categories of inventory that are excluded in the scope of IAS 2 only, namely:

- **IFRS 15:** Work in progress under construction contracts, inclusive of directly related service contracts
- **IAS 32, IFRS 9 and IFRS 7:** Financial instruments
- **IAS 41:** Agriculture produce at the point of harvest, and biological assets related to agricultural activities.

In a manufacturing environment, there are customarily a number of different inventories. This chapter will focus on some of the underlying issues regarding the valuation of inventory, especially in the manufacturing environment.

Figure 3.1 shows the flow of different categories of inventory from the supplier to the customer.

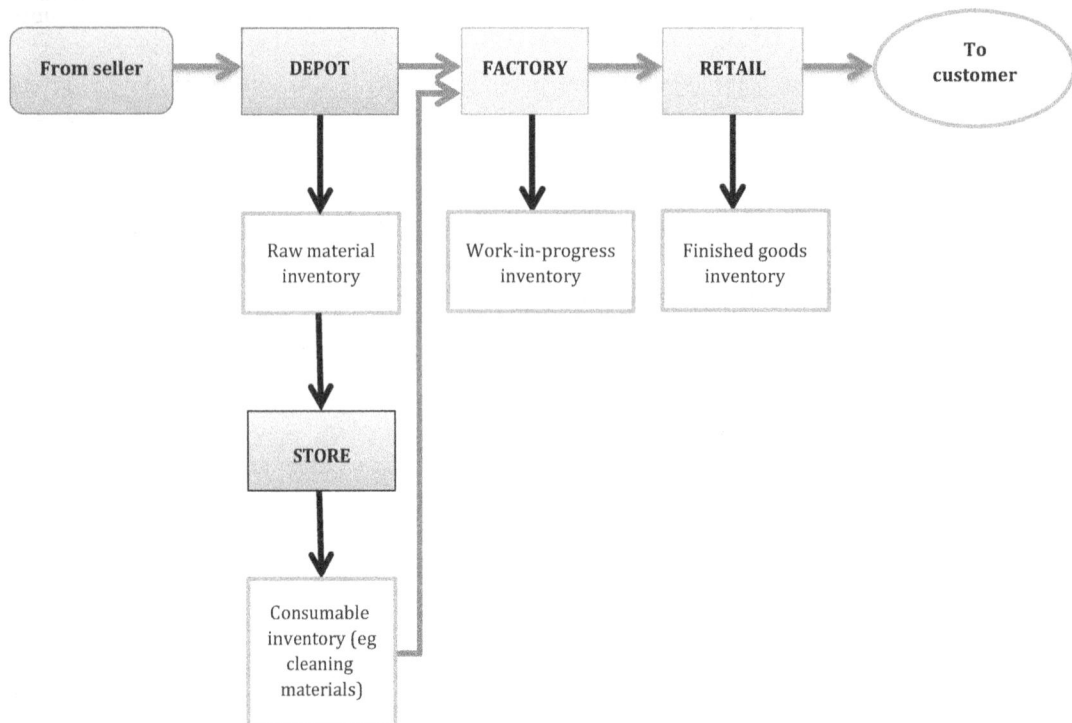

Figure 3.1: The flow of inventory in a manufacturing business

3.3 INVENTORY MOVEMENT

The movement of inventory can be accounted for using one of the following two different inventory systems:

1. Periodic inventory system
2. Perpetual inventory system.

3.3.1 Periodic inventory system

Under the periodic inventory system, the inventory account is updated periodically (ie monthly, quarterly, half-yearly or annually). Most companies using the periodic inventory system would rely on periodic stock takes, conducted by companies to determine the value of their inventory at a given time. The periodic inventory system works on the basis that the purchase of inventory during the course of business is allocated to a purchases account, which is a temporary account, and then transferred to the inventory account once a stock take has been conducted to update the value of inventory. The purchases account is regarded as an expense, so all merchandise that is purchased for cash or credit would be charged to the purchases account during the period. The journal entry for the purchase account would be: debit purchases and credit bank or trade and other payables account. So, all purchases of merchandise will automatically accumulate in the purchases account.

When inventory is sold, the revenue account in the statement of profit and loss and comprehensive income is affected. However, the actual inventory records relating to inventory on hand cannot be adjusted until the balance is either calculated or a physical inventory count is done to determine the value of the inventory on hand. As mentioned above, this assessment and recording of inventory on hand is done on a periodic basis, which could be either monthly, quarterly, half-yearly or annually. Thus, the value of inventory is not available on a continuous basis but only once the inventory count has been performed. Hence, the cost of sales account will not be updated until the inventory count is performed. When using this method, transport costs of goods purchased are recorded on a separate transport costs account.

The trading section of the statement of profit or loss and comprehensive income would be presented as follows when using the periodic inventory system:

MHLONGO LTD
Statement of profit and loss and comprehensive income for the year ended 28 February 2019

Revenue	XXX
Less: Cost of sales* (*balancing figure*)	(XX)
Opening inventories	XX
Add: Purchases	XX
Add: Transport costs	XX
Less: Closing inventories	(XX)
GROSS PROFIT	**XXX**

So if, for example, you purchase bottled water from a service station shop at a cost of R15,00 cash and the shop uses a periodic inventory system, the following accounts will be affected (ignoring VAT):
- Cash/bank increases
- Revenue increases.

3.3.2 Perpetual inventory system

Under the perpetual inventory system, the inventory account is updated on a continuous basis. The perpetual inventory system shows the movement of inventory as and when the inventory is purchased and sold. Hence, the cost of sales account is also always updated and there is no need to calculate it at the end of the period. When inventory is sold, the selling price is credited to the revenue account and debited to trade and other receivable or bank/cash account. The cost price of the goods sold is simultaneously charged (credited) to the inventory account and debited to the cost of sales account. The balance in the inventory account is thereby updated to reflect the current value of inventory on hand on a transaction by transaction basis.

In order to operate the perpetual inventory system, the business requires a sophisticated, good quality accounting software package and the latest barcode scanning equipment, which is relatively expensive. Nevertheless, these accounting software packages will support better management of an entity's inventory, which will help them identify shortages and surpluses of inventory determined during physical inventory counts. When using this method, transport costs of goods purchased are incorporated into the inventory account.

The trading section of the statement of profit or loss and comprehensive income would be presented as follows when using the perpetual inventory system:

MHLONGO LTD

Statement of profit and loss and comprehensive income for the year ended 28 February 2019

Revenue	XXX
Less: Cost of sales	(XX)
GROSS PROFIT	**XXX**

So if, for example, you purchase bottled water from a service station shop at a cost of R15,00 cash and the shop uses a perpetual inventory system, the following accounts will be affected (ignoring VAT):
- Cash/bank increases
- Revenue increases
- Inventory decreases
- Cost of sales increases.

Refer to Example 3.1 for a practical understanding of the journal entries for periodic and perpetual inventory systems.

EXAMPLE 3.1 Happy Malevu Spaza Shop (periodic and perpetual inventory system)

Happy Malevu Spaza Shop in Gugulethu sells groceries to the surrounding area and schools. Miss Malevu, the owner, checked the store room and realised that the teabags were out of stock, so she went to a nearby wholesaler and purchased 10 boxes of teabags for R30 each on 1 April 2019, for which she paid cash. On 11 April 2019, one of her customers bought three boxes of teabags for the Gugulethu community drive function happening over the weekend and paid R120 cash. On 19 April 2019, a second customer, Mr Pangwa, purchased four boxes of teabags for a wedding function and paid R40 cash for each box.

REQUIRED:

Ignoring all VAT implications, prepare the journal entries for the above transactions only using:

1. the periodic system
2. the perpetual system.

EXAMPLE 3.1 Solution – Happy Malevu Spaza Shop

Journal entries for Happy Malevu Spaza Shop

1. The periodic system

		R	R
1 April 2019	Dr Purchases (10 × R30)	300	
	Cr Cash		300
11 April 2019	Dr Cash (3 × R40)	120	
	Cr Revenue		120
19 April 2019	Dr Cash (4 × R40)	160	
	Cr Revenue		120

2. The perpetual system

		R	R
1 April 2019	Dr Inventory	300	
	Cr Cash		300
11 April 2019	Dr Cash	120	
	Cr Revenue		120
	Dr Cost of sales (3 × R30)	90	
	Cr Inventory		90
19 April 2019	Dr Cash	160	
	Cr Revenue		160
	Dr Cost of sales (4 × R30)	120	
	Cr Inventory		120

At the end of April 2019, a physical stock count is carried out and three boxes of teabags are found to be on hand. How did we get three boxes on hand?

Teabags: 10 boxes purchased – 3 boxes sold – 4 boxes sold = 3 boxes (on hand)

From the above information, you are now required to prepare the statements of profit or loss account, assuming there were no other transactions for the month of April, one based on the periodic system and one based on the perpetual system.

Happy Malevu Spaza Shop
Statement of profit or loss and comprehensive income for the month of April 2019

Periodic system	R	Perpetual system	R
Revenue (120 + 160)	280	Revenue (120 +160)	280
Cost of sales	(210)	Cost of sales (90 + 120)	(210)
O/inventories (0) + purchases (300)			
C/inventories (3 × 30 = 90)			
Gross profit	**70**	**Gross profit**	**70**

The gross profit is the same for both the periodic and perpetual inventory system. The difference is that the periodic system requires a stock count to complete the profit or loss account, whereas the perpetual system does not.

The gross profit is known for each sale immediately by the calculation of cost of sales, so for sale 1, gross profit is R120 – R90 = R30 and for sale 2, gross profit is R160 – R120 = R40.

3.4 COST FORMULAS FOR THE TRANSFER OF INVENTORY

There are three cost formulas for the transfer of inventory in a manufacturing concern, briefly discussed below (IAS 2, par 24, 27):

- **Weighted average cost formula:** The cost of each item is calculated based on the weighted average cost per unit at the beginning of a period and the cost of similar value inventory purchased or produced at the end of the period.
- **First in, first out (FIFO) cost formula:** This formula deals with manufactured or purchased inventory that is bought first (oldest inventory) and sold first (eg fruit, vegetables, cellphones).
- **Specific identification cost formula:** There are specific costs that are attributable to dissimilar value of inventory (eg custom-made handbags).
- **Standard costing cost formula:** This may be employed when there is an estimated cost and if it is reviewed on a regular basis.
- **Retail cost formula:** When the cost of inventory is reduced by gross profit percentage, this can be used if other cost formulas are not working.

3.5 DISCOUNTS

Discounts are an important part of any entity and there are many different types of discount, especially in the manufacturing environment. Customers and debtors are often faced with an array of discounts. Discounts need to be taken into consideration as they will automatically be deducted from the cost of inventory as follows:

- **Trade/bulk discounts**: These are discounts normally given by suppliers or wholesalers to regular customers, who will buy in bulk to break up and sell on to their own customers, probably the users. Trade discounts are usually shown on an invoice that is recorded net of trade discounts by the seller. For example, goods to the value of R2 000 that are subject to a 20% trade discount would be recorded net at R400 (R2 000 less 20%) in the books of the seller.
- **Cash discounts:** These are discounts offered to customers that choose to pay cash rather than purchase on credit. This can be viewed as an incentive discount for paying promptly in cash. The accounting treatment is the same as for trade discounts in the books of the seller business so the revenue is recorded net of cash discounts.
- **Settlement discounts:** These are more complex and estimated but can be seen as an incentive when the account is paid on time. The customer purchases on credit and the transaction has an impact on the trade and other receivables account. Therefore, if a customer pays within a certain period of time, which could be around 30 days, the customer will get a settlement discount (eg 3%). However, if same customer pays the account around 60 days, the customer cannot receive a settlement discount and will have to pay the gross amount for the inventory purchased. The business needs to review and make a judgement call as to whether there is certainty that the settlement will be granted at the time of the transaction.
- **Target rebates:** These are discounts (rebates) paid to customers on achieving targets. The business that is buying inventories may receive a rebate (set off against inventory or against income). However, accounting for these rebates can be quite complex due to uncertainties involved in reaching targets, and target rebates will therefore not be discussed any further in this chapter.

EXAMPLE 3.2 Settlement discounts (Mandonsela Ltd)

Consider the following table in the books of Mandonsela Ltd, the seller, where a R10 000 sales invoice is considered (excluding VAT):

	Certainty – Aphiwe	Uncertainty – Bonga
	R	R
Sales invoice amount	20 000	20 000
10% settlement discount at transaction date	(2 000)	0
Revenue recognised	18 000	20 000
Settlement discount (payment date)	0	(2 000)
Cash payment	18 000	18 000

Required:

Prepare the journal entries for Aphiwe and Bonga.

EXAMPLE 3.2 Solution – Mandonsela Ltd

Now consider the journal entries for the above:

	Certainty – Aphiwe		Uncertainty – Bonga	
	Debit	Credit	Debit	Credit
Transaction date	R	R	R	R
Dr Accounts receivable	20 000	2 000		20 000
Cr Provision for settlement discount		18 000	20 000	
Cr Revenue				
Payment date: *Aphiwe pays on time, but the Bonga account is deferred.*				
Dr Cash/bank	18 000		20 000	
Dr Settlement discount	0		0	
Dr Provision for settlement discount	2 000		0	
Cr Accounts receivable		20 000		20 000
Payment date: *Both Aphiwe and Bonga pay promptly.*				
Dr Cash/bank			18 000	
Dr Settlement discount	18 000		2 000	
Dr Provision for settlement discount	0		0	
Cr Accounts receivable	2 000	20 000		20 000

Note:

In the profit and loss account, the revenue account is always shown NET of any settlement discount given. Revenue would therefore be shown as R18 000 (R20 000 – R2 000). In the case of Bonga, where no settlement discount was given as payment was delayed, the revenue will be shown as R20 000.

Therefore, in the statement of financial position, the trade and other receivables account will be shown NET of the provision for settlement discount where the amount is still outstanding at statement of financial position date.

3.6 COST OF INVENTORY
The cost of inventory shall comprise all costs of purchases, costs of conversion and other costs incurred in bringing the inventory to its present location and condition (IAS 2, paras 10, 11).

3.6.1 Cost of inventory purchased for resale
Historically, the cost of inventory is calculated as follows:
- Purchase price (excluding VAT)
- Import charge/duties
- Other levies
- Transport and handling charge (carriage inwards)
- Other direct costs of acquisition

Minus
- Trade discounts
- Rebates received
- Other similar items.

The cost of inventory excludes the following:
- **Abnormal emission costs:** This includes raw materials, other production costs and labour during the production process. However, it should be noted that these can be indirectly included in COST OF SALES.
- **Fixed costs:** These production costs are not allocated to the production process based on normal capacity.
- **Storage costs:** Unless such costs are necessary in bringing the inventories to their location and condition, they are excluded.
- **Administrative costs:** These are costs that are NOT related to bringing inventory to its location and condition.

3.6.2 Cost of conversion in a manufacturing concern

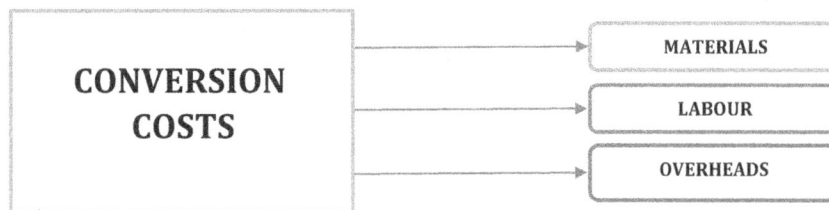

Figure 3.2: Cost of conversion framework

The conversion cost of inventory includes costs directly related to the unit of production, such as direct material and direct labour. It also includes a systematic allocation of fixed and variable production overheads that are incurred in converting materials into finished goods (IAS 2, par 12).

3.6.3 The cost of a manufactured product
It is necessary to identify the goods to be included in inventory at the end of the financial period as well as the other costs associated with them. The cost of normal spillage forms part of conversion costs.

The cost of a product is made up of the following three components:
1. **Materials**: Raw materials or direct materials can be directly identified with each unit of production which is recorded separately.
2. **Labour**: Direct labour can be directly identified with each unit of production which is recorded separately. Labour such as cleaning and general administrative costs cannot be directly identified with a unit of production and are therefore classified as indirect labour, which is part of overheads.
3. **Direct materials and direct labour:** These are considered to be variable costs because they change in accordance with the level of production.

All manufacturing costs that are NOT direct material costs or direct labour costs are classified as **overheads (production overhead costs)**:
- **Variable overheads:** These are production costs that change directly or almost directly with the level of production. These costs can be directly related to the product being manufactured (eg indirect materials and indirect labour).

- **Fixed overheads:** These are production costs that do not vary with level of production and are related to the operation of the business as a whole. These costs are not directly related to the product being manufactured (eg factory rental, factory wages, depreciation and maintenance of factory, and salaries of permanent staff).

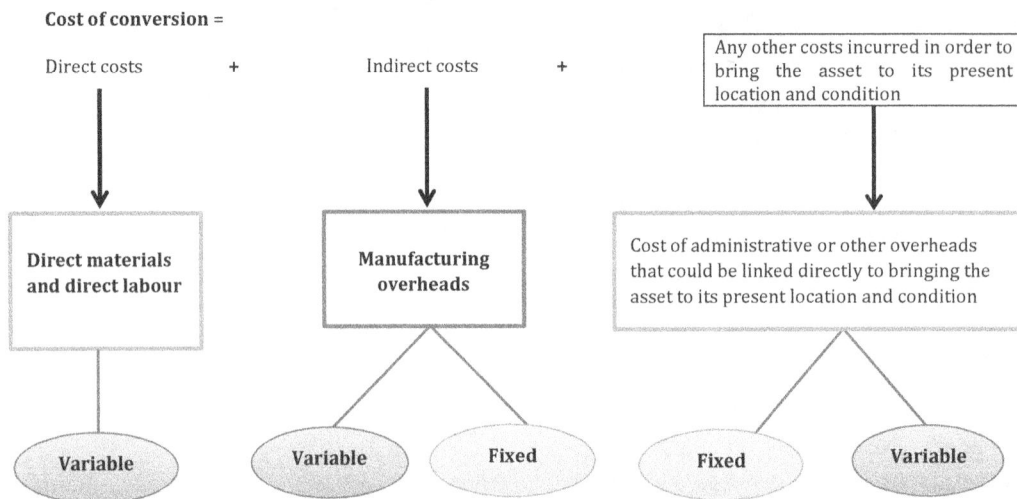

Cost of conversion =

Direct costs   +   Indirect costs   +

Any other costs incurred in order to bring the asset to its present location and condition

| Direct materials and direct labour | Manufacturing overheads | Cost of administrative or other overheads that could be linked directly to bringing the asset to its present location and condition |

Variable   Variable   Fixed   Fixed   Variable

Figure 3.3: Conversion cost of inventory

In terms of IAS 2 par 16, the cost of conversion includes the cost of manufacture related to work in progress and finished goods as follows:
- Direct costs of manufacture (direct labour and direct material)
- Indirect costs of manufacture (fixed manufacturing overheads and variable manufacturing overheads)
- Any other costs necessarily incurred in order to bring the asset to its present location and condition (where even administrative overheads could be included if directly linked to bringing the asset to a condition and location enabling it to be used or sold).

Costs which are not closely related to the purchased or conversion of inventories should be expensed in the period in which they are incurred.

The following must always be expensed:
- Abnormal amount of wastage
- Storage costs (unless these are directly related to the production process).

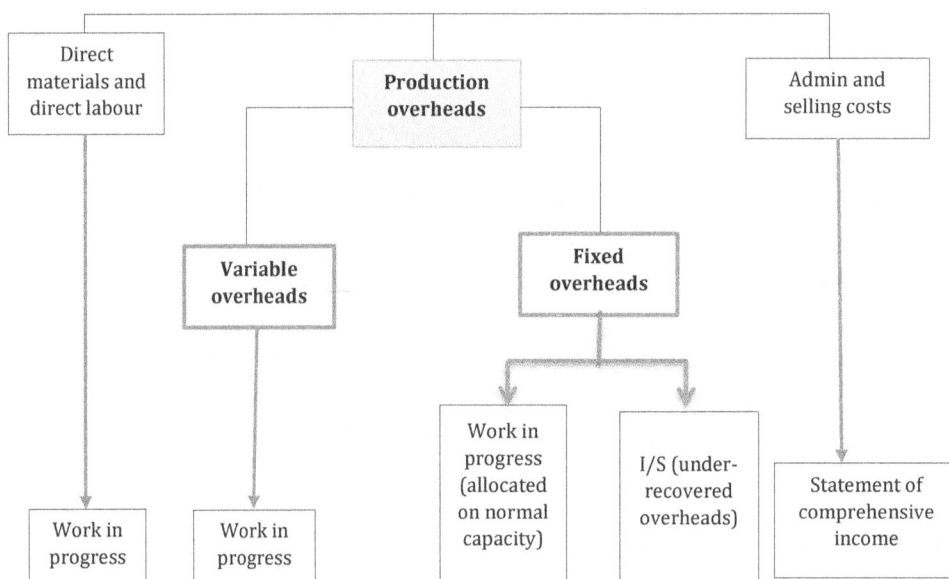

Direct materials and direct labour   Production overheads   Admin and selling costs

Variable overheads   Fixed overheads

Work in progress   Work in progress   Work in progress (allocated on normal capacity)   I/S (under-recovered overheads)   Statement of comprehensive income

Figure 3.4: Allocation of costs

Figure 3.4 demonstrates how costs are allocated between work in progress, which is a classification of inventory and a current asset line item, or to the profit and loss account as an expense.

Allocation of costs (to assets or to expenses)

As shown in Figure 3.4, variable costs such as direct material, direct labour and the variable portion of the overheads can be included in asset work in progress. However, difficulties arise in the allocation of the fixed portion of the factory overheads to the asset work in progress due to under-absorption (*budgeted greater than actual*) and over-absorption (*budgeted less than actual*).

3.7 COST OF A MANUFACTURED PRODUCT (cost per unit)

To determine the value of inventory to be shown as a current asset, the cost of each unit of inventory has to be calculated as follows:

Cost price per unit = Variable cost per unit + Fixed cost per unit

3.7.1 Calculation of the variable cost per unit

This is a relatively simple calculation because the cost of direct material, direct labour and the variable portion of manufacturing overheads can be associated directly with the manufacturing of the product. The variable cost per unit or variable manufacturing costs are all the costs per unit in total that vary with production. The following are some variable costs:

- **Indirect costs:** For example, indirect materials and indirect labour
- **Direct costs:** For example, direct labour
- **Purchase costs:** For example, direct materials or raw materials.

EXAMPLE 3.3 Calculation of variable cost per unit (Mxolisi & Rudra Dutt Ltd)

Mxolisi & Rudra Dutt Ltd are new owners of a furniture manufacturing business in Lenasia, Gauteng. Assume that all manufacturing overheads are fixed and that 100 units of furniture inventory manufactured uses the following:

- 100 factory labour hours (at R30 per hour), and
- 55 kg of mahogany wood raw material at R105 per kg (excluding VAT).

REQUIRED:

Calculate the variable cost per unit of inventory.

EXAMPLE 3.3 Solution – Mxolisi & Rudra Dutt Ltd

The variable manufacturing cost per unit of inventory is:

Direct labour	100 hrs × R30	R3 000
Direct material	55 kg × R105	R5 775
Variable cost per unit		**R8 775**

Therefore, a variable cost of R8 775 will be included to arrive at the cost of each manufactured product.

3.7.2 Calculation of the fixed cost per unit

Fixed costs per unit are manufacturing cost that do not vary with level of production. In order to calculate the fixed cost per unit, the **total fixed manufacturing cost** has to be allocated to the **actual number of products** manufactured. However, this will cause a problem as the **actual** products manufactured are only known at the **end of the year**, while a rate for the fixed cost per unit is required at the **beginning of the year**. The purpose of the fixed cost per unit is quoting, budgeting and interim reporting.

During the year, fixed manufacturing overhead costs are allocated to products on the basis of '**normal capacity**' (IAS 2, par 13). So, the number of products that can reasonably be expected to be manufactured under normal circumstances reflect the normal level of production. The following are the two fixed manufacturing cost rates which can be used:

1. **Budgeted fixed cost per unit** for the *beginning* of the year
2. **Actual fixed cost per unit** for *end* of the year.

Calculation of the budgeted fixed cost per unit (normal capacity)

This calculation is based on the expected level of production under normal circumstances, **budgeted for the year**. The fixed costs can be determined at the beginning of the year because these costs are not expected to change. The budgeted fixed cost can be calculated at the beginning of the year using the following formula:

$$\text{Budgeted fixed application rate} = \frac{\text{Fixed manufacturing overheads}}{\text{Budgeted (normal) level of product}}$$

Note: As previously mentioned, there is a need to calculate the budgeted fixed cost per unit or budgeted application rate for interim reporting, quoting and budgeting purposes. The purpose of this formula is to ensure that we allocate the correct amount of fixed costs to the inventory account at the beginning of the year. So, *why is this rate important?*

It is not possible to merely **ADD** all the fixed costs such as factory depreciation, factory rent, etc, to the inventories account of the statement of financial position at the *beginning of the year*. This would indicate that we already have an inventory amount (current assets) in the statement of financial position from fixed costs without any manufacturing or production of inventory in the factory. It is important to note that as per IFRS, this allocation is **NOT** allowed since there is no evidence of inventory being manufactured. In addition, it is NOT possible to sell fixed costs such as factory depreciation, factory rent, etc, as inventory.

Therefore, to support this stance, the fixed manufacturing costs are **debited** to a suspense account instead of the inventory account. The suspense account is utilised when we are unsure of which elements (asset, owner's equity, liabilities, income, expense) to debit or credit.

The following is a sample example presentation of a suspense account in the General ledger:

Dr Fixed manufacturing cost suspense account Cr

Budgeted	Actual

Calculation of actual fixed cost per unit (end of the year)

Actual manufacturing overheads are the amounts actually spent during a given period as shown by records of the enterprise at the end of the period. The actual fixed cost per unit rate would depend on the actual level of inventory produced in any one period and can only be calculated at year end. The actual cost per unit will be used to calculate the actual value of inventories that would have been produced at a given period.

$$\text{Actual fixed application rate} = \frac{\text{Fixed manufacturing overheads}}{\text{Greater of: budgeted or actual production}}$$

3.7.3 Under-absorption (if budgeted production > actual production)

When there is a decrease in production, the fixed production overheads allocated per unit do not increase, so the unallocated overheads are expensed in the period in which they were incurred (IAS 2, paras 12–14). In the event that budgeted production is **greater** than actual production, the fixed overhead application rate is calculated using **budgeted** production since this avoids inventory being overstated as a result of company inefficiencies (under-productivity). The amount is expensed instead as it would be incorrect to debit or add too much fixed cost to the inventory account. Therefore, this illustrates that we used less fixed cost and rather over-spent or over-budgeted.

EXAMPLE 3.4 Fixed manufacturing costs (under-absorption)

Fixed manufacturing overheads	**R400 000**
Normal expected production	**400 000 units**
Actual production	**275 000 units**
Fixed non-manufacturing overheads	**R50 000**

REQUIRED:

1. Calculate the budgeted fixed cost per unit or budgeted fixed application rate.
2. Calculate the actual fixed cost per unit or actual fixed application rate.
3. Journalise the above.
4. Post to the ledger.

EXAMPLE 3.4 Solution

1. Budgeted fixed application rate/budgeted fixed cost per unit rate (normal absorption rate)

$$\frac{\text{Fixed manufacturing overheads}}{\text{Budgeted production}}$$

$$= \frac{\text{R400 000}}{\text{400 000 units}}$$

= R1,00 per unit

The above R1,00 per unit will be used to quote to customers, for budgeting and when drafting interim financial statements. The purpose of interim drafting of financial statements is to have something to present to the bank or investors when raising short- or long-term loans.

2. Actual fixed application rate/actual fixed cost per unit rate (actual absorption rate)

$$\frac{\text{Fixed manufacturing overheads}}{\text{Greater of budgeted/actual production}}$$

Fixed manufacturing overheads $\frac{}{\text{Budgeted production}}$ $= \frac{\text{R400 000}}{\text{400 000 units}}$ = R1,00 per unit (normal budgeted production)	Fixed manufacturing overheads $\frac{}{\text{Actual production}}$ $= \frac{\text{R400 000}}{\text{275 000 units}}$ = R1,50 per unit (actual production)

At the end of the year, we will compare the normal budgeted production to the actual production and select the lowest production unit, which is the actual production. Since the budgeted production of 400 000 units is greater than the actual production of 275 000 units, the result is a decrease in company's efficiency or productivity.

3. Journal entries

	Dr	Cr
During the year Fixed manufacturing costs (suspense) Bank/trade and other payables *Fixed manufacturing overheads incurred: given*	400 000	400 000
Inventories Fixed manufacturing costs (suspense) *Allocation of fixed manufacturing overheads to inventory over the year: 275 000 × R1 (BFCPU)*	275 000	275 000
At the end of the year Fixed manufacturing overhead expense (E) Fixed manufacturing costs (suspense) *Expensing of the balance of the fixed manufacturing overhead suspense account at year end*	125 000	125 000
Fixed non-manufacturing overhead expense (E) Cash/bank *Payment of non-manufacturing fixed overheads*	50 000	50 000

Note: The conceptual framework states that the value of the asset should represent the probable future economic benefits expected to flow from the current asset. It would be unfavourable to allocate all the fixed manufacturing costs to inventory account due to **under-productivity**. Thus, this value of R125 000 (as per Example 3.4) is abnormal wastage in production capacity and must be **expensed**. If this amount of R125 000 is NOT expensed, then inventory will be over-valued.

4. General ledger entries

Bank

		Fixed manuf. costs (suspense)	400 000
		Fixed non-manufacturing overheads expense	50 000

Fixed manufacturing overheads/costs expense

Bank	400 000	Inventory	275 000
		Fixed manufacturing overheads expense	**125 000**
	400 000		400 000

Inventory

Fixed manufacturing costs (suspense)	275 000	Balance c/d	275 000
	275 000		**275 000**

Fixed manufacturing overheads expense

Fixed manufacturing cost (suspense)	125 000		
Bank	50 000		

3.7.4 Over-absorption (if budgeted production < actual production)

The fixed manufacturing overheads allocated per unit of production are reduced when there is an abnormally high production level, to ensure that inventory is not measured above cost (IA 2, paras 12–14). In the event that budgeted production is **less** than actual production, the budgeted fixed overhead allocation rate (BFOAR) will be higher than the actual fixed overhead allocation rate (AFOAR) per unit, which in essence means that we produced more than expected.

The budgeted fixed application rate is used to absorb fixed overheads into the cost of the inventory during the course of the year. The fixed manufacturing overheads will be over-absorbed into the cost of inventory by the end of the year due to over-productivity. The extra inventory, if sold, can be transferred to cost of sales (COS) (expense) OR if the inventory is on hand, it can be reversed from the inventory account. This chapter will focus on inventory on hand so the over-production will be reversed. The actual fixed application rate is calculated using actual production since this avoids inventory being shown at a value above cost.

EXAMPLE 3.5 Fixed manufacturing costs (over–absorption)

Fixed manufacturing overheads	R400 000
Normal expected production (units)	400 000
Actual production (units)	800 000
Fixed non-manufacturing overheads	R50 000

REQUIRED:

1. Calculate the budgeted fixed cost per unit or budgeted fixed application rate.
2. Calculate the actual fixed cost per unit or actual fixed application rate.
3. Journalise the fixed manufacturing costs.
4. Post to the ledger.

EXAMPLE 3.5 Solution

1. Budgeted fixed application rate (normal absorption rate)

$$\frac{\text{Fixed manufacturing overheads}}{\text{Budgeted production}}$$

$$= \frac{\text{R400 000}}{\text{400 000 units}}$$

= R1,00 per unit

2. Actual fixed application rate (actual absorption rate)

$$\frac{\text{Fixed manufacturing overheads}}{\text{Greater of budgeted/actual production}}$$

$$= \frac{\text{R400 000}}{\text{800 000 units}}$$

= R0,50 per unit

It should be noted that although the budgeted fixed application rate (BFAR) of R1,00 per unit is used throughout the year for quoting customers and for producing interim financial statements, the value for inventory at the end of the year would use the actual fixed application rate of R0,50 per unit instead.

Reason: If we used the BFAR of R1,00 per unit when actual production was 800 000 units, then R800 000 (800 000 units × R1,00) would have been the fixed overhead included in inventory (ie to be shown at a value that exceeds cost). There would be excessive fixed overheads included in the inventory account, also known as over-allocation. However, this is not possible as the fixed overheads incurred were only R400 000. Therefore, the fixed overheads are allocated in full to inventories as the budgeted production < actual production.

3. Journal entries

	Dr	Cr
During the year Fixed manufacturing costs (suspense) Bank/creditor *Fixed manufacturing overheads incurred: given*	400 000	400 000
Inventory Fixed manufacturing costs (suspense) *Allocation of fixed manufacturing overheads to inventory over the year:* *800 000 × R1 (BFAR)*	800 000	800 000
At year end Fixed manufacturing costs (suspense) Inventory ***Reversal** of fixed manufacturing costs transferred to the inventory account*	400 000	400 000
Fixed non-manufacturing overheads expense Bank/cash *Payment of non-manufacturing fixed overheads*	50 000	50 000

4. General ledger entries

Bank

		Fixed manufacturing costs (suspense)		400 000
		Fixed non-manufacturing overheads		50 000

Fixed manufacturing costs (suspense)

Bank	400 000	Inventory		800 000
Inventory	400 000			
	800 000			400 000

Inventory

Fixed manufacturing costs (suspense)	800 000	Fixed manufacturing costs (suspense)	400 000
		Balance c/d	400 000
	800 000		800 000

Fixed non-manufacturing overheads (E)

Bank	50 000		

3.8 VALUATION OF INVENTORY AT YEAR END

Although the conceptual framework states that an asset should be measured at an amount representing future economic benefits expected to be derived from the asset, the standard governing inventory disallows the measurement of inventory above cost. Therefore, unlike other assets, even if inventory is expected to render future economic benefits in excess of its costs, it may never be valued above cost.

In essence, the inventory cost will be reflected at a higher amount and will eventually be sold at a loss due to over-valuing of the inventory. So, from a revenue perspective, it will have an impact on future economic benefits. Thus, inventory is generally written-down to net realisable value on an item by item basis (IAS 2, paras 28–33)

3.8.1 Accounting policy for inventory

Inventory shall be measured at lower of cost or net realised value (IAS 2, par 9).

If the net realisable value at the end of the year is lower than price for the goods, then the net realisable value should be used in the valuation of inventories. So, at the end of each financial year, inventory should be tested for write-down (impairments) by calculating the net realised value and comparing the amount to the cost of inventory.

The following is a sample example presentation of an extract accounting policy note for inventory (IAS 1, paras 54–102):

Thabisile Nomthi LTD

EXTRACT from notes for the year ended 28 February 2019

Note 3: Accounting policy

3.1. INVENTORY
Inventory shall be measured at lower of cost and net realised value using the following methods:
Raw materials – FIFO method
Work in progress – FIFO method
Finished goods – FIFO/weighted average method

3.8.2 Inventory write-downs

The amount of inventory write-downs to net realisable value and all inventory losses will be recognised as an expense in the period the write-down or loss of inventory occurs (IAS 2, paras 34–35). As per IFRS, any write-down of inventory to net realisable value is an expense in the relevant financial period and should be disclosed as part of the cost of inventory expensed. It is important to note that these write-downs may be required if inventory is damaged, obsolete or if the competitive selling price has decreased.

Note: If the net realisable value is **lower** than cost, the inventory must be written down to this lower amount. This is the concept of prudence: recognising losses as soon as they happen rather than waiting for them to be incurred.

3.8.3 Net realisable value (NRV)

The cost of inventory may not be recovered if the inventory is damaged, becomes exclusively or partly obsolete, or if its selling price has dropped, selling costs have increased and estimated cost to complete (work in progress) has increased. Hence, such inventory shall be written down to net realisable value (IAS 2, paras 28–33).

Net realisable value can be defined as follows: estimated selling price (in the ordinary course of business) less costs incurred to make the sale. For example:
- Cost to complete the inventories (eg work in progress)
- Trade discounts

- Advertising costs
- Sales commission
- Transport/packaging/carriage costs (eg transport/carriage inwards).

Recognition as an expense in the financial statements (IAS 2, paras 34–35)

According to the IFRS framework, the following should be recognised as expenses in the statement of profit and loss and comprehensive income of a related period:
- Carrying amount of inventory sold (referred to as cost of sales)
- Write-downs to net realisable value
- Inventory losses (damage, obsolete)
- Fixed non-manufacturing overheads/costs
- Abnormal amounts of wasted materials, labour and overheads
- Allocation of inventory to other asset accounts (constituent of self-constructed asset).

EXAMPLE 3.6 Lower of cost and net realisable value (NRV)

Zolile Ltd is a plastic manufacturing business situated in Springfield Field Park, Durban, KwaZulu-Natal. After a brief discussion with his accountant, there was a need to assess inventory on an item-by-item basis so that inventory did not exceed the lower of cost or net realisable value. The following was assumed regarding inventory:
- The business has plastic inventory on hand at year end 31 December 2018 which it expected to be able to sell in the ordinary course of business for R2 500.
- In order to sell this inventory, the company expects to incur selling costs of R500 and further costs of R700 to complete this inventory.
- The cost of the inventory is R1 600.
- The business utilises the perpetual inventory system.

REQUIRED:

1. Calculate the net realisable value (NRV).

2. Calculate any possible write-down.

3. Journalise any write-down.

4. Show the effect of the write down in the financial statements for the year ended 31 December 2018.

EXAMPLE 3.6 Solution

1. Calculation of net realisable value (NRV)

	R
Estimated selling price	2 500
Less: Estimated selling costs	500
Less: Estimated costs to complete	700
Net realisable value	**1 300**

2. Calculation of write-down of inventory

	R
Cost	1 600
Net realisable value	1 300
Inventory write-down (cost needs to be reduced to NRV)	**300**

3. Journal entry

	Dr R	Cr R
Cost of sales/write down of inventories (expense)	300	
Inventory (current asset)		300
Write-down of inventory to net realisable value (160 – 130)		

4. Effect of write-down in the financial statements (extract)

Statement of profit or loss and other comprehensive income for the year ended 31 December 2018

Note		2018	2017
		R	R
Revenue		XXX	XXX
Cost of sales	**(XX + 300)**	**(X)**	**(X)**
Other income		X	X
Other expenses		(X)	(X)
Profit before taxation		XX	XX

5. Notes for the year ended 31 December 2018 (extract)

	2018	2017
	R	R
Note 3: Profit before tax		
Profit before taxation is stated after taking into account the following separately disclosable item:		
Expenses Write-down of inventory	300	

Note: If the net realisable value is **greate**r than cost, then no adjustment would need to be made. Valuation of inventory to a net realisable value that is higher than cost is not allowed since any increase in value will have an impact on gross profit and thus will result in the recognition of gross profit before the sale can take place. In addition, any increase in value should only effect gross profit when revenue is actually recognised and inventory has been sold. When the write-down or reversal of write-down forms part of normal trading then the inventory write-down may be included in cost of sales expense.

3.8.4 Reversal of a previous write-down

At the end of each period, a new evaluation is done for the net realisable value of all inventories on hand. If the net realisable value of an item previously written down to below cost has recovered to cost or above, the inventory write-down should be reversed in the current period. According to IAS 2 (par 34–35), any reversal of write-down from an increase in net realisable value will be recognised as a decrease in cost of sales (expense) in the year of the reversal of write-down of inventory. Such reversal is limited to the amount of the original write-down amount which is inventory cannot be valued above cost. Therefore, write-downs and reversals should be separately disclosed.

It should be noted that revenue from the sale of inventory is recognised only when inventory is sold and cannot be recognised before. If we were to value inventory above cost, then a gain would be recognised in the current year, which would represent the future profit on the future sale of the inventory. This is not possible as revenue would then be recognised before it was earned, which is NOT permissable as per the standard.

EXAMPLE 3.7 Reversal of previous write-down of inventories

As per Example 3.6, Zolile Ltd in the previous year (2018) had written down inventory on an item-by-item basis after a systematic check by the accountant revealed that inventory needed to be written down to net realisable value. In 2019, the manufacturing concern has inventory on hand at the end of the year that was already written down in 2018 to a net realisable value of R1 300 (its original cost was R1 600).

REQUIRED:

Calculate, journalise and disclose the write-back or reversal of write-down (if any), assuming that the net realisable value of this inventory at the end of the current year is:

1. R1 500
2. R1 800.

CORE PRINCIPLES OF ACCOUNTING

EXAMPLE 3.7 Solution

1. Net realisable value for R1 500

	R
Carrying amount (from 2018)	1 300
Net realisable value (R1 500) limited to the cost (R1 600)	1 500
Reversal of previous write-down	200

Journal entry

	R	R
	Dr	Cr
Inventories (current asset) Cost of sales (3.7.1.)	200	
Reversal of previous write-down of inventories		200

Extract to the statement of profit or loss and other comprehensive income for the year ended 31 December 2019

	Note	2019	2018
		R	R
Revenue			
Cost of sales (XX – 200)		XXX	XXX
Gross profit		(X)	(X)
Other income		XX	XX
Other expenses		X	X
Profit before taxation		(X)	(X)
		XX	XX

Note for the year ended 31 December 2019

	2019	2018
	R	R
Note 9: Profit before tax		
Profit before taxation is stated after taking into account the following separately disclosable items		
Income		
Reversal of previous write-down of inventory	200	

2. Calculation for NRV = R1 800

	R
Carrying amount	1 300
Net realisable value (R1 800) is limited to the cost (R1 600)	1 600
Reversal of previous write-down	300*

Journal entry

	R	R
	Dr	Cr
Inventories (current assets)		
Cost of sales (from *)	300	
Reversal of previous write-down of inventory		300

Extract of statement of profit or loss and comprehensive income for the year ended 31 December 2019

	2019	2018
	R	R
Revenue		
Cost of sales (XX – 300)	XXX	XXX
Gross profit	(X)	(X)
Other income	XX	XX
Other expenses	X	X
Profit before tax	(X)	(X)
	XX	XX

Notes for the year ended 31 December 2019

	2019	2018
	R	R
Note 10: Profit before tax		
Profit before taxation is stated after taking into account the following separately disclosable items		
Income		
Reversal of previous write-down of inventory	300	

3.8.5 Disclosure

The financial statements shall disclose the following (IAS 2, par 36):
- The inventory amount recognised as an expense in the financial period
- The write-down of inventory recognised as an expense in the financial period
- The reversal of write-down of inventory that is recognised as a decrease in the amount of inventory recognised as an expense in the financial period.

3.9 SUMMARY

The chapter commenced with a fundamental understanding of previous knowledge on inventory relative to the different cost formulas, and inventory movements from the perpetual and periodic inventory system perspective. Thereafter, the chapter discussed conversion costs and the importance of proper cost allocation in a manufacturing concern. In addition, there was a detailed explanation and focus on the allocation of fixed costs linked to the measuring of inventory. Lastly, the chapter discussed the most appropriate way to account for the valuation of inventory at the end of the period and its impact on the financial statements.

EXERCISES

Exercise 3.1

1. What are the four categories of inventory with which you are familiar?
2. Which of the above categories of inventory would you expect to find in a service entity, a trading entity and a manufacturing entity, respectively?
3. A second-hand car dealer purchased a vehicle for the purpose of selling it at a profit.
   a) Can the car be classified as an asset?
   b) Will this car be regarded as a current or non-current asset? Why?
   c) What if this business was an insurance company and the car was given to one of its salespeople to visit clients? How would this car then be classified, as a current asset or a non-current asset?
   d) Which fact did you use to decide whether it was a current or non-current asset?

Exercise 3.2

A business provides the following information for its January 2019 month of trading:
- There was trading inventory to the value of R5 000 at the beginning of the month.
- Trading inventory purchased for cash amounted to R12 000 for the month.
- Sales, all for cash, amounted to R20 000 (cost price of the goods was R10 500).
- At 31 January 2019, a physical stock take revealed that the value of trading inventory on hand was R7 000.

REQUIRED:

1. Show the journal entries to record the above transactions using each of the following (ignore VAT):
   a) The perpetual inventory system
   b) The periodic inventory system
2. What are the differences between the results produced?

Exercise 3.3

1. Thulani Mbhense is planning on buying a pack of 10 new USB memory sticks for R500 to sell to students at a school in Kwa-Mashu, Natal. If there is a 20% mark-up on cost price, at what price will each USB stick be sold?
   a) If Thulani bought 5 boxes of USB sticks and sold each stick at the planned selling price, what is the gross profit percentage of cost?
   b) What is the gross profit percentage of selling price?
   c) Why is there a difference between the gross profit percentage on cost price and the gross profit percentage on selling price?
   d) Is there a difference between the concepts 'mark-up' and 'gross profit'?
2. If a pair of denim jeans is advertised for R171 (inclusive of VAT at 15%), could you calculate the amount of VAT included in the R171? If the shop selling the jeans has a policy to mark up all jeans at cost plus 50%, could you calculate the cost of the jeans to the shop?

Exercise 3.4 Akona Jewellers

Akona Jewellers, a business specialising in imitation jewellery consisting of silver rings, gold-plated earrings and copper bangles, provides the following information about silver rings for the month of January 2019:
- 1 Jan purchased 100 silver rings @ R1,00 each.
- 5 Jan purchased 200 silver rings @ R1,30 each.
- 20 Jan sold 150 silver rings @ selling price R1,50 each.

REQUIRED:

1. Calculate the value of closing inventory of silver rings using the first-in, first-out basis.
2. Calculate the value of closing inventory of silver rings using the weighted average cost basis.
3. Is there a difference in the value of closing inventory of silver rings?
4. Will the difference in value have any impact on the trading results?

Exercise 3.5

You are supplied with the following information for a newly established manufacturing entity:

Budgeted production	1 000 units
Actual production	500 units
Budgeted fixed non-manufacturing overheads	R1 000
Budgeted fixed manufacturing overheads	R40 000
Prime costs per unit	R12 per unit

REQUIRED:

1. Calculate the budgeted fixed application rate at the beginning of the year.
2. Calculate the actual fixed application rate at the end of the year.
3. Post to the general ledger account.

Exercise 3.6

You are supplied with the following information for a newly established manufacturing entity:

Budgeted production	1 000 units
Actual production	1 500 units
Budgeted fixed non-manufacturing overheads	R1 000
Budgeted fixed manufacturing overheads	R40 000
Prime costs per unit	R12 per unit

REQUIRED:

1. Calculate the budgeted fixed overhead application rate at the beginning of the year.
2. Calculate the actual fixed overhead application rate at the end of the year.
3. Post to the ledger accounts.

Exercise 3.7 Ntuli & RudraDutt Papers Ltd

Ntuli & RudraDutt Papers Ltd is an SME manufacturing business in its first year of operation in Cape Town. The company specialises in the manufacturing of plastic screen covers for laptops and is the supplier to most of the South African and sub-Saharan markets. The company plans on manufacturing mobile plastic parts in the near future since the current product might become obsolete due to newer laptop screen cover technologies in the region.

The accountant has reviewed the inventory at the end of the year being 28 February 2019 and there is 1 000 units of finished goods of this product on hand. It should be noted that these 1 000 units of finished goods on hand at the end of the year were sold for an amount of R7 000 after year end but before approval of the financial statements for 28 February 2019.

The production for the company's year of operation is as follows:

	UNITS
Budgeted sales	20 000
Budgeted production	40 000
Actual production	25 000
Actual sales	24 500

It could be assumed that:

- the cost of finished goods was R5 000
- the company had work in progress on hand at the end of the year with a cost of R300 000
- the fixed manufacturing overhead or cost account had an amount of R40 000
- the work in progress required another R15 000 in costs to be incurred in order to be completed
- the company plans to complete the work in progress and sell it at a mark-up of 20% on cost with the cost to sell estimated at R65 000.

REQUIRED:

1. Calculate the value of inventory and any possible write-down of inventory for each of the following for the year ended 28 February 2019:
   a) Work in progress
   b) Finished goods.
2. Provide the journal entries for the year ended 28 February 2019.

Exercise 3.8 SABELO & RAM Interior Ltd

Sabelo & Ram Interiors Ltd is a manufacturing business in Phoenix Industrial Park, Durban, KwaZulu-Natal. It is a BEE compliant company that specialises in the manufacturing of kitchen cupboards and granite tops for the kitchen sector. The owners are unsure of the best way to value inventory at year end, hence have requested advice and guidance from you as the new accountant regarding the valuation in accordance with International Financial Reporting Standards (IFRS).

Sabelo & Ram Interiors Ltd have given you the following information relative to finished goods at 30 June 2019:

Inventory items	Net realisable value	Cost price
	R	R
	2019	2019
KITCHEN CUPBOARDS		
Top cupboards	70 000	62 000
Bottom cupboards	60 000	70 000
GRANITE TOPS		
Capricorn granite	114 000	109 000
Emerald pearl granite	80 000	72 000

REQUIRED:

1. Calculate the values at which inventory can be measured for the following:
   a) Top cupboard
   b) Bottom cupboard
   c) Capricorn granite
   d) Emerald pearl granite

2. Calculate any possible write-down of inventory items.

3. Disclose the value of inventory in the following notes to the financial statements of Sabelo & Ram Interior Ltd for the year ended 30 June 2019:
   a) Accounting policy for inventories
   b) Inventories
   c) Profit before tax

(*It should be noted that raw materials are valued on the weighted average cost basis and amounted to R35 500. There is no work in progress.*)

Exercise 3.9 Nzimande (Pty) Ltd

Nzimande (Pty) Ltd is a plastics factory in Gauteng near Midrand that started operations on the 1 March 2019 with a financial year ending 31 December 2019. The business budgeted the following fixed costs for the period:

	R
Plant and equipment depreciation (40% on manufacturing; 60% administrative office equipment)	400 000
Wages (60% for factory; 40% for administrative)	200 000
Factory manager's salary per annum	200 000

A new supervisor, Mr Bonga Siyabonga, was employed in the company and earned a salary of R35 500 per annum. The supervisor was directly involved in administrative duties, with little of his time spent in the plastics factory. The company allocates fixed overheads based on units produced.

Nzimande Ltd was in its first year (10 months) of operation at year end and the following information relates to the allocation of budgeted and actual costs:

	Units
Budgeted production for the year	40 000
Budgeted sales for the year	30 000
Actual production for the year	24 000
Actual sales for the year	20 000

REQUIRED:

1. Calculate the fixed manufacturing cost for the year ended 31 December 2019.
2. Calculate the budgeted fixed application rate to be used when valuing inventories at year end.
3. Prepare the following ledger entries for the year end 31 December 2019:
   a) Fixed manufacturing cost suspense account
   b) Inventories account
   c) Fixed overhead expense account.

Exercise 3.10 Dlomo and Dlamini Ltd

Dlomo and Dlamini Ltd is a company in Phoenix Industrial Park, KwaZulu-Natal, Durban. The company supplies parts to many retail stores in the surrounding area for the repair of dishwashing machines and fridges. The company financial statements were checked on 30 June 2019 and the following inventory items were noted to be on hand:

Product type	Net realisable value per unit	Units on hand	Cost per unit
	R	Unit	R
Water pipes	100,50	250	82,50
Compressors	123,00	1 800	135,00
DW motors	105,00	750	127,50
F motors	120,00	2 200	96,00
Timers	202,50	1 000	225,00

REQUIRED:

1. Calculate the total value of closing inventories that would appear on the statement of financial position of Dlomo and Dlamini Ltd at 30 June 2019.
2. Calculate any write-down of inventory for product type.
3. Provide the journal entry for the combined items that were written down.

Exercise 3.11 Siyabonga Ltd

Siyabonga Ltd is a paper manufacturing company in Limpopo in its first year of operation. Siyabonga Ltd manufactures one product of printing paper with 1 000 units of finished goods of this product on hand at 30 June 2019. The new accountant, Miss Siphesande Ntuli, is unsure of how to treat fixed overheads and has left the fixed overhead costs for the year in the fixed manufacturing cost account. She has given you the following information:

Budgeted sales	70 000 units
Budgeted production	40 000 units
Actual production	50 000 units
Actual sales	49 000 units
Fixed manufacturing overhead account	R80 000
Closing balance of finished goods	R4 500

Closing balance of labour and other conversion costs (R4 per unit)	R2 500
Closing balance of materials (R6 per unit)	R2 000

There were 1 000 units of inventory on hand at the end of the year which were sold for R7 550 after the end of the year (event after reporting period), but before approval of the financial statements for the year ended 30 June 2019.

REQUIRED:

1. Calculate the cost of finished goods.

2. Calculate any write-down/reversal of write-down of finished goods for the year ended 30 June 2019.

3. Prepare the profit before taxation note in the financial statements for the year ended 30 June 2019.

CHAPTER 4

FINANCIAL INSTRUMENTS: SHARE CAPITAL

LEARNING OUTCOMES

After studying this chapter, you should be able to:

- Define the following terms:
  - Financial instrument
  - Financial asset
  - Financial liability
  - Equity instrument.
- Differentiate between the following:
  - Ordinary shares and preference shares
  - Cumulative and non-cumulative preference shares
  - Participating and non-participating preference shares
  - Redeemable and non-redeemable preference shares.
- Understand the following changes affecting share capital:
  - Issue of ordinary shares
  - Conversion of shares
  - Rights issue
  - Share splits
  - Share consolidations
  - Capitalisation issues
  - Share buy-backs (s48) and the Solvency and liquidity test (s46).
- Understand and apply the principles in respect of redemption of preference shares.
- Understanding the principles in respect of distributions to equity holders.

PREAMBLE

Mr Mhlongo (known as Njomane) has been running his family business for 20 years. The business has grown very fast over the years and the family seeks funding for expansion purposes. Njomane spoke to a corporate lawyer who advised him about issuing shares in the company to raise more funds. The concept of issuing shares is a new one to Njomane. He has heard that there are different types of shares and they have different rights, and he is confused about which shares to issue, as he does not want the shareholders to have a share in his family business forever. His plan is to repay some of them in the future when the business is able to fund itself. He was referred to you, as an accountant, for advice.

4.1 INTRODUCTION

The aim of this chapter is to explain principles affecting the share capital of a company, which are equity instruments. Equity instruments are classified as financial instruments, hence the chapter will firstly discuss what a financial instrument is according to IFRS 32 *Financial instruments – presentation*. A financial instrument is a contract that gives rise to a financial asset of one entity and a financial liability or equity instrument of another entity.

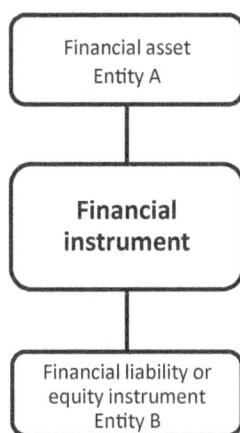

Figure 4.1: Definition of a financial instrument

Source: Adapted from IFRS 32 Financial instruments – presentation

For example, if entity A issues shares to entity B, entity A will recognise equity in its books and entity B will recognise investment. The transaction will have resulted in a financial asset for entity B and equity for entity B, therefore it is a financial instrument.

At initial recognition, financial instruments are classified as a financial asset, financial liability or equity instrument. The classification is based on the substance of the transaction, considering the stipulations in the contractual arrangement and not the legal form.

This chapter provides more insight into the different types of equity instrument and financial liability that arise from issuing of shares.

4.2 DEFINITIONS (IAS 32, par 11)

A **financial asset** is any asset that is:
- Cash
- An equity instrument of another entity (eg Investment in shares)
- A contractual right
  - to receive cash or another financial asset from another entity (eg Trade receivables); or
  - to exchange financial assets or financial liabilities with another entity under conditions that are potentially favourable to the entity (eg Purchased call option); or
- A contract that will or may be settled in the entity's own equity instruments and is:
  - a non-derivative for which the entity is or may be obliged to receive a variable number of the entity's own equity instruments
  - a derivative that will or may be settled other than by the exchange of a fixed amount of cash or another financial asset for a fixed number of the entity's own equity instruments. For this purpose, the entity's own equity instruments do not include instruments that are themselves contracts for the future receipt or delivery of the entity's own equity instruments
  - puttable instruments classified as equity or certain liabilities arising on liquidation classified by IAS 32 as equity instruments

Financial liability is any liability that is:
- A contractual obligation:
  - to deliver cash or another financial asset to another entity (eg Trade payables); or
  - to exchange financial assets or financial liabilities with another entity under conditions that are potentially unfavourable to the entity (eg A written put option); or
- A contract that will or may be settled in the entity's own equity instruments and is
  - a non-derivative for which the entity is or may be obliged to deliver a variable number of the entity's own equity instruments; or
  - a derivative that will or may be settled other than by the exchange of a fixed amount of cash or another financial asset for a fixed number of the entity's own equity instruments.

Equity instrument is any contract that evidences a residual interest in the assets of an entity after deducting all of its liabilities. Equity can also be described as the capital contributions made by the owners (or shareholders) of the business **plus** the gains and losses that are retained in the business.

4.3 DIFFERENT TYPES OF SHARES

When a company needs funds for expansion in the business, it can obtain them from either equity or liability. The company can either issue new equity instruments in the form of shares or take on a financial liability in the form of a debt instrument. According to the new Companies Act 71 of 2008 (hereafter referred to as the 'Companies Act'), shares can be divided into two categories, namely ordinary shares and preference shares. The classes of shares and the number of shares of each class that a company is authorised to issue must be stated in the memorandum of incorporation (MOI).

4.3.1 Ordinary shares

Ordinary shares are the type of shares that give the holders voting powers. The holders of these shares receive distributions in the form of a dividend, decided upon by the board of directors. The dividend is not fixed and the company has no obligation to distribute the dividend or to repay the capital, therefore the shares are always classified as equity.

Par value and no-par value shares

Par value shares have a standard nominal rand value at which the company can issue the shares, whereas the no-par value shares have no rand value attached to them and the directors can decide the price at which they can issue the shares. Although the directors can decide on the price, the Companies Act requires that if the company is issuing no-par value shares, the price that is determined by the directors should be an adequate consideration. The issue of no-par value shares is credited to a share capital account and forms part of the company's equity.

According to the Companies Act, companies that are registering for the first time on or after May 2011 can no longer have par value shares, only no-par value shares. However, companies that are already registered can keep the par value shares or pass a special resolution to convert those shares into no-par value shares.

4.3.2 Preference shares

Preference shares are the type of shares that give their holders preference over ordinary shareholders in relation to distribution of profits or the returns on capital upon the winding up of the company. Preference shareholders are usually entitled to a fixed dividend and their dividend has to be paid before the ordinary shareholders can be entitled to a dividend. There are different types of preference shares and this has an impact on whether the preference shares are classified as equity or liability.

Redeemable and non-redeemable preference shares

According to the Companies Act, shares can be issued with an aim to redeem them in the future and this must be authorised by the MOI. If preference shares are non-redeemable, they are classified as equity. If preference shares are classified as redeemable at the option of the company, they are also classified as equity as the company does not have an obligation to redeem the shares. However, if the preference shares are redeemable at the option of the shareholder, the company has an obligation to redeem, therefore they are classified as a liability.

Cumulative and non-cumulative preference shares

The difference between cumulative and non-cumulative preference shares is the treatment of dividends and the claim that the holders have towards these dividends. Holders of cumulative preference shares have a claim towards the fixed preference dividend. The dividend accrues to them whether the entity is able to pay it or not; it accumulates until such time that the entity is able to pay.

The holders of non-cumulative preference shares do not have a claim towards the dividend; if the entity is unable to pay the fixed dividend, the holders forfeit it as it does not accumulate.

Participating and non-participating preference shares

The difference between participating and non-participating preference shares lies in the right to participate in the company's profit after the fixed dividends have been paid to shareholders. Non-participating preference shareholders are only entitled to their fixed dividend and after the dividend has been paid, they cannot participate in the profits of the company. Participating preference shareholders can participate in the profits of the company after the fixed dividend has been paid.

Convertible preference shares

Convertible preference shares are shares that give the holders the option to convert them into ordinary shares at a specified time.

4.4 DISTRIBUTIONS TO EQUITY HOLDERS

Shareholders are entitled to receive distributions (dividends) declared by the company and in a case where the company is liquidated, they are entitled to their share of the net assets. Before a company makes distributions to its shareholders, the requirements of section 46 of the Companies Act must be satisfied. Section 46 stipulates that no distribution should be made to shareholders unless:

- there is a legal obligation or court order to do so;
- the board has authorised the distribution by resolution;
- the solvency and liquidity test will be met afterwards; and
- the board has acknowledged, by resolution, that it has applied the solvency/liquidity test.

In terms of liquidity: the company will be able to settle their debts as they become due in the ordinary course of business for a period of 12 months after the test/distribution. In terms of solvency: the assets of the company (fairly valued) equal or exceed the liabilities (fairly valued).

The dividends can be in the form of cash, assets or shares. All distributions to owners of equity should be deducted from the equity of the company.

4.4.1 Cash dividend

When an entity declares a cash dividend, a liability account should be created until such a time that the dividend is paid. The journal entry to record the cash dividend is as follows:

Dr Dividends declared (SOCE)
    Cr   Shareholders for dividend FOFP *(liability)*

EXAMPLE 4.1

Company A had 15 000 issued ordinary shares on 1 January 2018. On 15 December 2018, the company declared a cash dividend of 20 cents per share to all its existing shareholders. The dividend was paid on 31 December 2018.

REQUIRED:

Prepare the journal entries to account for the dividends in the books of company A for the reporting period ended 31 December 2018.

EXAMPLE 4.1 Solution

	R	R
15 December 2018		
Cr Dividends declared: ordinary shares SOCE	3 000	
Dr Shareholders for dividend SOFP *(liability)*		3 000
Being declaration of dividend		
Note: The dividend is debited directly to the retained earnings in the statement of changes in equity. The liability will be reversed when the cash is paid.		
31 December 2018		
Cr Shareholders for dividend SOFP *(liability)*	3 000	
Dr Bank SOFP		3 000
Being cash payment of dividend		

4.4.2 Capitalisation issue

Capitalisation issue is a way of converting reserves into equity. As an alternative to the payment of cash dividends, some companies offer to distribute the dividend in the form of the issue of new shares to the shareholders. Shareholders are usually given a choice of receiving the full dividend in cash, or a portion or the whole of the dividend in the form of new shares.

EXAMPLE 4.2

Company A had a share capital of R3 million on 1 January 2018. The share capital consisted of 1 500 000 ordinary shares. The retained earnings on 31 December 2017 amounted to R1 200 000. On 31 March 2018, the company's directors resolved to make a capitalisation issue to all existing ordinary shareholders. The company will give each shareholder one share for every five shares held in the company. The shares were issued on 30 April 2018. The retained earnings opening balance was R1 200 000 on 1 January 2018. Profit after tax for the current year amounted to R1 800 000.

REQUIRED:

Prepare the Journal entries to account for the capitalisation issue in the books of company A for the reporting period ended 31 December 2018.

EXAMPLE 4.2 Solution

	R	R
31 March 2018		
Dr Retained earnings SOCE	600 000	
Cr Capitalisation reserve SOCE		600 000
*(1 500 000/5 = 300 000 * 2)*		
30 April 2018		
Dr Capitalisation reserve SOCE	600 000	
Cr Share capital SOCE		600 000

Effect on the statement of changes in equity

	Share capital	Retained earnings	Total
Opening balance	3 000 000	1 200 000	4 200 000
Total comprehensive income		1 800 000	1 800 000
Capitalisation issue	600 000	(600 000)	0
Dividends	0	0	0
Closing balance	3 600 000	2 400 000	6 000 000

4.5 CHANGES TO SHARE CAPITAL

4.5.1 Issue of ordinary shares

A company can issue new shares during a reporting period should a need for funds arise and if it has enough authorised share capital. Before a company can issue new shares, all the requirements of the Companies Act regarding specific rights and obligations associated with the different types of share must be met. The shares will be classified as an equity instrument and will be measured at the fair value of the cash or other resources received or receivable net of direct costs of issuing the equity instruments as follows:

Application date (before issue)

Once the applications for the shares are opened, all the cash received will be debited to the bank account and a temporary liability account will be created. The temporary account is called the 'application and allotment account'. The journal entry will be as follows:

Dr Bank   xxx
    Cr Application and allotment   xxx

Proceeds received from applicants for new shares

Issue date
Once the shares have been issued, this account should be cleared to zero and the amount should be allocated to the share capital account as follows:

Dr Application and allotment account   xxx
    Cr Share capital   xxx

Allocation of new shares to applicants

Share issue costs
According to the Companies Act, all share issue costs (directly attributable to the share issue, for example legal fees, accounting fees, underwriting costs, printing, etc) should be netted off against the consideration received when the shares are issued. The share capital account should be debited accordingly. All other costs (eg preliminary costs which were incurred upon the formation of the company) are expensed in profit or loss.

Dr Share capital   xxx
    Cr Bank/payable   xxx

Over-subscription
When shares are oversubscribed, the company has two options. It can choose either to accept the full subscription or to refund the oversubscription. However, the authorised share capital should be taken into account when choosing the first option. Should the subscription be in excess of its authorised share capital for that specific class of shares, the company may make a recommendation to the board for the share capital to be increased. The company may also decide to do a refund of the oversubscribed shares.

EXAMPLE 4.3
On 1 February 2018, company A resolved to offer 100 000 shares to the public at R2 per share; applications for these shares were opened on the same date. By 31 March 2018, which was the closing date for applications, R240 000 had been received from the applicants. The company did not need the funds so it decided to refund the oversubscription. The shares were allotted (issued) on 1 April 2018.

REQUIRED:
Prepare the journal entries to account for the share issue in the books of company A for the reporting period ended 31 December 2018.

EXAMPLE 4.3 Solution

	R	R
Before shares are issued		
31 March 2018		
Dr Bank SOFP	240 000	
Cr Application and allotment SOFP		240 000
Being consideration received from applicants		
1 April 2018		
Dr Application and allotment SOFP	240 000	
Cr Share capital SOCE		200 000
Cr Bank SOFP		40 000
Being the allotment of shares and refund of oversubscription of shares on issue date		

EXAMPLE 4.4

On 1 February 2018, company A resolved to offer 100 000 shares to the public at R2 per share; applications for these shares were opened on the same date. By 31 March 2018, which was the closing date for applications, R240 000 had been received from the applicants. The company needed the funds from the oversubscription so it decided to accept all the applications. The shares were allotted (issued) on 1 April 2018. The company has enough authorised share capital to cover the oversubscription.

REQUIRED:

Prepare the journal entries to account for the share issue in the books of company A for the reporting period ended 31 December 2018.

EXAMPLE 4.4 Solution

	R	R
Before shares are issued		
31 March 2018		
Dr Bank SOFP	240 000	
Cr Application and allotment SOFP		240 000
Being consideration received from applicants		
01 April 2018		
Dr Application and allotment SOFP	240 000	
Cr Share capital SOCE		240 000
Being the allotment of shares on issue date		

Underwriters

Before a company issues shares, it can enter into an agreement with underwriters to buy all the shares which are not subscribed for. Companies are able to underwrite a share issue with a group of underwriters, who usually charge a set percentage of the value of all the shares under offer. Underwriters are considered to be a form of insurance should the shares be undersubscribed; the underwriters are obliged in terms of their agreement to purchase any shares not applied for at the closing date.

EXAMPLE 4.5

On 1 February 2018, company A resolved to offer 100 000 shares to the public at R2 per share, applications for these shares were opened on the same date. By 31 March 2018, which was the closing date for applications, R180 000 had been received from the applicants. The shares were allotted (issued) on 1 April 2018. The share offer was underwritten at a cost of 5%, paid in cash on issue date, and the underwriters bought all the remaining shares. The company incurred other share issue costs of R2 000 which were also paid in cash.

REQUIRED:

Prepare the journal entries to account for the share issue in the books of company A for the reporting period ended 31 December 2018.

EXAMPLE 4.5 Solution

	R	R
Before shares are issued		
31 March 2018		
Dr Bank SOFP	200 000	
Cr Application and allotment SOFP		180 000
Cr Application and allotment SOFP *(underwriters)*		20 000
Being consideration received from applicants		
01 April 2018		
Dr Application and allotment SOFP *(underwriters)*	20 000	
Dr Application and allotment SOFP	180 000	
Cr Share capital SOCE		200 000
Being the allotment of shares on issue date		
Dr Share capital *(underwriters' commission)*	10 000	
Dr Share capital *(share issue costs)*	2 000	
Cr Bank SOFP		12 000
Being the recognition of share issue costs		

4.5.2 Rights issue

When a company issues shares, it can decide to give preferential rights to its existing shareholders to subscribe to the shares first at a specific price, lower than the market price, within a specified period. If a shareholder chooses not to buy the shares, they can sell the right to somebody else. The journal to account for a rights issue is the same as the normal issuing of shares.

EXAMPLE 4.6

On 1 June 2018, the directors of company A resolved to offer a rights issue of two new ordinary shares for every five ordinary shares held, at R5 per share. The company had 200 000 ordinary shares at R6 per share in issue on that date. The current market price immediately before this issue was R10 per share. All the shareholders had accepted the offer by the last day of the offer, which was 30 June, and the shares were issued on the same date.

REQUIRED:

Prepare the journal entries to account for the rights issue in the books of company A for the reporting period ended 31 December 2018.

EXAMPLE 4.6 Solution

	R	R
30 June 2018		
Dr Bank SOFP	400 000	
Cr Share capital SOCE		400 000
Rights issue to ordinary shares		
*(200 000/5 * 2 = 80 000 shares)*		
*(80 000 * 5)*		

4.5.3 Share splits

With a share split, a company increases the number of shares by subdividing the existing shares and proportionately decreasing the value per share. No cash or other asset is transferred to the company; there is no change in the total owner's equity and in the share capital account. Therefore, no journal entry is required.

EXAMPLE 4.7

Company A has 100 000 ordinary shares originally issued at R20 per share. The directors of the company decide to split the shares into 200 000 shares of R10 each.

The value of share capital *before* the split is 100 000 × R20 = R2 000 000

The value of share capital *after* the split is 200 000 × R10 = R2 000 000

No journal entry will be processed as the transaction only affects the number of shares and the price per share, which increases from 100 000 to 200 000; the price per share decreasesd from R20 to R10. There is no change in the value of share capital, which remains as R2 000 000. After a share split, the number of shares will be more, the share price will be less, and the share capital will remain the same.

Although the effect of the share split will not necessarily be noticeable on the company's statement of changes in equity itself, the share split must still be disclosed in the notes to the financial statements in order to explain the change in the number of shares, as this change will have an impact on future dividends.

4.5.4 Share consolidations

A share consolidation is the opposite of a share split as per paragraph 4.5.3. A share consolidation happens when a company reduces the number of shares to increase the price per share. This usually happens when an entity thinks their share price is too low. Just like with a share split, there is no journal entry required for this transaction as there is no change in the share capital of the company.

EXAMPLE 4.8

Company A has 100 000 ordinary shares originally issued at R20 per share. The directors of the company decide to consolidate the shares into 50 000 shares of R40 each.

The value of share capital *before* the share consolidation is 100 000 × R20 = R2 000 000

The value of share capital *after* the split is 50 000 × R40 = R2 000 000

No journal entry will be processed as the only change is number of shares, which decreases from 100 000 to 50 000; there is no change in the value of share capital, which remains as R2 000 000. After a share consolidation, the number of shares will be less, the share price will be more, and the share capital will remain the same.

A share consolidation should be disclosed in the notes to the financial statements.

4.5.5 Share buy-backs (share repurchase) (s85)

A company can buy back its own shares from the market to reduce its share capital. The share buy-back should be done according to the provisions of the Companies Act. A company can undertake a share buy-back for various reasons such as the following:
* Improving the company's capital structure and increasing shareholder value
* Improving the company's financial ratios such as return on assets (ROA) and return on equity (ROE)
* the company feeling that its share price has been reduced unfairly by the market.

Before a company can buy back its own shares, it must satisfy the requirements of s46 and s48 of the Companies Act, and the memorandum of incorporation must allow such a buy back. Section 48 of the Companies Act stipulates as follows:
* After the buy-back, there must be shares in existence other than redeemable or convertible shares.
* A share buy-back must also satisfy the requirements of s46 of the Companies Act (discussed in par 4.5 as part of distributions).

After the share buy-back, all the shares that have been bought back must be cancelled and added back to the authorised number of shares. This means that the share capital account must be reduced by the value of the shares bought back.

EXAMPLE 4.9

On 15 January 2018, company A decided to buy back 50 000 of its own shares for R2,50 each. As of 1 January 2018, the company had 150 000 issued ordinary shares, which were initially issued at R2 each. Assume that all the requirements for a share buy-back were met.

REQUIRED:

Prepare the journal entries to account for the share buy back in the books of company A for the reporting period ended 31 December 2018. *Show the effect of the share buy back on the Statement of changes in equity.*

EXAMPLE 4.9 Solution

	R	R
15 January 2018		
Dr Share capital SOCE	100 000	
Dr Retained earnings SOCE	25 000	
Cr Bank SOFP		125 000
Share buy-back of 50 000 shares at R2,50		

The effect on the statement of changes in equity

	Class A share capital R	Retained earnings R	Total R
Balance at 1 January 2018	300 000	xxx	xxx
Share buy-back	(100 000)	(25 000)	(125 000)
Total comprehensive income		xxx	xxx
Dividends	xxx	xxx	xxx
Balance at 31 December 2018	200 000	xxx	xxx

4.5.6 Redemption of preference shares

Under the Companies Act, the redemption of preference shares is classified as a distribution to shareholders, hence the s46 requirements must be met before the shares can be redeemed. Upon the redemption of the shares, the company must pay the holders all the distributions (dividends) that have accrued to them.

Redemption at a nominal amount

When preference shares are redeemed at a nominal amount, it means they are redeemed at the value they were initially issued for, ie their nominal value.

EXAMPLE 4.10

On 30 September 2018, company A's directors resolved to redeem the preference shares, which were classified as equity. On that date, the company had 50 000 preference shares in issue. The preference shares were originally bought at R5 per share and were to be redeemed at their nominal value of R5 per share. The shares were redeemed on 30 November 2018.

REQUIRED:

Prepare the journal entries to account for the redemption of preference shares in the books of company A for the reporting period ended 31 December 2018.

EXAMPLE 4.10 Solution

	R	R
30 September 2018		
Dr Redeemable preference share capital SOCE	250 000	
Cr Preference shareholders SOFP*(liability)*		250 000
Being the obligation to redeem the preference shares		
30 November 2018		
Dr Preference shareholders SOFP*(liability)*	250 000	
Cr Bank SOFP		250 000
Being payment to preference shareholders		

Redemption at a discount

When preference shares are redeemed at a discount, it means they are redeemed at a value lower than their nominal value.

EXAMPLE 4.11

On 30 September 2018, company A's directors resolved to redeem the preference shares, which were classified as equity. On that date, the company had 50 000 preference shares in issue. The preference shares were originally bought at R5 per share and were to be redeemed at R3 per share. The shares were redeemed on 30 November 2018.

REQUIRED:

Prepare the journal entries to account for the redemption of preference shares in the books of company A for the reporting period ended 31 December 2018.

EXAMPLE 4.11 Solution

	R	R
30 September 2018		
Dr Redeemable preference share capital SOCE	250 000	
Cr Retained earnings SOCE		100 000
Cr Preference shareholders SOFP*(liability)*		150 000
Being the obligation to redeem the preference shares		
30 November 2018		
Dr Preference shareholders SOFP*(liability)*	150 000	
Cr Bank SOFP		150 000
Being payment to preference shareholders		

Redemption at a premium

When preference shares are redeemed at a premium, it means they are redeemed at a value higher than their nominal value.

EXAMPLE 4.12

On 30 September 2018, company A's directors resolved to redeem the preference shares, which were classified as equity. On that date, the company had 50 000 preference shares in issue. The preference shares were originally bought at R5 per share and were to be redeemed at R7 per share. The shares were redeemed on 30 November 2018.

REQUIRED:

Prepare the journal entries to account for the redemption of preference shares in the books of company A for the reporting period ended 31 December 2018.

EXAMPLE 4.12 Solution

	R	R
30 September 2018		
Dr Redeemable preference share capital SOCE	250 000	
Dr Retained earnings SOCE	100 000	
Cr Preference shareholders SOFP*(liability)*		350 000
Being the obligation to redeem the preference shares		
30 November 2018		
Dr Preference shareholders SOFP*(Liability)*	350 000	
Cr Bank SOFP		350 000
Being payment to preference shareholders		

4.5.7 Financing the redemption of preference shares

The redemption of preference shares can be funded through various sources such as new debt instruments or equity instruments. For example, a company can obtain a loan from the bank to finance the redemption.

EXAMPLE 4.13

On 31 December 2018, the directors of company A decided to redeem all the preference shares at a premium of R1,20 per share. The company had 50 000, 5% issued redeemable preference shares on that date. The shares were issued at R4 per share. The redemption would be financed through:
- the issue of 25 000 ordinary shares at R4 per share
- a 10% short term loan with ZBD Bank for the balance.

Dividends on preference shares for the year which were declared on 31 December 2018 are still unpaid.

REQUIRED:

Prepare the journal entries to account for the redemption of preference shares in the books of company A for the reporting period ended 31 December 2018.

EXAMPLE 4.13 Solution

	R	R
31 December 2018		
Dr 5% redeemable preference share capital SOCE	200 000	
Dr Retained earnings SOCE (premium)	60 000	
Dr Retained earnings SOCE (dividends)	10 000	
Cr Preference shareholders SOFP		270 000
Being the obligation to redeem the preference shares		
Dr Bank SOFP	270 000	
Cr Share capital: ordinary shares SOCE		100 000
Cr Loan from ZBD bank SOFP		170 000
Being the issue of ordinary shares and obtaining of loan		

Calculations

How much is owed?	R
Shares (50 000 × R4)	200 000
Premium (50 000 × 1,20 cents)	60 000
Dividends (50 000 × R4 × 5%)	10 000
	270 000
Finance plan (funds)	
Ordinary shares (25 000 × R4)	100 000
10% short-term loan	170 000
	270 000

4.6 SUMMARY

The focus of this chapter was mainly on explaining principles relating to the share capital of a company. The chapter also provided the definition of a financial instrument in order to give some background on equity instruments. Changes in share capital and the redemption of preference shares which were treated as equity were discussed in detail.

EXERCISES

Exercise 4.1 Luna Ltd

Luna Ltd has 500 000 ordinary authorised shares. The company was founded on 1 January 2017. The founders subscribed for 300 000 ordinary shares at R3 each. On 1 June 2018, Luna Ltd offered a further 200 000 of its authorised ordinary shares to the public, payable in full on application, at R3,50 per share. Applications closed on 31 July at which time applications totalling R875 000 had been received. The shares were allotted on 5 August 2018.

On 31 October 2018, Luna Ltd declared a dividend of 10 cents per share to the ordinary shareholders. The dividends were paid on 29 February 2019.

The following information was provided:

	2018	2017
	R	R
Retained earnings		80 000
Profit for the year	65 000	

REQUIRED:

1. State whether the following are true or false:
   a) Share issue costs are netted off against the consideration received (share capital account) when shares are issued.
   b) If redeemable preference shares are redeemable at the option of the shareholder, they are classified as liabilities.
2. Prepare the journal entries to account for the share issue and the dividends in the books of Luna Ltd for the reporting period ended 31 December 2018.
3. Prepare the statement of changes in equity for the reporting period ended 31 December 2018.

Exercise 4.2 Monte Ltd

Monte Ltd has 1 000 000 authorised ordinary shares. The company was founded on 1 July 2017. On that date the shareholders who started the company subscribed for 500 000 ordinary shares at R3 each. Monte Ltd also have 200 000 5% issued preference shares which were classified as redeemable at R2 per share. The company has a 30 June year end.

They also offered a further 200 000 authorised ordinary shares to the public, payable in full on application, at R3,50 per share. The company received full subscription for these shares and they were allotted on 01 May 2019.

On 25 May 2019, Monte Ltd declared a dividend of 25 cents per share to ordinary shareholders. The dividends were paid on 30 August 2019.

On 31 May 2019, the directors resolved to redeem the preference shares at a premium of R1,50 per share. The preference dividend for the current year has been declared and paid.

Assume that the retained earnings on 1 July 2018 were R800 000 and that the net profit before tax for the year ended 30 June 2019 was R600 000, with tax amounting to R120 000.

REQUIRED:

1. Provide the necessary journal entries in order to account for the redemption of preference shares.

   Prepare the statement of changes in equity for Monte Ltd for the year ended 30 June 2019.

Exercise 4.3 Lusaka Ltd

Lusaka Ltd had an authorised share capital of 25 000 ordinary shares and 10 000 issued shares issued for a total value of R150 000 as of 1 January 2019.

On 1 January 2019, the entity decided to offer 10 000 ordinary shares to the public at a cost of R10 per share.

The share offer closed on 23 January 2019, by which time applications had been received for 9 500 shares. The share offer was underwritten at a cost of 5% and share issue expenses amounted to R3 000. The shares were issued on 30 March 2019. The underwriter's commission and the share issue were paid for in cash.

Retained earnings amounted to R300 000 as of 1 January 2019 and the profit after tax amounted to R200 000 on 31 December 2019. The company has a reporting period ending 31 December 2019.

REQUIRED:

1. State whether the following are true or false:
   a) Share capital is the capital contributed by the shareholders to a company, which is then used as part of the financial resources to generate profits.
   b) The company must ensure that it meets the liquidity and solvency test when shares are redeemed.
   c) Share issue costs are expensed in profit or loss.
   d) An entity can never distribute assets other than cash as dividends to its shareholders.

2. Prepare the journal entries to record the share issue in the books of Lusaka Ltd.

3. Prepare the statement of changes and equity of Lusaka Ltd for the year ended 31 December 2019.

Exercise 4.4 BWG Ltd

BWG Ltd is a retail company based in Johannesburg. The company has a reporting period ending 31 March 2019. On 1 February 2019, the company obtained a loan from ABC bank. The total amount was used to buy 10 000 redeemable preference shares from DEF Ltd at R50 per share on 1 February 2019. The shares are redeemable at the option of the company.

REQUIRED:

1. Discuss whether the above preference shares will be classified as equity or liability in the books of BWG Ltd.

2. Show the effect of the above transaction on the accounting equation in the books of BWG and DEF as follows. Include **effect**, **amount** and **account description**.

Transaction	A =	OE +	L
Example	+ 100 000 receivables	+ 100 000 sales	

Exercise 4.5 Queen Bee Ltd

The following balances were extracted from the accounting records of Queen Bee Ltd on 30 June 2018, before taking into account the transactions below:

	R
400 000 ordinary shares of no-par value	400 000
400 000 6% redeemable preference shares of no-par value	400 000
Retained earnings	200 000
Bank	220 000

Redeemable preference shares:

- The redeemable preference shares are redeemable at a premium of 25 cents per share at the option of the company.
- The directors have decided to redeem the preference shares of the company on 30 June 2018.
- The redemption of the preference shares will be financed as follows:
  - A long-term loan of R400 000 raised on 30 June 2018, repayable on 30 June 2020
  - The issue of as many ordinary shares as is necessary at an issue price of R2 a share (there are 3 million authorised shares still available for issue)
  - The directors have the power to issue the unissued authorised shares.
- Preference dividends are always declared and paid on 30 June of each year, from the bank account and not financed from the redemption. The preference dividends declared on 30 June 2018 will, together with the share issue expenses of R20 000, be paid out of currently available cash resources. No ordinary dividends were declared in 2018.
- The directors are satisfied that after redeeming the preference shares, the company will be in compliance with the requirements of the Companies Act.

REQUIRED:

Prepare the journal entries to record all the above transactions relating to the redemption of preference shares.

Exercise 4.6 Big Echo Ltd

Below is an extract from the trial balance of Big Echo Ltd as of 29 March 2019:

	Debit	Credit
	R	R
Ordinary share capital		1 000 000
10% redeemable preference share capital		240 000
Retained earnings		520 000
Bank	640 000	
Land and buildings	1 200 000	
Creditors		80 000

Additional information:

1. Authorised share capital consists of:
   - 1 200 000 ordinary shares of no-par value, R2 400 000
   - 240 000 10% redeemable preference shares of no-par value.
2. The directors decided to redeem the preference shares on 31 March 2019 at a premium of 25 cents per share.
3. The redemption will be financed through:
   - the issue of 125 000 ordinary shares at a premium of 25 cents per share, and
   - the raising of a 10% short-term loan with Zanadu Bank for the balance.
4. Dividends on preference shares for the year are still unpaid, and a dividend of 10 cents per share was declared on 31 March 2019.
5. Share issue costs associated with the new issue of shares amounted to R8 900.

REQUIRED:

1. Record the journal entries relating to the new issue and redemption of preference shares.

2. Prepare the statement of changes in equity of Big Echo Ltd after the redemption on 31 March 2019.

Exercise 4.7 New York Ltd

The following information relates to New York Ltd during the year ended 28 February 2019. Directors' resolution to approve the rights issue during the financial year: *The directors resolved to offer a rights issue of 2 new ordinary shares for every 4 ordinary shares held, at R10,50 per share.*

Additional information:

1. The company has 400 000 shares in issue, each issued at R3.

2. The current market price immediately before this issue is R18.

3. All the shareholders had accepted the offer by the last day of the offer.

REQUIRED:

Prepare the journal entry/entries relating to the transaction mentioned above for the year ended 28 February 2019.

Exercise 4.8 Parkhill Ltd

The following is an extract from the accounting records of Parkhill Ltd on 1 November 2018:

Authorised shares	R
350 000 ordinary shares of no-par value	
70 000 8% preference shares	
Issued share capital	
200 000 ordinary shares at R2 each	400 000
70 000 8% preference shares at R2 each	140 000
Retained earnings	325 000
Bank	90 000
Trade creditors	50 000
Motor vehicles	120 000

Additional information:

1. The preference shares were issued on 1 May 2014, redeemable on 30 April 2019 at a premium of 20 cents per share in accordance with the original terms of issue.
2. Preference shares are redeemable at the option of the company.
3. The board of directors decided to exercise the option and redeem the preference shares on 31 October 2019.
4. The redemption is to be financed as follows:
   - An issue of 40 000 ordinary share at a price of R2,50 each
   - The issue of 10 000 6% debentures at R3 each
   - The balance of cash from the bank account.
5. The preference shares were redeemed on 31 October 2019 at a premium of 20 cents per share.
6. The preference dividends must still be accounted for.
7. Share issue costs of R5 500 and debenture issue expenses of R3 000 were incurred and paid.
8. At year end, a capitalisation issue of one share for every four ordinary shares held was made out of retained earnings at the market price of R3 per share.
9. The directors are satisfied that company assets, fairly valued, exceed the company's liabilities and that the company will be able to pay its debts as they become due.

REQUIRED:

Prepare all journal entries relating to the information provided above for the year ended 31 October 2015.

Exercise 4.9 Peek-a-Boo Ltd

Peek-a-Boo Ltd is a company that installs security gates and bars. The financial year end is 28 February. Peek-a-Boo Ltd has been in operation for the last 10 years.

The following are extracts from the financial statements of Peek-a-Boo Ltd:

Extract from statement of changes in equity of Peek-a-Boo Ltd for the year ended 28 February 2017

	R
Equity (closing balances)	7 140 000
Ordinary share capital	1 080 000
10% preference share capital	300 000
Revaluation surplus	60 000
Retained earnings	5 700 000

Total comprehensive income earned for the year ended 28 February

	2019	2018
	R	R
Profit for the year	660 000	558 000
Other comprehensive income	30 000	0
Revaluation surplus	30 000	0
Total comprehensive income for the year	690 000	558 000

Additional information:

1. Ordinary share capital
   - Ordinary share capital issued at 1 March 2016 consisted of 1 080 000 shares of no-par value. The authorised share capital has remained unchanged at 3 000 000 since incorporation.
   - On 1 June 2017, 120 000 additional ordinary shares were issued at R2,40 each. The share issue costs for this issue amounted to R6 000 and are not taxable.
   - On 30 November 2018, the directors authorised a capitalisation issue of 1 share for every 4 shares held at the current market price of R1 each.
   - An ordinary dividend of 10 cents per share was declared on 31 January 2019. No dividend was declared for the financial year ended 28 February 2018.

2. Preference share capital
   - The preference shares are not redeemable.
   - The preference share capital issued on 1 March 2017 consisted of 60 000 shares of no-par value. All the authorised preference share capital has been issued.
   - The dividends are paid on 15 November every year.

REQUIRED:

1. List two classes of equity that a company may issue.
2. Explain any two different ways in which a company can *increase* its number of issued shares.
3. Explain the difference between share issue costs and preliminary costs.
4. Prepare the statement of changes in equity of Peek-a-Boo Ltd for the years ended 28 February 2018 and 28 February 2019.
5. Prepare the share capital note for the years ended 28 February 2018 and 28 February 2019 in the books of Peek-a-Boo Ltd.

CHAPTER 5

REVENUE FROM CONTRACTS WITH CUSTOMERS
(IFRS 15)

LEARNING OUTCOMES

After studying this chapter, you should be able to:

- Identify the overall objective and the scope of the standard on IFRS 15 *Revenue from contracts with customers*.
- Identify and define the elements of revenue.
- Recognise (understand when to record revenue earned to depict the transfer of promised goods or services to customers).
- Measure (know how to calculate the amount of revenue earned).
- Present and disclose revenue in the financial statements, including disclosure in the notes.
- Apply the IFRS 15 *Revenue from contracts with customers* principles in a calculation or discussion scenario by referring to the five-step process as set out in that standard.

PREAMBLE

Mr Mhlongo (known as Njomane) heard in passing from two business consultants' discussion that the International Accounting Standard Board (IASB) has revised the old revenue standard (IAS 18) and replaced it with a new standard on revenue (IFRS 15). It is important for Njomane, as a business owner, to understand the revised standard as it will affect how revenue will have to be recognised going forward. Therefore, Njomane comes to you for business advice.

5.1 INTRODUCTION

Revenue is the income received by a company from its sales of goods or the provision of services. It is important to note that revenue does not necessarily mean cash received. The revenue recognition principle (the accrual basis of accounting) states that revenue should be recognised and recorded when it is earned. In other words, an entity should not wait until revenue is collected to record it in their books. This is because revenue can be recorded without actually being received. Revenue represents a key figure for the users of financial statements in that it forms a major leading factor in the assessment of the financial performance for a company or business. IFRS 15 *Revenue from contracts with customers* provides a detailed set of principles and concepts regarding the recognition criteria for revenue, the measurement of revenue, and the presentation and disclosure in terms of IFRS.

The overriding principle in this new standard is that any business or company should recognise revenue to depict the transfer of promised goods or services to customers in an amount that reflects the consideration to which the entity expects to be entitled in exchange for those goods or services.

5.2 OBJECTIVE OF IFRS 15

The standard establishes principles and concepts that a business ought to apply in order to recognise and present information in the financial statements regarding the:

- nature
- amount
- timing, and
- uncertainty

of revenue and cash flows as a result of a contract with a customer.

5.3 APPLICATION OF THE STANDARD

IFRS 15 is applicable for all periods starting on **1 January 2018 or later**. IFRS 15 applies only to contracts that are between the **entity** and a **customer**.

The following are **excluded** from the provisions of IFRS 15:

- Leases (IAS 17 or IFRS 16)
- Financial instruments and other rights and obligations within the scope of IFRS 9 (IAS 39), IFRS 10, IFRS 11, IAS 27 and IAS 28
- Insurance contracts (IFRS 4)
- Non-monetary exchanges between entities within the same business to facilitate sales.

5.4 DEFINITIONS

The following terms are applicable in IFRS 15 *Revenue from contracts with customers* and the meanings are briefly explained.

A **customer** is defined as a party in a contract for the purchase of goods or services, arising from the supplier's ordinary activities, with the intention to exchange the purchase for a consideration.

A **contract** is an agreement between two or more parties, which creates enforceable rights and obligations. A contract asset is an entity's right to consideration in exchange for goods or services, which the entity has transferred to a customer when that right is subject to something other than the passage of time (eg the entity's future performance).

A **contract liability** is an entity's obligation to transfer to a customer goods or services for which the entity has received consideration (or the amount is due) from the customer.

Income is an increase in economic benefits during the accounting period in the form of inflows or enhancements of assets, or a decrease of liabilities that results in an increase in equity, other than those relating to contributions from equity participants.

A **performance obligation** is a promise in a contract with a customer to transfer either a good or a service (or a bundle of goods or services) that is distinct or a series of distinct goods or services that are substantially the same and that have the same pattern of transfer to the customer.

Revenue is income arising in the course of an entity's ordinary activities.

The **stand-alone selling price** is the price at which an entity would sell a promised good or service separately to a customer.

The **transaction price** is the amount of consideration to which an entity expects to be entitled in exchange for transferring promised goods or services to a customer, excluding amounts collected on behalf of third parties (eg VAT).

5.5 FIVE STEPS FOR REVENUE RECOGNITION

The application of the core principle in IFRS 15 is carried out in five steps:

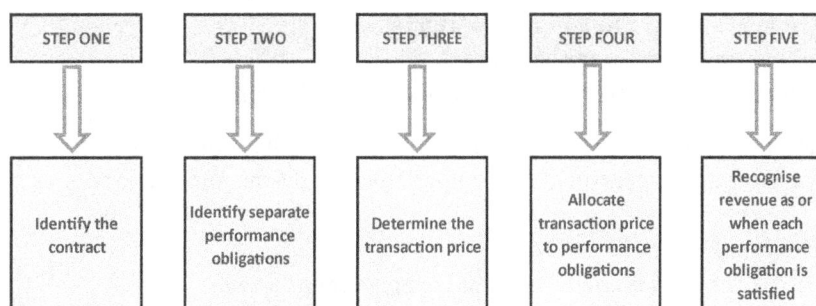

STEP ONE	STEP TWO	STEP THREE	STEP FOUR	STEP FIVE
Identify the contract	Identify separate performance obligations	Determine the transaction price	Allocate transaction price to performance obligations	Recognise revenue as or when each performance obligation is satisfied

Figure 5.1: The five-step process

5.5.1 Step 1: Identify the contract with the customer

The following five criteria should be present before applying the provisions of IFRS 15:

1. The contract should be approved by all parties in question. The approval should be in writing, orally or in accordance with other customary business practices, and the parties to it should be committed to performing their respective obligations (IFRS 15.12).

2. Each party's rights to the goods and/or services transferred are identified (IFRS 15.11).

3. The payment terms for the goods/services to be transferred can be identified.

4. The contract has a commercial substance (the contract should represent an arm's length transaction between two willing parties).

5. It is probable that an entity will collect the consideration – the entity must assess the purchaser's capability and resolution to redeem the amount payable (this encompasses evaluating whether they are financially sound).

The contract should meet all five criteria before applying the provisions of IFRS 15. If it does not meet all five criteria, a different standard that is applicable to the transaction should be used. A contract does not exist if each party to the contract exercises its unilateral enforceable right to terminate a wholly unperformed contract without compensating the other party (or parties).

A contract is wholly unperformed if both of the following criteria are met:

1. The entity has not yet transferred any promised goods or services to the customer.

2. The entity has not yet received, and is not yet entitled to receive, any consideration in exchange for promised goods or services (IFRS 15.12).

If the contractual requirements of IFRS 15 have not been met yet, but the entity has received consideration, this does not automatically mean that the consideration received is revenue, even if it is non-refundable.

Recognise consideration received as revenue only if:
- there are no remaining obligations to deliver goods and services, including substantially all of the consideration has been received, plus the consideration is non-refundable; OR
- the contract was terminated, plus consideration received is non-refundable (IFRS 15.15).

EXAMPLE 5.1 Gusheshe Ltd
Assessing the existence of a contract

Gusheshe Ltd sells new and used motor vehicles. In the agreement to sell a motor vehicle to a client, Gusheshe Ltd evaluates the certainty and substance of a contract with the customer. In the process of evaluating the contract, Gusheshe Ltd should take into account features such as the following:
- The customer's credit-worthiness by performing a credit check on the customer
- The customer's obligation and accountability to the contract, which can be identified by the deposit paid up-front by the customer
- Gusheshe Ltd's prior experience with similar contracts and customers under similar situations
- Gusheshe Ltd's intention to enforce its contractual rights
- The payment terms and conditions of the contract
- Whether the receivable from the customer is subject to future subordination.

In the case where Gusheshe Ltd discovers that it is unlikely to receive the consideration to which it has a right, the obligation in the contract to transfer control of the motor vehicle to the customer does not exist.

EXAMPLE 5.2 Thuto Mobile Phones (Pty) Ltd
Assessing the existence of a contract: no written sales agreement

Thuto Mobile Phones (Pty) Ltd procures mobile phones and other electronic accessories from China. Before the end of its financial year, the entity sold and delivered a consignment of its inventory to a client in Botswana. Thuto Mobile Phones (Pty) Ltd has previously entered into a sale agreement with this customer and both parties would sign a contract for each sale transaction. The contractual agreement for this particular sale was signed by Thuto Mobile Phones (Pty) Ltd only – the client's representative has not yet signed the agreement.

However, Thuto Mobile Phones (Pty) Ltd is not overly concerned with this issue due to the fact that both entities had telephonically agreed to the sale agreement as per their ordinary business practice. The client has in the past always honoured the obligation to pay for the goods delivered, even though in this case they have not signed the contract yet.

Therefore, even though there is not a legally binding agreement, we can conclude that a contract exists (based on past practice) and the client's capability and determination to pay. Therefore, Thuto Mobile Phones (Pty) Ltd can apply the provisions as laid out in IFRS 15 to sales made up to the year end.

Combination of contracts

IFRS 15 *Revenue from contracts with customers* provides that an entity may combine two or more contracts in the following scenarios:

1. The entity has a portfolio of contracts (or performance obligations) with similar traits, and it reasonably expects that the effects on the financial statements of applying this standard to the portfolio would not differ materially from applying this standard to the individual contracts (or performance obligations) within that portfolio (IFRS 15.04).
2. The entity entered into two or more contracts at or near the same time with the same customer (or related parties of the customer) and one or more of the following criteria are met:
   (i)   The contracts are negotiated as a package with a single commercial objective.
   (ii) The amount of consideration to be paid in one contract depends on the price or performance of the other contract.
   (iii) The goods or services promised in the contracts (or some goods or services promised in each of the contracts) constitute a single performance (IFRS 15.17).

EXAMPLE 5.3 Khumalo IT Developers

Combination of contracts

Khumalo IT Developers entered into an IT contract to develop and install accounting software for company A. Two weeks later, in a totally different contract, Khumalo IT Developers signed a contract with company B to offer them similar accounting software. Both companies A and B are subsidiaries of company X. Throughout the course of the negotiations with the CEO of company X, Khumalo IT Developers had made a price concession for both companies A and B, agreeing to sell its accounting software at a discount if company B purchased the software as well.

Khumalo IT Developers can conclude that the two contracts should be combined. This is due to the fact that company A is related party to company B, and the two separate contracts with the two parties were signed in almost a similar period, and the terms and conditions were concluded as a single commercial package. Khumalo IT Developers, furthermore, has to evaluate if the sale of the same accounting software represents a single performance obligation.

EXAMPLE 5.4 Sithole Engineers

Combination of contracts

Sithole Engineers sold mining equipment to Simunye Anglore Ltd, a mining company based in Marikana. The equipment was delivered and assembled on site and was certified as ready for use by Sithole engineers on date of delivery. After 30 days, the two entities entered into a separate agreement for Sithole Engineers to modify the equipment and enhance its operational functionalities.

Even though they are carried out a month apart, the two contracts were entered into around a similar period, therefore the two contracts can be combined and be considered a single performance obligation. In applying the provisions of IFRS 15, Sithole Engineers can conclude that these two separate contracts were executed as a package with a single commercial objective. Consequently, the two agreements constitute a single contract.

Contract modification

The accounting treatment for modification of a contract relies on whether distinct goods or services are added to the contract, including the associated pricing in the modified arrangement. A contract modification is a change in the scope or price (or both) of a contract that is approved by the parties to the contract. The modification either creates new or changes existing enforceable rights and obligations of the parties to the contract.

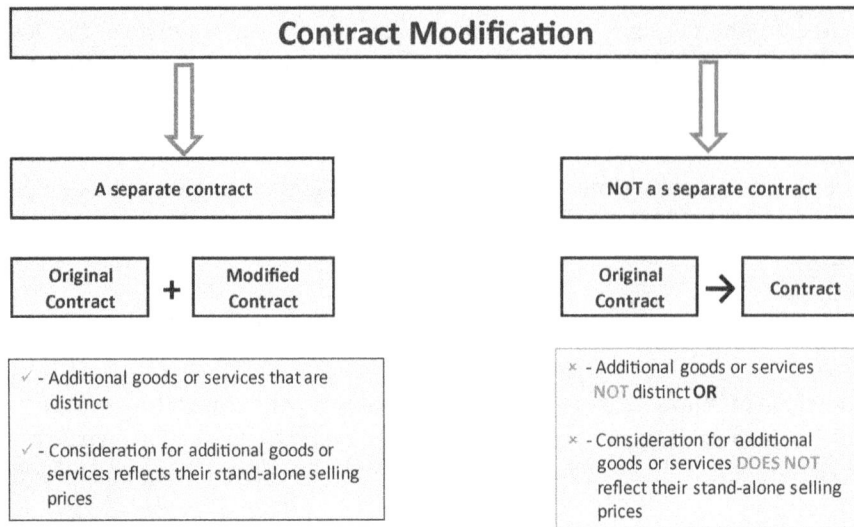

```
                          Contract Modification

        ┌─────────────────────────┐         ┌─────────────────────────┐
        │   A separate contract   │         │  NOT a s separate       │
        │                         │         │       contract          │
        └─────────────────────────┘         └─────────────────────────┘

   ┌──────────┐  +  ┌──────────┐      ┌──────────┐  →  ┌──────────┐
   │ Original │     │ Modified │      │ Original │     │ Contract │
   │ Contract │     │ Contract │      │ Contract │     │          │
   └──────────┘     └──────────┘      └──────────┘     └──────────┘
```

√ - Additional goods or services that are distinct

√ - Consideration for additional goods or services reflects their stand-alone selling prices

× - Additional goods or services NOT distinct **OR**

× - Consideration for additional goods or services DOES NOT reflect their stand-alone selling prices

Figure 5.2: Contract modification

In instances of significant uncertainty about enforceability, professional judgement would have to be sought in assessing if the right and obligations arising from the contract still continue to exist for the justification of enforcing the provisions of IFRS 15.

EXAMPLE 5.5 Gauteng Buses Ltd
Identifying a contract modification

Gauteng Buses Ltd is an experienced manufacturer of buses. The entity enters into an agreement to manufacture 33 (50-seater) new buses as part of the Gauteng Province Bus Transport Initiative (GPBTI) in the inner city and the surrounding areas. Gauteng Busses Ltd agrees to manufacture the 33 buses for the government and commences the work on 1 January of year 1. On 30 June of the same year, the government notifies Gauteng Buses Ltd to amend the specifications of the new buses to increase their seating capacity from 50 to 65.

Gauteng Buses Ltd ascertains that in order to change the specifications, it would have to procure the services of specialist engineers to develop and manufacture the new buses and would also have to buy specialised materials and parts from overseas.

To decide whether to account for the contract modification, Gauteng Buses Ltd will make an assessment if it has established new or changed existing, enforceable rights and obligations under the contract. In executing this assessment, Gauteng Buses Ltd has to consider the following:

- Even though Gauteng Buses Ltd and the government have not effected the modification of the contract terms as they relate to the amended design and construct specifications, increased materials and labour needed to realise the construction of the new modifications, amendments of such processes are normal.
- Will the government compensate Gauteng Busses Ltd for the incremental costs?
- Gauteng Buses Ltd must consider the enforceability of the obligation of the government to pay for additional costs.
- It is reasonable for Gauteng Buses Ltd to expect that the government should consent to and have the financial resources to pay the additional charges due to the amendment of the specifications.

In instances of major uncertainty regarding enforceability of the contract, written approval would be needed to endorse a conclusion that the parties to the contract have approved the modification.

5.5.2 Step 2: Identify the performance obligations in the contract

Performance obligation is any good or service that the entity promises to transfer to the customer. It can be either:

- a single good or service, or a bundle that is distinct; or
- a series of distinct goods or services that are substantially the same and have the same pattern of transfer.

An important feature of a performance obligation is based on the term *'distinct'*. In substance, it refers to separable, or separately identifiable. The performance obligations must be identified at the inception of the contract. This can be done by determining the goods or services promised in a contract with a customer and identifying as a performance obligation each promise to transfer to the customer. A good or service that is promised to a customer is distinct if both of the following are met:

1. The customer can benefit from the good or service either on its own or together with other resources that are readily available to the customer.

2. The entity's promise to transfer the good or service to the customer is separately identifiable from other promises in the contract (ie the good or service is distinct within the context of the contract).

Promises in contracts with customers

According to IFRS 15, a promise is 'granting a right to goods or services to be provided in the future'.

All goods or services promised to a customer as a result of a contract give rise to performance obligations because those promises were made as part of the negotiated contract between the entity and its customer. Promises (performance obligations) include not only those expressly stated in a contract but may also include those implied by past business practice or instances where a valid expectation has been created in the mind of the customer (constructive obligation).

In order to recognise the revenue, the following two criteria need to be met:

1. The performance obligation must be satisfied over time.

2. The same method would be used to measure the entity's progress towards complete satisfaction of the performance obligation to transfer each distinct good or service in the series to the customer.

EXAMPLE 5.6 Island Life (Pty) Ltd
Performance obligations

Island Life (Pty) Ltd sells grass-cutting motorised equipment to a client and also offers maintenance services on the sale for a specified period. The agreement gives rise to two performance obligations: (1) the sale of the equipment, and (2) the service, which will be provided over an agreed period of time.

Promised goods or services might not represent performance obligations if those promises did not exist at the time that the parties entered into to the contract. Performance obligations do not include activities that an entity must undertake to fulfil a contract unless those activities transfer a good or service to a customer.

A service provider may need to perform various administrative tasks to set up a contract. The performance of those tasks does not transfer a service to the customer as the tasks are performed. Therefore, those set-up activities are not a performance obligation.

EXAMPLE 5.7 High End Security Services (Pty) Ltd
Performance obligations

A security company, High End Security Services (Pty) Ltd, provides guarding and security services to a client for an agreed period of 12 months. The security company will not have 12 separate performance obligations but only one, as the service is substantially the same every month and has the same pattern of transfer to the customer.

EXAMPLE 5.8 Intuthuko IT Consultants (Pty) Ltd
Explicit and implicit promises in a contract

Intuthuko IT Consultants (Pty) Ltd sells computers and provides IT services to its clients and customers. In order to increase its revenue, the entity decides to offer maintenance services for all purchases made for 'no cost' to the customer. The 'sales promotion', ie the maintenance services, have improved the revenue of the entity, even though the customers can choose not to use the added service offered to them.

REQUIRED:
Discuss whether the maintenance service is a performance obligation.

EXAMPLE 5.8 Suggested solution – Intuthuko IT Consultants (Pty) Ltd

Due to the fact that the provision of maintenance services is a promise to transfer goods or services in the future and is part of the negotiated exchange between Intuthuko IT Consultants (Pty) Ltd and the customer, Intuthuko IT Consultants (Pty) Ltd determines that the promise to provide maintenance services is a performance.

Intuthuko IT Consultants (Pty) Ltd concludes that the promise would represent a performance obligation regardless of whether the customer exercised the option to use the maintenance service.

Consequently, Intuthuko IT Consultants (Pty) Ltd can allocate a portion of the transaction price to the promise to provide maintenance services.

EXAMPLE 5.9 King Star Tech
Performance obligations

King Star Tech sells home electronic items to the public from its warehouse in Midrand. King Star Tech has historically provided maintenance services on products sold to their clients for no additional consideration. The contractual agreement on the sale of their electronic items does not explicitly promise maintenance services nor does it define the terms and conditions for this service.

REQUIRED:

Explain whether the maintenance service provided by King Star Tech to its customers is a performance obligation in accordance with IFRS 15 *Revenue from contracts with customers.*

EXAMPLE 5.9 Suggested solution – King Star Tech

On the basis of King Star Tech's ordinary business practice, it determines at contract inception that it has made an implicit promise to provide maintenance services as part of the negotiated exchange with the customer.

King Star Tech's actions through past practice of providing these maintenance services has created a valid expectation that it will continue to provide the same services to its customers.

Consequently, King Star Tech identifies the promise of maintenance services as a performance obligation to which it allocates a portion of the transaction price.

5.5.3 Step 3: Determine the transaction price

The **transaction price** is the amount of consideration to which an entity expects to be entitled in exchange for transferring promised goods or services to a customer, excluding amounts collected on behalf of third parties (eg VAT). A party to contract does an estimation of the transaction price at the commencement of the contract, as well as the variable consideration, and revises the amount with the latest estimate at each reporting period if there are amendments in the terms and conditions of the contract. The following will be considered by the entity when recognising the amount of revenue: variable consideration, constraining estimates in variable consideration, significant financing component, non-cash consideration and consideration payable to a customer.

Variable consideration

If the consideration promised includes a variable amount, an entity estimates the amount of consideration to which the entity will be entitled in exchange for transferring the promised goods or services to a customer. Promised consideration can also vary provided it is dependent on something that is undetermined or unknown.

EXAMPLE 5.10 MTM Ltd
Variable consideration

MTM Ltd enters into contractual agreements with clients to offer internet data using different offerings or packages. The standard contractual agreement with a customer is for a minimum period of two years. The contract specifically states that any client who uses any data over and above the contracted agreement will be charged a fee for extra usage.

Due to the fact that both MTM Ltd and the client have signed and agreed to the terms and conditions of the contract, the additional charges create a variable consideration. Therefore, MTM Ltd should estimate the amount of the additional data fees when the contract is commenced in order to establish the transaction price.

Determining the amount of variable consideration

A party to a contract should assess which specific method can be employed to determine the amount of the consideration it will collect from the contract.

Expected value method

A party to a contract should give regard to the sum of probability-weighted amounts for a variety of feasible consideration amounts. The expected value method gives rise to practical and achievable amounts of variable consideration provided or supposing the entity has entered into many contracts that have identical features or attributes.

EXAMPLE 5.11 Lebone Opticals

Estimate of variable consideration: expected value

Lebone Opticals enters into an agreement with an optometrist to sell them designer spectacle frames for R700 per unit. The terms and conditions do not stipulate the minimum purchase quantities the optometrist can make. However, in order to incentivise the optometrist to be a repeat client, the contract stipulates that the optometrist is entitled to a rebate for the purchases made in the year. Based on Lebone Opticals past experience for similar contractual offerings, it projects the undermentioned results.

No of units bought	Rebate for each unit	Likelihood
0–12 000	8%	40%
12 001–24 000	15%	35%
24 001+	25%	25%

Lebone Opticals has ascertained, through analysis, that the expected value method presents the most reliable and appropriate estimate of the amount of consideration which it will collect. Therefore, it forecasts the amount of the rebate to be:

$$= (8\% \times 40\%) + (15\% \times 35\%) + (25\% \times 25\%)$$
$$= 14,7\%$$

Therefore, Lebone Opticals estimates the transaction price to be R597,10 (R700 × (1 – 0,147)) per unit.

Most likely amount

The entity considers the single most likely amount from a range of possible consideration amounts. This will apply if the amount of the variable consideration has two or more possible outcomes.

EXAMPLE 5.12 Shisanyama Foods

Estimate of variable consideration: most likely amount

Shisanyama Foods signed a contract with Bizzy Corner Restaurants to supply them with basting sauces for their meat products. The two entities agreed to a fixed price of R38 per bottle of basting sauce. The contract provides for a yearly retrospective discount or refund provided to a purchaser – ie Shisanyama Foods will reduce the amount charged to Bizzy Corner Restaurants provided they buy 700 units or more. The rebate amount will be R1,10 for each bottle purchased in that year. The contract does not oblige the client to purchase a minimum quantity of bottles. However, Shisanyama Foods estimates that Bizzy Corner Restaurants will purchase approximately 900 units annually. The rebate due to the client will be calculated as follows:

Number of units purchased	Rebate
0–700	No rebate
701+	R1,10

Immediately after signing the contract, Bizzy Corner Restaurants placed an order for 180 bottles. Shisanyama Foods must assess the probability of Bizzy Corner Restaurants buying more than 700 based on historical sales data for similar customers and should also estimate annual sales, taking into account the current market conditions. This is because the rebate arrangement in the contract represents a variable consideration. Subsequent to determining the variable consideration, an entity has an option to add the whole amount or a portion of it in the transaction price.

The entity will have to exercise sound judgement when making the determination of the variable consideration. It must also pay particular attention and exercise rationale to all the details and finer points in the contract.

Constraining estimates in variable consideration

The entity should include variable consideration (eg bonus) in the transaction price only when it is highly probable that it can keep it.

EXAMPLE 5.13 The Billion Group
Applying the constraint: consideration based on occupancy of property

The Billion Group is a property development company. The entity bought land and obtained approval to develop a rental accommodation village in central Johannesburg. The Billion Group then signed a contract with ENYE Properties, a property agency, to market the development to potential residents for rental amount of R3 400 per unit. This amount is based on occupancy levels on completion.

At completion date, the Billion Group estimates that the variable consideration amounts to R2 500 provided they apply the expected value method. The Billion Group then applies the constraint guidance and takes into consideration the following:
• ENYE Properties is inexperienced with such contracts.
• The Billion Group has no power or control over the number of occupied units.
• The entity will not be able to find a solution to the lack of certainty for an extended period of time.
• The set of different possibilities is huge.

For these reasons, the Billion Group makes a decision that the variable consideration must be limited to a nil amount. The Billion Group should re-evaluate its decisions at the end of each financial year until such a time when they find a solution to the uncertainty.

Significant financing component

The promised amount of consideration is adjusted for the effects of the time value of money if the timing of payments agreed to by the parties to the contract provides the customer or the entity with a significant benefit of financing the transfer of goods or services to the customer. The aim of modifying the contracted amount of consideration for a significant financing component is to recognise revenue at an amount that depicts what the cash selling price of the promised good or service would have been had the entity collected the cash sale simultaneously when control of that good or service was transferred by the entity to the customer. The discount rate used is comparable to a rate that would be expressed in a different financing transaction between the entity and the customer at the commencement of the contract.

Non-cash consideration

The transaction price for contracts in which a customer promises consideration in a form other than cash is measured at fair value of the non-cash consideration. Supposing an entity is unable to determine an appropriate estimate of fair value based on sound and professional judgement, in consequence it should use the estimated selling price of the promised goods or services. If a customer does not remit cash to the entity, the entity will recognise the revenue when control over those goods or services is transferred to the entity.

Consideration payable to a customer

An entity accounts for consideration payable to a customer as a reduction of the transaction price and, therefore, of revenue. An entity should determine the amount that is due to the customer and make a resolution regarding whether the amount constitutes a subtraction from the transaction price, an outlay for distinct goods or services, or a combination of the two.

Right of return

An entity may sell (ie transfer control of) an item to a customer but also allow the customer to return the item and receive a refund of cash or a credit to be applied against future purchases or another item in exchange. Therefore, an entity should record the following:
• Revenue for those items it does not expect to be returned
• A refund liability for the consideration it expects to return
• An asset and corresponding adjustment to cost of sales.

EXAMPLE 5.14 Astral Ltd
Right of return
Astral Ltd sells computer hardware and software to its customers. During the current year the entity sold 1 000 computers to its clients and customers. Each computer was sold for R8 500 with a cost price of R5 200. Based on past experience, Astral Ltd expects 55 of the computers to be returned by customers for a full refund.

Note that the returns are in terms of a returns policy offered for any defective products which are returned within the warranty period of 12 months after the date of sale.

REQUIRED:
Prepare the journal entries that Astral Ltd would record in respect of the sales made for the year.

EXAMPLE 5.14 Suggested solution – Astral Ltd
Recognising the sale:

	R	R
Dr Bank (SFP)	8 500 000	
Cr Revenue (PL)		8 032 500
Cr Refund liability (SFP)		467 500

(945 × R8 500) = R8 032 500
(55 × R8 500) = R467 500

Recognising the costs:

	R	R
Dr Cost of sales (PL)	5 200 000	
Cr Inventory (SFP)		5 200 000

(1 000 × R5 200) = R5 200 000

	R	R
Dr Right of return asset (SFP)	286 000	
Cr Cost of sales (PL)		286 000

(55 × R5 200) = R286 000

5.5.4 Step 4: Allocate the transaction price to the performance obligations

The transaction price is assigned to every single performance obligation – every single specific good or service – in order to reflect the amount of consideration to which the entity expects to collect from the customer in relation to the transfer of promised goods or services to the customer. The transaction price is allotted to every single performance obligation as part considered in comparative relation to its stand-alone selling price.

A **stand-alone selling price** is a price at which an entity would sell a promised good or a service separately to the customer.

The best way to determine a stand-alone selling price is simply to take **observable selling prices** and if these are not available, **estimating them**. Suitable methods for estimating the stand-alone selling price of a good or service include the following:

Adjusted market assessment approach: An entity can assess the market in which it sells goods or services and estimate the price that a customer in that market would be willing to pay for those goods or services. That approach might also include referring to prices of the entity's competitors of similar goods or services and adjusting those prices as necessary to reflect the entity's costs and margins.

Expected cost plus a margin approach: An entity estimates the expected costs of satisfying a performance obligation and adds a suitable margin for that good or service.

Residual approach: An entity may estimate the stand-alone selling price by referring to the total transaction price less the sum of the observable stand-alone selling prices of other goods or services promised in the contract.

EXAMPLE 5.15 Mercedez Bens Ltd
Allocate transaction price to performance obligation in the contract
Mercedez Bens Ltd, a car manufacturer, enters into a contract with a customer to supply three vehicles: a K class sedan, a D series convertible and a GDC 4×4 vehicle. Mercedez Bens Ltd concludes that the items are distinct and therefore three performance obligations exist, and that the goods will most likely be delivered at different times. The total transaction price is R1,7 million.

Mercedes Benz Ltd regularly sells each item separately and has established stand-alone prices as follows:

K class sedan	R550 000
D series convertible	R750 000
GDC 4×4	R900 000
TOTAL	**R2 200 000**

REQUIRED:
Perform an allocation of the transaction price to the individual performance obligations.

EXAMPLE 5.15 Suggested solution – Mercedes Benz Ltd
Mercedes Benz Ltd allocates the transaction price of R1,7 million to the performance obligations as part considered in comparative relation to its stand-alone selling price as part considered in comparative relation to its stand-alone selling prices as per below:

K class sedan	425 000	550 000/2 200 000 × R1 700 000
D series convertible	579 545	750 000/2 200 000 × R1 700 000
GDC 4×4	695 455	900 000/2 200 000 × R1 700 000
	R1 700 000	

Because the delivery of the vehicles to the client will occur at various or different dates, Mercedes Benz Ltd will have to do an approximate calculation for the stand-alone selling price of every single vehicle. Revenue will be recognised at a point in time as control of each vehicle is delivered to the customer.

5.5.5 Step 5: Recognise revenue when (or as) the entity satisfies a performance obligation
The standard is a control-based model. The standard extends a control-based method to all engagements. IFRS 15 adopted the use of the principle of control to recognise an asset from the accounting framework to help assess when a good or service is transferred to a customer. 'Control' in the conceptual framework refers to the entity having control over the economic benefits that would be derived from the use of the asset. The term 'transferred' indicates 'delivered' within a frame of reference for the sale of goods and 'performed' within frame of reference of contracts for rendering services.

A performance obligation is satisfied (and revenue is recognised) when a **promised good or service is transferred to a customer**. A good or service is 'transferred' when or as the customer obtains control of it. The benefits of an asset are the potential cash flows (inflows or savings in outflows) that can be obtained directly or indirectly in many ways, such as by:
- using the asset to produce goods or provide services
- using the asset to enhance the value of other assets
- using the asset to settle liabilities or reduce expenses
- selling or exchanging the asset
- pledging the asset to secure a loan
- holding the asset.

A performance obligation can be satisfied or control may be transferred either:
- over time – in this case, control is passed to the customer over some period of time; or
- at the point of time – in this case, control is retained by the supplier until it is transferred at some moment.

Performance obligations satisfied over time

An entity transfers control of a good or service over time and, therefore, satisfies a performance obligation and recognises revenue over time, if one of the following criteria is met:

- The customer simultaneously receives and consumes the benefits provided by the entity's performance as the entity performs (eg auditing services).
- The entity's performance creates or enhances an asset (work in progress) that the customer controls as the asset is created or enhanced (eg developing a structure at a customer's premises).
- The entity's performance does not create an asset with an alternative use to the entity and the entity has an enforceable right to payment for performance completed to date (eg building a unique or customised asset which can only be used by the customer). An entity only being able to build an asset with no other possible different use than what the customer wants to use it for would mean the asset was developed at the instruction of the customer. The agreement will normally have an arrangement giving some financial protection against the possibility of financial loss should the customer end the agreement.

Consequently, to show that a customer controls a resource which has no other possible use as it is being made, an entity should evaluate if it has an enforceable right to collect any payments for performance finished to date. In doing this evaluation, the entity must reflect if it qualifies for any consideration for execution performance finished to date should the agreement be terminated by the customer for any grounds except for the entity's inability to proceed with its performance obligations.

EXAMPLE 5.16 Wealth Property Developers
Applying the over-time criteria: sales of real estate – no alternative use and enforceable right to payment
Wealth Property Developers bought land in order to develop homes in a gated luxurious security estate, called Ebotse. The entity entered into binding sales agreements with different customers in order to build them houses. Each house has its own unique plan, has different sizes, and the following information is standard in each contract:

- The client has to pay a 10% non-refundable deposit of the contract price.
- The deposit is made seven days after the contract is signed.
- The customer will pay in instalments as different stages of the development are completed.
- The contract has cumbersome terms and conditions that prevent Wealth Property Developers from offering the house to another client.
- If the client fails to make the promised progress payments when they are due, then the developer has a right to all of the consideration promised in the contract if it completes the construction of the house.
- The courts have previously upheld similar rights that entitle developers to require the customer to perform, subject to the entity meeting its obligations under the contract.

EXAMPLE 5.16 Suggested solution – Wealth Property Developers
At contract inception, the developer ascertains that in view of the fact that it is legally prohibited from making a sale offer of the house to a different customer, the house has no other different ways it can be used. Moreover, should the client default on its obligations then the developer would have an enforceable right to all of the consideration promised under the contract. As a result, the developer recognises revenue from the construction over time.

Measuring progress towards complete satisfaction of a performance obligation
For each performance obligation satisfied over time, an entity recognises revenue over time by measuring the progress towards complete satisfaction of that performance obligation to depict the transfer of control of goods or services promised. Progress towards complete satisfaction of a performance obligation satisfied over time is re-measured at the end of each reporting period. As circumstances change over time, an entity updates its measure of progress to reflect any changes in the outcome of the performance obligation.

In some circumstances (early stages of a contract), an entity may not be able to measure the outcome of a performance obligation reasonably, but it may still expect to recover the costs incurred in satisfying the performance obligation. In these circumstances, the entity recognises revenue only to the extent of the costs incurred which are recoverable, until such time that it can reasonably measure the outcome of the performance obligation.

In recognising revenue over time, the entity will choose one of the following methods that best reflects the progress towards satisfying that performance obligation:

- **Output methods:** Measure progress by evaluating the extent of output delivered to date (eg time elapsed, units produced, surveys of performance to date)

- **Input methods:** Measure progress by considering the entity's efforts/inputs in satisfying the obligation (eg costs incurred, machine hours lapsed, etc).

REQUIRED:

Explain how will Wealth Property Developers treat the sale of houses in their accounting records.

EXAMPLE 5.17 Debt Collections Ltd

Recognition over time

Debt Collections Ltd enters into a contract to provide monthly debt collections from overdue clients for a customer for one year. Debt Collections Ltd will do the following:

- Reconcile and prepare debtors statements for all customers who are six months in arrears.
- Get a court judge approval to garnish all debtors who owe the client.
- Make collections for the amounts that are due in that month and deposit the amounts in the client's bank account.
- List the debtors who have had an outstanding amount for more than nine months with the credit bureau.
- Receive a monthly service fee of 25% of collections made.

REQUIRED:

Does Debt Collections Ltd 'qualify' to recognise revenue over time in terms of IFRS 15?

EXAMPLE 5.17 Suggested solution – Debt Collections Ltd

The promised debt collection services are accounted for as a single performance obligation since they form a 'series' of distinct goods and services that are substantially the same and have the same pattern of transfer to the customer (IFRS 15.22(*b*)).

Debt Collections Ltd is able to prove that control of the goods and services are transferred to the customer over time as:

- the customer simultaneously receives and consumes the benefits of Debt Collections Ltd collection of the outstanding debt from clients (IFRS 15.35(*a*))
- another entity would not need to re-perform the collection from the clients (which also demonstrates that consumption of services has been simultaneous)

Consequently, the entity concludes that the best measure of progress towards complete satisfaction of the performance obligation over time is a time-based measure and it recognises revenue as a percentage of the collections made in the month.

Performance obligations satisfied at a point in time

If a performance obligation is not satisfied over time, an entity satisfies the performance obligation at a point in time. To determine the point in time at which a customer obtains control of a promised asset and the entity satisfies a performance obligation, the entity considers the requirements for control and the indicators of the transfer of control, which include, but are not limited to, the following:

- The entity has a present right to payment for the asset.
- The customer has legal title to the asset.
- The entity has transferred physical possession of the asset.
- The customer has the significant risks and rewards of ownership of the asset.
- The customer has accepted the asset (IFRS 15.38).

EXAMPLE 5.18 Novus Ltd

When amounts are received but do not meet recognition criteria as yet

On 12 March 2020, Novus Ltd signed an agreement with Sussex Ltd to deliver a product on 1 May 2020. The agreement provides that either party can terminate the contract by giving a seven-day notice to the other party. A consideration of R450 000 needed to be paid up-front on 30 March 2020. Sussex Ltd paid the R450 000 on 30 March 2020. The product was transferred by the seller to the buyer on 31 March.

REQUIRED:

Provide the journal entries for the above transaction in the books of Novus Ltd.

EXAMPLE 5.18 Suggested solution – Novus Ltd

1/3/2019

	R	R
Dr Cash (SFP)	450 000	
Cr Contract liability (SFP)		450 000

Entity receives cash before satisfaction of performance obligation

31/3/2019

Dr Contract liability (SFP)	450 000	
Cr Revenue (P/L)		450 000

5.6 CONTRACT COSTS

IFRS 15 provides a guidance about two types of costs related to a contract: costs to obtain the contract and costs to fulfil the contract.

5.6.1 Costs to obtain a contract

Those are the incremental costs to obtain a contract. In other words, these costs would not have been incurred without an effort to obtain a contract, for example legal fees, sales commissions and similar. These costs are not expensed in profit or loss, but instead are **recognised as an asset** if they are expected to be recovered.

5.6.2 Costs to fulfil a contract

If the costs incurred in fulfilling a contract with a customer are not within the scope of another standard (IAS 2 *Inventories*, IAS 16 *Property, plant and equipment* or IAS 38 *Intangible assets*), an entity recognises an asset from the costs incurred to fulfil a contract only if those costs meet all of the following criteria:

- The costs relate directly to a contract or to an anticipated contract that the entity can specifically identify.
- The costs generate or enhance resources of the entity, which will be used in satisfying performance obligations in the future.
- The costs are expected to be recovered (IFRS 15.95).

5.7 AMORTISATION

An entity should amortise or rationally allocate the costs it has incurred to secure and fulfil its contractual obligations based on a formula that is logical and in agreement with the manner that reflects the transfer of the good or service to which the asset is connected.

EXAMPLE 5.19 Pastellex

Amortisation: specifically anticipated contracts

Pastellex signs an agreement with a customer to manage the airplanes owned by the customer and used for business purposes for a period of 10 years. Pastellex pays initial costs of R500 000 to get the business ready. The initial money expended by Pastellex to get the business ready does not transfer goods or services to the customer. Based on past experience with the customer, Pastellex expects the new contract to be extended for another three years, bringing the total contract period to 13 years.

EXAMPLE 5.19 Suggested solution – Pastellex

Pastellex will capitalise the initial set up costs of R500 000 as an asset as a part of the asset management system and will subsequently amortise that asset over the expected period of the contract, ie 13 years. The write-off of these costs is based on using a rational method in line with the sequence of satisfaction of the performance obligation.

REQUIRED:

Explain how will Pastellex treat the transaction in their accounting records.

5.8 IMPAIRMENT

An entity should recognise an asset at its carrying amount, however, if the carrying amount is more than the future economic benefits that are expected to be derived from the asset, the asset must be impaired. For example, an entity would write off (eliminate) a trade receivable due to the customer's inability to pay the amount owed. The write-off of the amount that is uncollectable is an impairment. The statement of financial position will be reporting a lower, more realistic amount of its accounts receivable (assets).

5.9 PRESENTATION

An entity should separately present contract assets, contract liabilities and receivables due from customers in its statement of financial position. An entity will present a contract either as a contract asset or a receivable when it transfers control over goods or services to a client or customer if the customer has not paid the consideration. A contract asset is a vendor's right to consideration in exchange for goods or services that the vendor has transferred to a customer, when that right is conditional on the vendor's future performance. A receivable is a vendor's unconditional right to consideration, and is accounted for in accordance with IFRS 9 *Financial instruments* or IAS 39 *Financial instruments: recognition and measurement*. In accordance with the requirements of IAS 1 *Presentation of financial statements*, a vendor presents or discloses revenue from contracts with customers separately from the vendor's other sources of revenue.

5.9.1 Statements of profit or loss and cash flows

IFRS 15 does not clearly identify any specific reporting requirements for presentation of items linked to contracts with customers in the statement of profit or loss and in the statement of cash flows.

5.9.2 Disclosures

The standard provides that sufficient information should be included in the disclosures to allow the users of financial information to understand the nature, amount, timing and uncertainty of revenue and cash flows arising from contracts with customers.

IFRS 15 provides that an entity should disclose, distinctly from other sources of revenue, revenue recognised from contracts with customers and all impairment losses recognised on contract assets arising from contracts with customers.

5.9.3 Disaggregation of revenue

IFRS 15 provides that an entity should disaggregate revenue arising from contracts with customers between various classifications which reflect that the nature, amount, timing and uncertainty of revenue and cash flows are affected by economic factors.

EXAMPLE 5.20 Induna (Pty) Ltd

Disaggregation of revenue

Induna (Pty) Ltd creates these groupings when reporting in its annual financial statements: information and communications technology (ICT), logistics and personal health care products. When Induna (Pty) Ltd composes the information pack for its investor presentations, it disaggregates the revenue based on the location of its market, the group of related products that are marketed under a single brand name, and the timing of revenue recognition.

SEGMENTS	Information and communications technology (ICT)	Logistics	Personal health care products	TOTAL
Primary geographic markets				
South Africa	1 100	2 360	5 360	8 820
Botswana	410	860	1 110	2 380
Swaziland	810	360	–	1 170
	320	3 580	6 470	12 370
Major goods/services				
Desktop computers and laptops	1 010			1 010
Printers	770			770
Maintenance and repairs	540	600		1 140
Trucks		1 500		1 500
Cars		1 480		1 480
Hair care products			3 100	3 100
Skin care products			3 370	3 370
	2 320	3 580	6 470	12 370
Timing of revenue recognition				
Goods transferred at a point in time	1 780	2 980	6 470	11 230
Services transferred over time	540	600		1 140
	2 320	3 580	6 470	12 370

Contract balances

In terms of IFRS 15, an entity should disclose the following in its financial statements:

- The opening and closing balances of contract assets, contract liabilities and receivables from contracts with customers
- The amount of revenue recognised in the current period that was included in the opening contract liability balance
- The amount of revenue recognised in the current period from performance obligations satisfied (or partially satisfied) in previous periods (eg changes in transaction price)
- An explanation of how the entity's contracts and typical payment terms will affect its contract asset and contract liability balances
- An explanation of the significant changes in the balances of contract assets and contract liabilities, which should include both qualitative and quantitative information such as:
  - changes arising from business combinations;
  - cumulative catch-up adjustments to revenue (and to the corresponding contract balance) arising from a change in the measure of progress, a change in the estimate of the transaction price or a contract modification;
  - impairment of a contract asset; or
  - a change in the time frame for a right to consideration becoming unconditional (reclassified to a receivable) or for a performance obligation to be satisfied (the recognition of revenue arising from a contract liability).

Performance obligations

An entity provides the following information about its performance obligations:

- When the entity typically satisfies its performance obligations (eg on shipment, on delivery, as services are rendered or on completion of service)
- Significant payment terms (eg whether the contract has a significant financing component, the consideration is variable and the variable consideration is constrained)
- The nature of the goods or services that it has promised to transfer
- Obligations for returns, refunds and other similar obligations
- Types of warranties and related obligations
- The aggregate amount of the transaction price allocated to performance obligations that are unsatisfied (or partially unsatisfied) at the reporting date. The entity also provides either a quantitative (using time bands) or a qualitative explanation of when it expects that amount to be recognised as revenue.

5.10 SUMMARY

In this chapter, the overall objective and the scope of IFRS 15 *Revenue from contracts with customers* were discussed. The elements of revenue were identified, defined and discussed in detail, outlining the steps followed in the recognition of the revenue elements. The measurement and recognition criteria were also discussed. The chapter also looked into the guiding principles of presentation and disclosure of revenue in the financial statements.

IFRS 15 establishes a new set of principles and concepts regarding the approach to revenue recognition. These new principles and concepts have also resulted in changes regarding the measurement of revenue and the presentation and disclosure in terms of IFRS.

Effective date and transitional requirements

IFRS 15 is effective for annual reporting periods beginning on or after 1 January 2018. An entity's 31 December 2018 financial statements will need to be prepared applying the requirements of IFRS 15.

An entity can apply this standard in one of the following ways:

- **Option 1:** Fully retrospective application to each prior reporting period presented in accordance with IAS 8 *Accounting policies, changes in accounting estimates and errors*
- **Option 2:** Limited retrospective application. Retrospectively, with the cumulative effect of initially applying this standard at the date of initial application. An adjustment is made to the opening balance of retained earnings (or other component of equity, as appropriate). An entity would not restate comparative information and would recognise the cumulative effect of uncompleted contracts in the opening current year statement of financial position.

EXERCISES

Exercise 5.1 Lazarus Ltd

The following transactions took place at Lazarus Ltd:

1. On 4 February March 2019, Lazarus Ltd sold a fleet of vehicles to West End Bank for R13 million cash. Both parties signed an agreement that Lazarus Ltd would buy back the vehicles for R14,5 million cash on 1 June 2019. The vehicles would be put in a secure storage facility of the bank's choosing in Centurion, Pretoria.

   On 24 August 2019, Lazarus Ltd's motor parts division consigned engine parts to independent dealers for sale to third parties. These independent dealers are spread across the nine provinces of South Africa. The sales price to the dealers is Lazarus Ltd's market sales price to third parties. If any of the parts are not sold within 10 months after the date of consignment, the independent dealers are allowed to exercise the right to return these engines to Lazarus Ltd within 30 days after the expiry date.

REQUIRED:

Discuss how the above transactions should be accounted for in the books of accounts of Lazarus Ltd.

Exercise 5.2 Skeem Sam Ltd

Skeem Sam Ltd sells computer-based educational software packages meant for high schools. The package comprises the following subjects:

- Mathematics
- Accountancy
- Business studies
- Economics

The software package is sold:
- at price of R38 400 payable before delivery,
- with 15 days trial time, and
- without any maintenance support after trial time

As per practice, it takes about three weeks for the users to be proficient in the use of the package independent of any support from Skeem Sam Ltd. For practical expediency purposes, Skeem Sam Ltd has decided to provide an online support service for at least three months to its customers free of charge. This online support service has helped to increase the sales of its products.

However, for any maintenance and support services beyond the three-month period, Skeem Sam Ltd charges a nominal fee to the client of R750 per hour.

Skeem Sam Ltd also provides designing and development of customised software products for its clients. The terms and conditions for this additional service is that clients will be charged a standard fee of R1 200 per hour for this service.

First-year maintenance services are provided free of charge. Subsequent maintenance services are provided at the rate of 9% of the total contract price. Thereafter, for the next three years, maintenance services are provided at 6% of the contract price per annum.

REQUIRED:
Explain the considerations to be taken into account in determining accounting for revenue by Skeem Sam Ltd.

Exercise 5.3 ABC Ltd
ABC Ltd promises to sell 120 products to a customer for R12,000 (R100 per product). The products are transferred to the customer over a six-month period. The entity transfers control of each product at a point in time. After the entity has transferred control of 60 products to the customer, the contract is modified to require the delivery of an additional 30 products (a total of 150 identical products) to the customer. The additional 30 products were not included in the initial contract

REQUIRED:
Calculate the amount to be recognised as revenue:

1. When the price of additional products reflects the stand-alone selling price
2. When the price of additional products does not reflect the stand-alone selling price.

Exercise 5.4 DX Ltd
DX Ltd owns and operates radio stations. The main revenue stream is advertising revenue. Contracts are signed with various businesses for the sale of airtime. The account executives obtain these contracts and are compensated through a 5% commission on the total contract price for each new contract signed.

Executive B has obtained a new two-year advertising contract with the company.

Total contract costs related to this contract are as follows:
- Legal fees contract drafting = R10 000
- Commission paid to the account executive = R7 500
- Meals and entertainment incurred during the sales process = R1 750
- Creative director's time salary allocation to develop on-air advert = R1 500
- Amounts paid to external actors to record the on-air advert = R750
  Total costs = R21 500

REQUIRED:
Discuss whether to capitalise or expense each cost component.

Exercise 5.5 FX Ltd

A customer enters into a contract with a heavy-duty machine manufacturer for the purchase of a tractor for R10 million. All pieces of equipment sold by the manufacturer come with a one-year standard warranty that specifies the equipment will comply with the agreed-upon specifications and will operate as promised for a one-year period from the date of purchase.

In signing this contract, the customer also requests to purchase an additional R200 000 two-year warranty, commencing after the expiry of the standard one-year warranty.

REQUIRED:
Explain how you would treat the warranty.

CHAPTER 6

PROVISIONS AND CONTINGENCIES (IAS 37)

LEARNING OUTCOMES
After studying this chapter, you should be able to:
- Understand the underlying principles outlined in IAS 37 *Provisions and contingencies*.
- Use these principles to account for transactions affecting provisions and contingencies in the entity's accounting records.
- Disclose provisions and contingencies in the financial statements, to comply with the requirements of IFRS.

PREAMBLE
Mr Mhlongo (known as Njomane) is faced with a lot of uncertain transactions in his business. He has been wondering if transactions that are incomplete and uncertain are considered in the financial statements or whether they are only recognised once everything is confirmed. According to him, it does not help to speculate about business matters. He comes to you and asks whether you agree with him and tells you that for him, everything has to be in black and white, with no grey areas.

6.1 INTRODUCTION
There are transactions that take place in an entity where the amounts related to those transactions and/or the settlement of those amounts are uncertain or unknown.

When these transactions occur, the entity has to consider how best to capture them in the financial statements to ensure that all the affairs of the business are fairly presented. These transactions call for professional judgement. IAS 37 governs such transactions and gives guidelines on how to recognise them in the financial statements. If these kinds of transactions could influence the users of the financial statements when taking economic decisions, they are considered material and it is important to disclose them. These transactions could either be classified as provisions, contingent liabilities or contingent assets.

6.2 DEFINITION AND RECOGNITION OF A PROVISION
Provisions are defined as liabilities of which the amount and/or timing of settlement is unknown (IAS 37).

This is based on the definition of a liability, which is a present obligation arising from past events, settlement of which will result in an outflow of economic benefits from the entity. It must be probable that resources (economic benefits) will flow out of an entity and the amount can be measured reliably in order to recognise a liability in the accounting records. Therefore, provisions are liabilities of uncertain timing or amount. This means that for a provision to exist, a liability definition must be met fully.

If it is more likely (more than 50% chance) that a present obligation **DID** exist at the financial year end, then a provision is recognised. The transaction will be recorded in the accounting records of the entity as a **general journal** entry and will be disclosed under Liabilities in the **statement of financial position.**

NB: If these conditions are not met, then NO provision can be recognised.

6.3 DEFINITION AND RECOGNITION OF A CONTINGENT LIABILITY
There are two definitions for contingent liabilities:

1. Contingent liabilities are **possible** obligations that arise from past events and whose existence will be confirmed only by the occurrence or non-occurrence of one or more uncertain future event not wholly within the control of the entity.

2. Contingent liabilities are **present** obligations arising from past events where it is **NOT** probable that an outflow of resources (economic benefits) will be needed to settle the obligation, or the amount cannot be measured reliably (IAS 37).

If it less likely (less than 50% chance) that a present obligation DID exist at the financial year end, then a contingent liability cannot be recognised. The transaction will NOT be recorded in the books of the entity as a general journal entry. If the transaction is relevant or material, the details of the transaction will be disclosed as a NOTE, with a detailed description in the financial statements. If the possibility of the outflow of resources (economic benefits) is remote, then the transaction will be ignored.

6.4 DEFINITION AND RECOGNITION OF A CONTINGENT ASSET

Contingent assets are defined as **possible** assets that arise from past events and whose existence will be confirmed only by the occurrence or non-occurrence of one or more uncertain future events not wholly within the control of the entity (IAS 37).

If it is probable that there will be an inflow of economic benefits and the transaction is relevant or material, then the details of the transaction will be disclosed as a NOTE, with a detailed description in the financial statements. If the inflow of economic benefits is not possible or remote, then this transaction will be ignored.

EXAMPLE 6.1 Mpungose Refrigerators

Mpungose Refrigerators refurbishes and sells fridges within the Kwamakhutha area, near Amanzimtoti in KwaZulu-Natal. The fridges are sold with a refund policy that states that if a customer is not satisfied with the purchase, the goods may be returned for a full refund within 30 days of purchase. Sales for the year ended 28 February 2019 amounted to R250 000. Based on past experience, at 28 February 2019, a reliable estimate was made that 7% of sales would be returned for a full refund.

REQUIRED:

Explain whether a provision or contingent asset/liability should be reflected in the financial statements of Mpungose Refrigerators for the financial year ended 28 February 2019 in the form of a line item or a note, or if the refund policy should be ignored.

EXAMPLE 6.1 Suggested solution – Mpungose Refrigerators

Mpungose Refrigerators has a refund policy in place and is obligated to refund any customers who are dissatisfied with their purchases. Based on past experience of refunds this is an obligation. The sale of goods during the financial year ended 28 February 2019 is a past event. This event and the obligation of the policy make this a present obligation. Based on past experience, it is highly likely that 7% of sales will be refunded and the obligation can therefore be measured reliably at an amount of R17 500 (7% × R250 000).

A provision will be reflected as a line item under current liabilities in the financial statements of Mpungose Refrigerators for the financial year ended 28 February 2019.

Mpungose Refrigerators
General journal – 2019

Dr Refunds expense	R17 500	
Cr Provision for refunds		R17 500

Mpungose Refrigerators

Extract from statement of financial position as at 28 February 2019	**R**
Current liabilities	
Provision for refunds	17 500

EXAMPLE 6.2 Never say Never (Pty) Ltd

Never say Never (Pty) Ltd sells goods with a refund policy that states that if a customer is not satisfied with the purchase, the goods may be returned for a full refund within 30 days of purchase. Sales for the year ended 31 December 2019 amounted to R680 000. At 31 December 2019, it was not possible to estimate reliably possible returns and refunds.

REQUIRED:

Explain whether a provision or contingent asset/liability should be reflected in the financial statements of Never say Never (Pty) Ltd for the financial year ended 31 December 2019 in the form of a line item or a note or whether the refund policy should be ignored.

EXAMPLE 6.2 Suggested solution – Never say Never (Pty) Ltd

Never say Never (Pty) Ltd has a refund policy in place and is obligated to refund any customers who are dissatisfied with their purchases. Based on past experience of refunds, this is an obligation. The sale of goods during the financial year ended 31 December 2019 is a past event. This event and the obligation of the policy make this a present obligation. Since the obligation cannot be measured reliably, there will be no provision reflected in the financial statements, but a contingent liability needs to be disclosed in the notes to the financial statements of Never say Never (Pty) Ltd for the financial year ended 31 December 2019.

Never say Never (Pty) Ltd
Notes to the financial statements for the year ended 31 December 2019
Contingent liability

There is a refund that it is possible will need to be paid to customers when they return goods with which they are dissatisfied. The amount is currently not reliably measurable.

EXAMPLE 6.3 Amakhambi Ltd

The Department of Environmental Affairs passed a new legislation binding to all companies operating in the chemical industry. Amakhambi Ltd was notified in September 2019 by the local zoning commission that it must rehabilitate land on which chemicals had been stored, otherwise their operating licence would be revoked. Amakhambi Ltd hired a consulting firm to investigate the cost of rehabilitation, which was estimated at R29 million. Amakhambi Ltd has a December financial year end.

REQUIRED:

Explain whether a provision or contingent asset/liability should be reflected in the financial statements of Amakhambi Ltd for the financial year ended 31 December 2019 in the form of a line item or a note, or if the notification should be ignored.

EXAMPLE 6.3 Suggested solution – Amakhambi Ltd

Since the cost of the rehabilitation has been reasonably estimated by experts, and it is probable that the loss will occur, a present obligation exists at year end. Amakhambi Ltd has to account for a R29 million provision in the accounting books as follows:

Amakhambi Ltd
General journal – 2019

Dr Rehabilitation expense	R29 000 000	
Cr Provision for rehabilitation expense		R29 000 000
Amakhambi Ltd		
Extract from statement of financial position as at 31 December 2019		**R**
Current liabilities		
Provision for rehabilitation expense		29 000 000

6.5 ONEROUS CONTRACTS

An onerous contract is one in which unavoidable costs of fulfilling exceed the benefits from the contract. This occurs when a business has taken an assignment, only to find out in the middle of the contract that the contract will result in a loss. In a case like this, a provision should be made in the financial statements measured at the lower of:
- unavoidable costs of fulfilling the contract, and
- penalty for not meeting the obligations from the contract.

6.6 SUMMARY

This chapter dealt with the definitions, recognition criteria and the disclosure of provisions, contingent liabilities and contingent assets. A clear distinction was made between the different concepts to indicate the intricacies of each concept. Emphasis was drawn to the two types of definitions of contingent liabilities and their recognition criteria.

EXERCISES

Exercise 6.1 Lindela Ltd

On 30 June 2019, Lindela Ltd was notified that a third party may begin legal proceedings against it, based on a situation involving environmental damage to a site owned by Lindela Ltd. Based on the experience of other companies that have been subjected to this type of litigation in the area, it is probable that Lindela Ltd will have to pay R12 million to settle the litigation. Lindela Ltd has a December financial year end.

REQUIRED:

Explain whether a provision or contingent liability/asset should be reflected in the financial statements of Lindela Ltd for the financial year ended 31 December 2019 in the form of a line item or a note, or if the notification should be ignored.

Exercise 6.2 Games 'r Us

Games 'r Us, a local manufacturer of gaming stations, sells products to the local market. As part of customer service, the manufacturer provides a warranty to repair or replace its products one year after the sale. Using accumulated historical information, the manufacturer estimates that each gaming station sold results, on average, in R300 of warranty expense. During the current year ending 30 June 2019, Games 'r Us sold 3 000 gaming stations.

REQUIRED:

Explain whether a provision or contingent liability/asset should be reflected in the financial statements of Games 'r Us for the financial year ended 30 June 2019 in the form of a line item or a note, or if the warranty should be ignored.

Exercise 6.3 Yonela (Pty) Ltd

Yonela (Pty) Ltd is a consulting firm, specialising in engineering products and research and development. Just before the end of the financial year ending 30 June 2019, the company received a notice of a legal case from one of its competitors. The case is related to a potential infringement of the competitor's patent. The in-house legal counsel discussed the case with Yonela (Pty) Ltd's management, and based on the information available, concluded that the lawsuit was possible. However, there was not enough information to estimate the potential loss.

REQUIRED:

Explain whether a provision or contingent liability/asset should be reflected in the financial statements of Yonela (Pty) Ltd for the financial year ended 30 June 2019 in the form of a line item or a note, or if the notice should be ignored.

Exercise 6.4 New Age Computers Ltd

During 2018, New Age Computers Ltd manufactured and sold computers which were fitted with microchip C28. In November 2018, a new microchip, C 31, was introduced into the market, which doubled the storage capacity of the computer.

It was decided at a board meeting held on 30 November 2018 that in future only the C 31 microchip would be used. All the computers fitted with C28 microchip already sold before 1 December 2018 would be replaced. This was announced through advertisements in the media during December 2018. There were approximately 6 000 computers sold during 2018, and it is uncertain how many will be returned for a replacement and the cost of replacement cannot be measured.

REQUIRED:

Discuss how the transaction should be recognised in the financial statements of New Age Computers Ltd for the year ended 31 December 2018.

Exercise 6.5 – Qwemesha (Pty) Ltd

A claim of R10 million was initiated by Qwemesha (Pty) Ltd against Quaque Ltd on 1 July 2019, on the grounds of a trademark infringement. At the financial year end of Qwemesha (Pty) Ltd, 31 December 2019, legal advisors were of the opinion that the claim would probably succeed but they were not certain thereof.

REQUIRED:

Discuss how the transaction should be recognised in the financial statements of Qwemeshe (Pty) Ltd for the year ended 31 December 2019.

Exercise 6.6 Kwasuka (Pty) Ltd

On 30 June 2019, Kwasuka (Pty) Ltd is notified of a court decision, bringing to an end a protracted legal battle against it which was based on a situation involving environmental damage to a site owned by the company. The court has ruled against Kwasuka (Pty) Ltd, but has not yet made a decision on the legal costs of the case. Kwasuka (Pty) Ltd's legal team estimates they will be R12 million, based on their past experience.

REQUIRED:

Explain whether a provision or contingent liability/asset should be reflected in the financial statements of Kwasuka (Pty) Ltd for the financial year ended 31 December 2019 in the form of a line item or a note, or if the notification should be ignored.

Exercise 6.7 Pepcor Ltd

The following information relates to Pepcor Ltd, a JSE-listed company involved in the construction business, for the financial year ended 31 December 2018:

1. On 1 March 2018, Pepcor Ltd was awarded a government contract to construct a bridge in the Kwadukuza area (north coast) of Durban. The completion date of the project is 31 October 2020.

   Since the bridge is to be built over a river, the contract stipulates that the river and the area around the river must be restored to their original condition at the completion of the contract.

   Construction of the bridge commenced on 30 June 2018. Pepcor Ltd has a policy to restore the environment at each site where they have completed a project. This policy builds their image and promotes public relations.

   On 1 March 2018, the present value of the environmental restoration is estimated at R1 500 000.

2. Pepcor Ltd owes its employees an estimated amount of R455 000 in respect of past services. This will be paid out as long service costs. The payment date has not been decided.

REQUIRED:

Provide journal entries and reasons for the above information for the year ended 31 December 2018.

CHAPTER 7

INTANGIBLE ASSETS (IAS 38 and IFRS 3)

LEARNING OUTCOMES

After studying this chapter, you should be able to:

- Name and classify the overall objective and scope of the standard on intangible assets (IAS 38).
- Distinguish the recognition criteria.
- Identify the criteria for initial measurement.
- Discuss the treatment of internally generated goodwill as well as calculate purchased goodwill as per IFRS 3.
- Identify the criteria for subsequent measurement.
- Disclose these assets, including goodwill, in the annual financial statements and the notes in accordance with the requirements of IAS 38 and IFRS 3.
- Perform calculations on the basis of amortisation with depreciable amount and residual value; period and method of amortisation; and annual reviews (impairment testing).

PREAMBLE

Mr Mhlongo (known as Njomane) is having an argument with auditors relating to a list of customers of telecommunications his company bought for a significant amount of cash. The list contained the names, addresses and phone numbers of potential customers that Njomane intended to contact and offer his services. The auditors insist that the price paid for the customer list is an expense and should be recorded in the profit or loss section of the statement of comprehensive income. According to Njomane, the customer list perfectly meets the definition of an intangible asset. He argues that it has no physical substance, it is identifiable, the company controls it, the cost is reliably measurable and future economic benefits are expected.

This further sparks an argument regarding the Protection of Personal Information (POPI) Act, which was enacted in South Africa in 2013 to prevent companies from randomly contacting potential customers and to enforce consequences should a South African company behave in an irresponsible manner when collecting, processing, storing and sharing someone else's personal information.

Njomane comes to you for some clarification and explanation on intangible assets.

7.1 INTRODUCTION

The term *intangible* is defined as something that is 'unable to be touched' or 'not having physical substance'. This chapter therefore focuses on assets that have no physical substance, such as research and development, software, patents, trademarks, copyrights, brands, licences, training, etc. The fact that these assets are invisible makes it difficult to prove they exist and results in uncertainty in terms of recognition. Thus, most end up being expensed to the statement of profit and loss. The standard covering these invisible and untouchable assets is IAS 38 *Intangible assets*.

According to the conceptual framework, the contentious issue for intangible assets is the ability to meet the definition of an economic resource, in particular whether it has a potential to produce economic benefits. This creates a challenge when assessing the future cash flows associated with new products or technologies in the light of uncertainty.

There are further restrictions with the body of IAS 38, particularly in respect of research and development activities. The restrictions mean that certain entities do not feel confident in their ability to meet the criteria, resulting in certain development expenditures not being capitalised.

Intangible assets can be acquired in *four* distinct ways:

1. Purchase or separate acquisition
2. Acquisition as part of a business combination
3. Acquisition by way of government grant
4. Internally generated.

7.2 OBJECTIVE OF THE STANDARD

The standard's objective is to:

- guide the accounting treatment for intangible assets that are not dealt with expressly in another standard;
- stipulate that an entity can only recognise an intangible asset when it meets specific criteria;
- restrict how to measure the carrying amount; and
- specify the disclosure requirements (IAS 38.01).

7.3 SCOPE

IAS 38 prescribes the accounting rules of all intangible assets except for the intangible assets covered by another standard. This means that, should another standard prescribe the accounting treatment for a specific type of intangible asset, an entity should apply the prescribed standard instead of this standard (IAS 38).

Examples of intangible assets that are addressed by IAS 38 are:

- patents, trademarks and copyrights
- computer software
- recipes, formulae, models, designs and prototypes
- manufacturing and distribution licences
- mastheads and publishing titles
- fishing licences: import quotas
- brand names
- franchise rights
- broadcasting licences
- product development(R&D) costs
- customer lists
- right under licensing agreements for movies, video recording, plays, manuscripts, etc.

The following are excluded:

- Deferred tax covered by IAS 12
- Goodwill covered by IFRS 3
- Inventories covered by IAS 2
- Intangible assets held for sale covered by IFRS 5
- Goodwill arising from business combination (IFRS 3)
- Employee benefits covered by IAS 19
- Exploration and evaluation assets covered by IFRS 6
- Financial assets covered by IAS 32
- Expenditures for development and extraction of minerals, oils, natural gas and other non-regenerated resources.

7.4 DEFINITIONS

An **asset** is a resource controlled by an entity as a result of past events, and from which future economic benefits are expected to flow to the entity.

An **intangible asset** is an **identifiable non-monetary asset without physical substance** (IAS 38.08).

Monetary assets are monies held and assets to be received in fixed or determined amounts of money.

Research is the systematic investigation undertaken in order to establish facts and reach new conclusions.

Amortisation is the orderly allocation of the depreciable amount on an intangible asset over its useful life.

The **depreciable amount** is the gross carrying amount less residual value.

Residual value is the amount for which an entity would be able to sell the asset assuming it had already reached the end of its useful life.

Carrying amount is the cost price less accumulated depreciation.

The **fair value** is the price that would be accepted or paid due to an arm's length transaction between market participants.

An **impairment loss** is an amount by which the carrying amount of an asset or cash-generating unit (CGU) exceeds its recoverable amount of an asset.

Cash-generating unit is the smallest identifiable group of assets that generates combined cash inflows as a whole that cannot be attached to any one identifiable individual asset.

7.5 DEFINITION OF INTANGIBLE ASSET
An intangible asset is defined as an **identifiable non-monetary asset without physical substance**.

The asset meets the identifiable criteria when:
- it is separable, meaning the entity can separate it from the entity to sell it, transfer it, licence it, rent it or exchange it, either independently or unitedly with a linked contract asset or liability, regardless of the entity's intention to do so; or
- it originates from the contractual or statutory rights, irrespective of whether those rights are transferrable or separate from the entity or other rights and commitments.

Differentiation should be evident between an identifiable asset and goodwill (IAS 38.11).

Goodwill acquired in the business combination represents the payment in anticipation of future economic benefits from assets that are not capable of being individually identifiable (eg benefits that result from synergy between the identifiable assets acquired by the acquirer and acquiree) and separately recognised. Goodwill is therefore not considered to be an 'identifiable asset'.

Monetary assets are receivable in a fixed or determined amount of money (eg account receivable). All other assets are non-monetary.

An asset is a present economic resource controlled by the entity as a result of a past event. An entity's control of assets is emphasised by obtaining future economic benefits and restricting others' access to those benefits. Control exists because of enforceable legal rights. However, legal enforceability is not assurance for control since future economic benefits may be controlled somehow.

Those future economic benefits will include the income from products or services, cost gains or other gains developing from the asset's production by an entity (IAS 38.17).

When determining how to classify an asset with both intangible and tangible elements, an entity should assess which element is more significant. A patent, for instance, is without physical substance. The fact that the patent may be recorded in a physical document does not give rise to a material physical substance to the patent.

The standard (IAS 38) specifically prohibits the recognition of *internally generated* goodwill as it clearly fails the definition of intangible asset, ie it is not identifiable (it is neither separable nor does it arise from contractual or legal rights).

7.6 RECOGNITION AND INITIAL MEASUREMENT OF AN INTANGIBLE ASSET
In order to recognise an intangible asset, the reporting entity must be able to demonstrate that the item meets the definition of an intangible asset above, and the recognition criteria set out below.

This requirement applies to costs incurred initially to acquire or internally generate an intangible asset and those incurred subsequently to add, replace part of, or service it.

Recognition of an intangible asset as an asset depends on the probability of future economic benefits attributable to the entity's asset and measuring the cost reliably.

An entity shall assess the probability of expected future economic benefits using logical and endurable assumptions that represent management's best assessment of the probable set economic conditions that will exist over an asset's useful life (IAS 38.22).

An entity shall measure intangible assets initially at cost (IAS 38.24).

Costs incurred after an intangible asset is in the working condition necessary for its operation in the manner intended by management are *not* included in cost, but are expensed in the determination of profit and loss for the period. Once an intangible asset has been recognised, a basis of measurement is then assigned.

7.6.1 Separate purchase

If an intangible asset is bought independently, the asset's cost can usually be measured reliably, mainly when the cost is in the form of money or other monetary assets (IAS 38.26).

The cost of an intangible asset contains:
- its purchase price, including import charges and other non-refundable buying expenses after deducting trade concessions and rebates; and
- any directly attributable charges of preparing the asset for its planned use. These would include costs of employee benefits, professional fees and costs of testing whether the asset is functioning properly.

The probability criterion is always satisfied as the price paid for the intangible asset acquired reflects the expectations about the probability that future economic benefits embodied in the asset will flow to the acquirer.

Examples of expenditure that are not part of the cost of an intangible asset
The following are not included in the cost:
- Cost of introducing a new product service
- Cost of conducting business in a new area
- Administration and general overhead costs
- Costs incurred before the asset is brought into use but after the asset is capable of operating as intended
- Initial operating losses
- Costs of redeploying an intangible asset.

Classes of intangible assets
A class of intangible assets is a grouping of intangible assets that have a similar nature and use in the entity's operations. IAS identifies examples of separate classes of intangible assets, including brand names, mastheads and publishing titles, computer software, licences and franchises, copyrights, patents and other industrial property recipes, formulas, models, etc, and intangible assets under development.

7.6.2 Intangible assets acquired as a portion of a business combination

The value of an intangible asset received in a business combination, according to IFRS 3, is its fair value at the date of purchase. The acquirer in a business combination recognises an asset independently from goodwill, in-process research and the acquiree's development project if it meets an intangible asset's definition and can measure the fair value reliably.

An acquiree's in-process research and development project meets the definition of an intangible asset when:
- it meets the definition of an asset; and
- it is identifiable.

If the acquired intangible asset in a business combination is separable or arises from contractual or other legal rights, sufficient information should exist to measure reliably the fair value of the asset.

7.6.3 Intangible assets acquired by process of government grants

Following this standard, an entity may recognise both an intangible asset and the government grant initially at fair value. The entity's option is to recognise the asset initially at a nominal amount plus any expenditure directly linked to preparing the asset for its proposed use.

7.6.4 Substitution of assets

An entity may acquire one or more intangible assets in exchange for non-monetary assets or assets. The asset's cost, in this case, is measured at fair value unless the exchange transaction lacks economic substance. The asset lacks commercial substance if future cash flows are not expected to change as a result of this transaction. If the acquired asset is not measured at fair value, the cost is measured at the carrying amount of the asset given up.

A swap transaction has economic substance if the uncertainty, timing and price of the received asset's cash flows differ from the prospect, timing and cash flows of the transaction conveyed.

EXAMPLE 7.1

A company receives the right to a particular patent	R
Expected fees (including VAT)	17 100
Statutory fees (including VAT)	22 800
Distribution of management fees (capital in nature) (attributable to the acquisition)	35 000

The cost price is financed by the issue of 150 000 shares at R2,00 each. The shares were trading at R2,50 on the JSE.

REQUIRED:
Determine the total cost of the patent.

EXAMPLE 7.1 Solution

	R
Fair value of shares on JSE (150 000 × R2,50)	375 000
Expert fees (17 100 × 100/114)	15 000
Statutory Fees (22 800 × 100/114)	20 000
Management fees	35 000
	445 000

EXAMPLE 7.2

A company exchanges a computer program, Evolution, with a carrying value of R850 000, for another computer program, Quick Count, with a fair value of R950 000.

REQUIRED:
Recognise the cost of the computer software as at 30 June 2018 and 30 June 2019.

EXAMPLE 7.2 Solution

Quick Count is accounted for at R950 000 in the company's records and R100 000 will be recognised as a profit.

Suppose the fair value of Quick Count was R800 000. This indicates an impairment loss in terms of Evolution of R50 000 that will first be recognised before Quick Count is accounted for at R800 000.

7.7 COST OF AN INTERNALLY GENERATED INTANGIBLE ASSET

7.7.1 Internally generated goodwill

Goodwill contributes huge profits to the value of the business. Realistically, these profits might gradually decline as the market competition increases. The temporary nature of this intangible asset and its limited useful life result in it being treated in the same way as other non-current assets for accounting purposes and depreciated accordingly under (IAS 16). Goodwill is sometimes incorrectly referred to as an intangible asset.

An entity shall not recognise goodwill created internally as an asset (IAS 38.48). It is not recognised as an intangible asset because it is not an identifiable resource governed by the entity to measure the cost reliably. Internally created goodwill does not meet the definition of an asset nor the recognition criteria.

7.7.2 Internally created intangible assets other than goodwill

It is sometimes difficult to assess whether an internally generated intangible asset like a brand, customer list, publishing title or similar asset qualifies for recognition because it is difficult to determine if:
- there is a distinguishable asset that will produce future economic benefits; and
- the cost is reliable.

The standard prohibits the capitalisation of these assets because it is hard if not impossible to measure their cost reliably.

An asset's generation is classified into the research phase or development phase to assess whether the internally generated asset meets the recognition criteria (IAS 38.52).

Suppose the entity cannot separate the research phase from the development phase of the internal project to create an intangible asset. In that case, the entity treats the expenditure incurred as the research phase only (IAS 38.53).

The research phase
An entity shall not recognise intangible assets arising from research. It can recognise research expenditure as an expense when incurred (IAS 38.54). In the research phase of a project, an entity cannot prove that an intangible asset exists that will generate probable future economic benefits (IAS 38.55).

When examining competing products on the market, studying their features and trying to find weaknesses in order to better its own product, an entity cannot capitalise that expenditure, but must rather expense it to profit or loss.

Examples of research activities are activities aimed at acquiring new knowledge; the search, evaluation and final selection of alternatives; applications of research findings or other knowledge; the search for alternative materials, devices, products, processes, system or services; and the formulation, design, evaluation and final selection of possible alternatives for new or improved materials, devices, products, processes, systems or services.

The development phase
An intangible development asset is to be recognised if, and only if, the entity can prove **all** of the following:
- Probability of expected future economic benefits
- Management's intention to finish and use or sell the asset
- Existence of adequate and available resources to finish and utilise or dispose of the asset
- Ability to utilise or dispose of the asset
- Technical viability
- Reliable measure of expenditure.

Examples of development activities include the design, construction and analysis of pre-manufacturing or pre-utilise models; the designs of tools, jigs, moulds, etc.

Brands created within the entity, publishing titles, customer records and items similar in substance cannot be recognised as intangible assets because they cannot be separated from the cost of developing the company.

The cost of internally created intangible assets is the sum of expenditure incurred from when an intangible asset first meets the recognition criteria. The reinstatement of expenditure recognised as an expense in previous annual financial statements or interim financial reports is prohibited. The cost of an internally created intangible asset comprises all directly attributable costs necessary to create, produce, and prepare the asset to operate in the manner intended by management.

The examples of directly attributable costs are cost of materials and services in creating the intangible asset; salaries and wages; fees to register the statutory rights; and amortisation of patents and licences.

Expressly excluded from the cost are the selling and administration costs, other general overhead expenses unless they can be directly associated with providing the asset for use; identified inefficiencies and initial operating losses incurred before an asset achieves planned performance; and staff training.

EXAMPLE 7.3 My Property
My Property developed a new computer software package to use internally for property rentals. The expenses incurred are as follows:

	R
1 July 2018 to 31 May 2018	135 000
1 June 2018 to 30 June 2018	15 000
1 July 2019 to 30 June 2019	300 000

The following has been established:

1. On 1 July 2018, proof is provided that the software fulfils the recognition criteria as an intangible asset.
2. The recoverable value, including expected cash outflows to finish the package before it is ready for use, is R75 000 on 30 June 2018 and R285 000 on 30 June 2019.

REQUIRED:

Recognise the cost of the computer software as at 30 June 2018 and 30 June 2019.

EXAMPLE 7.3 Solution – My Property

On 30 June 2018

The cost of the computer software is R15 000 as recognised in the entity's records on 30 June 2018. That is the expenditure incurred since the date when the recognition criteria for an intangible asset were met.

R135 000 expenditure before 1 June 2018 is recognised as research expense. It will not be involved with the software package's cost recognised in the statement of financial position.

On 30 June 2019

My Property recognises the software as an intangible asset of R285 000 (R300 000 + R15 000 (2018) – R30 000 (impairment loss)). The entity can reverse loss in a subsequent period if the reversal requirement of an impairment loss is met.

EXAMPLE 7.4 Best of Times Games Ltd

Best of Times Games Ltd manufactures video games and is currently busy with five projects for which the following information is available:

Project	1	2	3	4	5
	R	R	R	R	R
Capitalised development cost brought forward	600	440	–	–	–
Research and development costs incurred during the year	–	90	125	181	98
• Salaries	–	70	60	150	80
• Directly attributable overheads	–	6	12	–	6
• Raw material	–	9	20	25	12
• Market research	–	–	25	6	–
• Patents and licences	–	5	8	–	–

Project 1:

This project is complete and commercial production commenced during the current reporting period. The directors are certain that the carrying amount of the capitalised costs will be covered through future sales of the product. Sales of the product amounted to 30 000 units for the year.

Estimates of future sales **in units (video games)** are as follows:

2012   40 000

2013   50 000

2014   60 000

It is estimated that no sales will take place after 2014.

Project 2:

Initially, this project was considered to be highly profitable, but as a result of the release of a similar product by Sony, which is more advanced that the envisaged product, the success of the project is now considered to be remote.

Project 3:

In previous years, R176 000 was initially recognised as an expense. Due to changes in the market, directors are now, after thorough market research, convinced that the project will in future earn income which exceeds the development costs. For this reason, the directors want to reverse the write-off.

Project 4:

The project satisfies the requirements for recognition of an intangible asset from 1 January and is estimated to continue for three years before the project is completed.

Project 5:

This project is new and activities have been limited to research and the formulation of product alternatives by engineers.

REQUIRED:

Disclose the research and development costs (expense and asset) in the financial statements for the year ended 31 December 2011. Show all your calculations. Notes, including the accounting policy note, are required.

EXAMPLE 7.4 Solution – Best of Times Games Ltd

1. Accounting policy

Research and development costs

Research costs are expensed when incurred. Development costs of technically feasible projects from which future economic benefits will flow to the company are capitalised and amortised over the periods during which benefits will be derived from the project based on estimated future sales, but limited to a period of five years. The amortisation will be based on the number of units produced in the reporting period divided by the expected number of units to be produced within the first five years since development.

2. Profit from operations

Profit from operations is shown after the following expenses:

	R	Calculations
Development costs – amortisation	100 000	*R100 (W1) project 1*
Expensed	188 000	*R90 (W1) project 2*
		+ R98 (W1) project 5
Impairment loss	530 000	*530 (W1) project 1*

3. Development costs

	R	
Balance at the beginning of the year	1 040 000	
Gross carrying amount	1 040 000	*R600 project 1*
		+ R440 project 2
Accumulated amortisation and impairment	–	*No project has been completed*
Development costs capitalised during the year	396 000	*R90 project 2*
		+ R125 project 3
		+ R181 project 4
Development costs impaired	(530 000)	*R530 (W1) project 2*
Development costs amortised	(100 000)	*R100 (W1) project 1*
Balance at the end of the year	806 000	

↳

Made up as follows:		806 000	
Gross carrying amount		1 436 000	*R600 project 1*
			+ R530 project 2
			+ R125 project 3
			+ R181 project 4
Accumulated amortisation and impairment		(630 000)	*R530 (W1) project 2*
			+ R100 project 1

WORKINGS:

W1 analysis of research and development costs

	Expense	Asset	Calculations
Balance at beginning of year	–	1 040 000	R600 + R440
Project 1			R600 000 × 30000/180 000 units
Amortisation	100 000	(100 000)	
Project 2		90 000	
Capitalised			
Impairment	(530 000)	(530 000)	R440 + R90
Project 3		–	
Amount which was initially expensed cannot be capitalised			
Current year's amount is capitalised		125 000	
Project 4		180 000	
All amounts capitalised			
Project 5	98 000		
All amounts expensed			
	728 000	**806 000**	

An intangible item's expenditure shall be recognised as an expense unless it forms part of the cost of an intangible item that meets the recognition criteria, or the item is acquired in the business combination and cannot be recognised as an intangible asset, and thus forms part of goodwill.

The following items are recognised as expenses:
- Research costs
- Expenses of start-up activities unless the expenditure includes the cost of an item of property, plant and equipment (IAS 16). Start-up costs may consist of:
  - legal and secretarial costs in establishing a legal entity;
  - costs to open a new facility or business; and
  - pre-operating costs (expenditure for starting new operations or launching new products or processes)
- Training costs
- Advertising and promotional costs
- Relocating or re-organising costs (IAS 38.69).

Expenditure on an intangible item that was initially recognised as an expense shall not be recognised as part of an intangible asset.

7.8 SUBSEQUENT MEASUREMENT

An entity shall choose either the cost model or the revaluation model as its accounting policy. If an intangible asset is recorded using the revaluation model, all other assets in its class shall also be accounted for using the same model, unless there is no active market for those assets.

7.8.1 Cost model

An entity shall carry an intangible asset at its cost less accumulated amortisation and any accumulated impairment losses.

7.8.2 Revaluation model

An intangible asset shall be carried at a revalued amount being the fair value at the date of revaluation less following accumulated amortisation and impairment loss. Determine the fair value by reference to an active market. Revaluations make such regularity that the asset's carrying amount does not materially differ from its fair value at the end of the reporting period. The revaluation model does not allow the revaluation of intangible assets that have not previously been recognised as an asset or the initial recognition of intangible assets at amounts other than their cost.

The revaluation model applies after initially recognising an asset at cost. However, suppose only part of the intangible asset cost is recognised as an asset because the asset did not meet the criteria for recognition until part of the process. In that case, the revaluation model may apply to the whole of that asset. The revaluation model can also apply to an intangible asset received by a government grant and recognised at a nominal amount.

Intangible assets' frequent revaluation depends on the volatility of the intangible assets' fair values being revalued.

If an intangible asset is revalued, any accumulated amortisation at the date of the revaluation is either:
- restated proportionally with the change in the asset's gross carrying amount so that the asset's carrying amount after revaluation equals its revalued amount; or
- eliminated against the gross carrying amount of the asset, and the net amount restated to the revalued amount of the asset (IAS 38.80).

EXAMPLE 7.5

	R
Cost of asset	300 000
Accumulated amortisation at 31 December 2018	50 000
Total useful life	12 years
Net replacement value at 31 December 2019	350 000

REQUIRED:
Apply the revaluation model for the determination of the fair value.

EXAMPLE 7.5 Solution
Alternative 1: Proportional increase in accumulated amortisation

	R
Carrying amount 31 December 2018 (300 000 – 50 000)	250 000
Net replacement value 1 January 2019 (350 000 + (350 000/9))	388 889
Revaluation surplus (388 889 – 250 000)	138 889
Gross replacement value (388 889 × 12/10)	466 667

	Revalued amount R	Carrying amount R	Revaluation R
Cost	466 667	300 000	166 667
Accumulated amortisation	(77 778)	(50 000)	(27 778)
Carrying amount	388 889	250 000	138 889

↪

Journal entry	Dr	Cr
	R	R
Dr Cost price (SFP)	166 667	
Cr Accumulated amortisation (SFP)		27 778
Cr Revaluation surplus (OCI)		138 889

Alternative 2: Elimination of amortisation

	R
Carrying amount 31 December 2018 (300 000 – 50 000)	250 000
Net replacement value 1 January 2019 (350 000 + (350 000/9))	388 889

Journal entry	Dr	Cr
	R	R
Dr Accumulated amortisation (SFP)	50 000	
Cr Cost price (SFP)		300 000
Dr Asset at revaluation amount (SFP)	388 889	
Cr Revaluation surplus(OCI)		138 889

Revalued intangible assets and all other assets in their class shall also be revalued unless there is no active market for those assets. In that case, the asset is carried at cost less accumulated amortisation and impairment losses (IAS 38.81). Suppose a revalued intangible asset's fair value can no longer be determined by reference to an active market. In that case, the asset's carrying amount shall be its revalued value at the last revaluation date by reference to the active market less any subsequently accumulated amortisation and any subsequent accumulated impairment losses (IAS 38.82).

The fact that an active market no longer exists may indicate that the asset may be impaired. If the fair value of the asset can again be determined by reference to an active market at a subsequent measurement date, the revaluation model is applied from that date (IAS 38.83-84).

An increase in an intangible asset's carrying amount due to revaluation shall be recognised on other comprehensive income and in equity under the revaluation surplus heading. However, a revaluation increase shall be recognised in profit or loss to the extent that it reverses a revaluation decrease (impairment loss) of the same asset previously recognised in profit or loss (IAS 38.85).

The profit or loss statement shall recognise a decrease in an asset's carrying amount due to revaluation. However, a revaluation decrease shall be recognised in other comprehensive income (debit) to the extent of any credit balance in the revaluation surplus regarding the asset. The decreased recognition in other comprehensive income reduced the amount accumulated in equity under the revaluation surplus heading (IAS 38.86).

The revaluation surplus in equity may be transferred directly to retained earnings when surplus on the asset's retirement or disposal is realised. Some of the surpluses are realised as the entity uses the asset. The amount realised is the difference between amortisation based on the revalued carrying amount of the asset and amortisation that would have been recognised based on the asset's historical cost.

EXAMPLE 7.6 BellTel Telecommunications Company
BellTel Telecommunications Company began researching and developing a wireless modem – one which truly did not have any wires, something they planned to call the 'Less-wire Wireless'. The following is a summary of the costs that the research and development (R&D) department incurred each year:

2017   R&D costs   R180 000

2018   R&D costs   R100 000

2019   R&D costs   R80 000

Additional information:

1. The costs listed above were incurred evenly throughout each year.
2. Included in the costs incurred in 2017 are administrative costs of R60 000 that are not considered to be directly attributable to the research and development process. The first two months of the year were dedicated to research. Development began from 1 March 2017, but all six recognition criteria for capitalisation of development costs were only met on 1 April 2017.
3. Included in the costs incurred in 2018 are administrative costs of R20 000 that are considered to be directly attributed to the research and development process.
4. Included in the costs incurred in 2019 are training costs of R30 000 that are considered to be directly attributed to the research and development process: in preparation for the completion of the development process, certain employees were trained on how to operate the asset.

REQUIRED:
Show all journals related to the costs incurred for each year ended 31 December 2017.

EXAMPLE 7.6 Solution – BellTel Telecommunications Company

31 December 2017		Debit	Credit
Administrative expense (E)		60 000	
Research expense (E)	$(180\,000 - 60\,000) \times 2/12$	20 000	
Development expense(E)	$(180\,000 - 60\,000) \times 1/12$	10 000	
Development: cost (A)	$(180\,000 - 60\,000) \times 9/12$	90 000	
Bank/liability			180 000
Research and development costs: all six criteria were met on 1 April 2017 and these costs will be capitalised after this date. Costs incurred before this date will be expensed. R&D costs are also expensed because they are not directly attributable to R&D.			
31 December 2018		**Dr**	**Cr**
Dr Development: cost (A)		100 000	
Cr Bank/liability			100 000
Development costs incurred (the administration costs of R20 000 are capitalised because they are directly attributable to the R&D project)			
31 December 2019		**Dr**	**Cr**
Dr Training expense (E)		30 000	
Dr Development cost	$(80\,000 - 30\,000)$	50 000	
Cr Bank/liability			80 000
Development costs incurred (training costs of R30 000 are expensed as they are expressly not allowed to be capitalised to the intangible asset)			

Comment:
- *Administrative costs are capitalised if they are directly attributable, otherwise they are expensed.*
- *Training costs are always expensed even if they are considered to be directly attributable.*
- *Research costs are always expensed.*
- *Development costs that are expensed due to being incurred before the recognition criteria were met may not be subsequently capitalised, even if the recognition criteria are subsequently met. They remain expensed.*

7.9 USEFUL LIFE, AMORTISATION AND IMPAIRMENT
7.9.1 Useful life
An entity shall assess whether the useful life of an intangible asset is finite or indefinite.

The useful life is indefinite when there is no foreseeable limit to the period over which the asset is expected to generate net cash inflows for the entity.

The term 'indefinite' does not mean infinite. The indefinite useful life of intangible assets requires future expenditure (eg advertising) to maintain their standard of performance. Such expenditure could be excessive (ie in excess of that required to maintain the asset's level of performance).

Intangible assets with finite useful life are amortised while those with indefinite useful lives are not.

The useful life of the intangible asset is determined by considering many factors, including:
- the expected usage of an asset;
- expected life cycles of an asset and unrestricted information on estimates of the useful life of similar assets that operate similarly;
- technical, technological, commercial or other kinds of obsolescence;
- the confidence of the industry in which the asset operates and changes in the market demand of the asset;
- expected effects by competitors or possible competitors;
- maintenance expenditure required;
- the period of control on the asset and legal limits on the use of the asset; and
- whether the useful life of an asset is dependent on the useful life of other assets of the entity.

The intangible asset's useful life arising from contractual or legal rights shall not exceed the period of the contractual or other legal rights but may be shorter depending on the period in which the entity expects to ice the asset. Suppose the contractual or other legal rights are conveyed for a limited term that can be renewed. In that case, the intangible asset's useful life shall include the renewal period(s) only if there is sufficient evidence to support the entity's renewal without a high cost.

The following factors indicate that an entity would be able to renew the contractual or legal rights without high cost:
- There is proof to renew the contractual or other legal rights.
- There is proof that conditions to obtain renewal will be satisfied.
- The cost to renew is not high compared with the future economic benefits.

7.9.2 Amortisation
Amortisation method
Amortisation is applicable only to those assets that have a finite useful life. Amortisation shall begin when the asset is available for use in the manner intended by management.

The amortisation method shall reflect the pattern in which the asset's future economic benefits are expected to be consumed by the entity. However, if that pattern cannot be established reliably, the straight line method should be used. The amortisation charge for each period shall be recognised in profit or loss unless this or another standard permits or requires it to be included in the carrying amount of another asset.

A variety of amortisation methods can be used to allocate the depreciable amount of the asset on a systematic basis over its useful life. These methods include the straight line method, the diminishing balance method and the unit of production method (IAS 38.98).

Residual value
The residual value of an intangible asset with finite useful life shall be assumed to be zero unless:
- there is a commitment to purchase the asset after its useful life finishes; and
- there is a dynamic market for the asset and:
  - a reference to that market
  - can determine the residual value; and
  - such a market will exist at the end of the useful life.

After deducting the residual value, the depreciable amount of an asset with finite useful life is determined. An other-than-zero residual value implies that an entity anticipates disposing of the intangible asset before the end of its economic life. Review of residual value is done at least at each financial year end. A change in the residual value is accounted for as a change in an accounting estimate by IAS 8.

Should the asset's useful life differ from previous estimates, the amortisation period shall change consequently. Suppose there has been a change in the expected consumption pattern. In that case, the amortisation method shall change to reflect the modified pattern.

The residual value of an intangible asset may increase to an amount equal to or greater than the asset's carrying amount. If it does, the asset's amortisation charge is zero unless and until its residual value subsequently decreases to an amount below the asset's carrying amount.

EXAMPLE 7.7 New Dawn Ltd

New Dawn Ltd developed a new product and capitalised an amount of R150 000 as development costs between 31 July 2017 and 31 December 2017. On 1 January 2018, the useful life of the development costs is expected to be five years.

On 31 December 2019, the following occur:
- A competitor introduces a new product that will shortly overtake the market held by the product of New Dawn Ltd.
- The management of the company estimate that the remaining life of their market is six months before it will be taken over by the product of the competitor.
- The recoverable amount of the asset is only R20 000.

REQUIRED:

1. Prepare relevant journal entries to recognise and amortise development costs for 2018.
2. Calculate the impairment loss of the development costs at the end of December 2019.

EXAMPLE 7.7 Solution – New Dawn Ltd

1.

31 July 2017–31 December 2017		Dr	Cr
Dr Development costs		150 000	
Cr Bank			150 000
Recognise development costs as an intangible asset			
31 December 2018			
Dr Amortisation (P/L)	(150 000/5)	30 000	
Cr Accumulated amortisation			30 000
Amortisation of development costs for 2018			
Note: The amortisation of the development costs can also be debited to cost of sales since it relates to the manufacture of the new product.			

2.

31 December 2019		Dr	Cr
Dr Amortisation (P/L)	(150 000 – 30 000)/4	30 000	
Cr Accumulated amortisation			30 000
Recognise amortisation for 2019			
Dr Impairment loss (P/L)	(150 000 – 60 000 – 20 000)	70 000	
Cr Accumulated amortisation			70 000
Recognise impairment loss as a result of the loss of market share			
Calculation of impairment loss			
Carrying amount (150 000 – 30 000 – 30 000)			90 000
Less: Recoverable amount			(20 000)
Impairment loss			70 000

7.10 INTANGIBLE ASSETS WITH INDEFINITE USEFUL LIVES

An intangible asset with an indefinite useful life shall not be amortised.

In accordance with IAS 36 *Impairment of assets*, an entity is required to test an intangible asset with an indefinite useful life for impairment by comparing its recoverable amount with its carrying amount annually, whenever there is an indication that the intangible asset may be impaired.

7.11 GOODWILL

Goodwill is an in intangible asset that occurs when a buyer acquires, wholly or partially, an existing business. It is not a separately identifiable asset and is not capable of being separated from the entity, or sold, transferred, or exchanged, either individually or together with a related contract.

It is only acquired through a whole or partial business purchase. Goodwill mainly represents that portion of the entire business value that cannot be assigned to other income-producing business assets.

Examples of acquired goodwill might include the company's brand name, customer relationships and patent proprietary technology.

Externally acquired or purchased goodwill arises when an entity's purchase price is more than the fair value of individual net assets. This excess is capitalised in the acquirer's books as purchased goodwill in terms of IFRS 3.

Purchased price paid – Net asset value = Goodwill

Remember that this is not self-created or internally generated. The company that generated or created goodwill will not be able to capitalise it as an asset in its books because it is not reliably measurable.

Should the company pay a purchase price that is less than the fair value of the net individual assets, this is recognised as a gain on bargain purchase.

If the fair value goes lower than the cost (what goodwill was purchased for), impairment should be recorded or lowered down to its fair market value.

Goodwill cannot be amortised because it is considered to have an indefinite useful life. An entity's management is responsible for valuing goodwill every year and determining if an impairment is required.

EXAMPLE 7.8 Shop 'n Go

Shop 'n Go acquired 100% of Ziza Spaza Shop, but paid more than the net market value. Ziza Spaza Shop's assets and liabilities at fair value are as follows.

Fair market value

Accounts receivable	R15 000
Accounts payable	R9 000
Inventory	R7 500

REQUIRED:

Calculate goodwill and show the journal entry for the purchase.

EXAMPLE 7.8 Solution – Shop 'n Go

Total net assets = R15 000 + R7 500 – R9 000
= R13 500

In order to acquire Ziza Spaza Shop, Shop 'n Go will pay R30 000. Hence, goodwill would be R16 500 (R30 000 – R13 500).

The journal entry in the books of Shop 'n Go to record the acquisition of Ziza Spaza Shop would be as follows:

Dr Accounts receivable	R15 000	
Dr Goodwill	R16 500	
Dr Inventory	R7 500	
Cr Accounts payable		R9 000
Cr Bank		R30 000

7.12 DISCLOSURE

7.12.1 General

An entity shall disclose each type of intangible asset, differentiating between internally generated intangible assets and other intangible assets and including the following:

- Whether the useful lives are indefinite or finite and, if finite, the useful lives or the amortisation rates used
- The amortisation methods used for finite intangible assets with useful lives
- The cost and any accumulated amortisation (and accumulated impairment losses) at the inception and end of the period
- Any amortisation of intangible assets in line with the statement of comprehensive income
- A reconciliation of the carrying value at the commencement and end of the period:
  - additions, indicating separately those from internal development, acquired separately and acquired from the business combination;
  - assets categorised as held for sale or included in a disposal group by IFRS 5 and other disposals;
  - rises and falls during the period arising from revaluations, and impairment losses recognised or reversed in other comprehensive income following IAS 36 *Impairment of assets* (if any);
  - recognition in profit and loss of impairment losses during the period following IAS 36;
  - reversed impairment losses in profit and loss during the period under IAS 36 (if any);
  - any amortisation recognised during the period;
  - net exchange differences arising on the translation into the presentation currency; and
  - other changes in the carrying amount during the period.

As already stated above, a class of intangible assets is a grouping of assets of a similar nature and use in an entity's operations.

Examples of separate classes may include:
- brand names;
- mastheads and publishing titles;
- computer software;
- licences and franchises;
- copyrights, patents and other industrial property rights, service and operating rights;
- recipes, formulas, models, designs and prototypes; and
- intangible assets under development.

The classes mentioned above are disaggregated into smaller or (more extensive) categories if this results in more relevant financial statements.

An entity discloses information on impaired intangible assets under IAS 36 *Impairment of assets,* in addition to the general disclosure requirements carrying amount during the period.

IAS 8 requires an entity to disclose the nature and amount of a change in an accounting estimate that has a material effect in the current period or is expected to have a material effect in subsequent periods. Such disclosure may arise from changes in:
- the assessment of an intangible asset's useful life;
- the amortisation method; or
- residual values (IAS 38.121).

An entity shall also disclose:
- for intangible assets assessed as having an indefinite useful life, the carrying amount of that asset, and the reasons supporting the assessment of indefinite useful life. In giving these reasons, the entity shall describe the factor(s) that played a significant role in determining that the asset has an indefinite useful life;
- a description, the carrying amount and remaining amortisation period of any individual intangible assets that are material to the entity's financial statements;
- for intangible assets required by way of a government grant and initially recognised at fair value:
  - the fair value initially recognised for these assets;
  - the carrying amount; and
  - whether they were measured after recognition under the cost model or revaluation model;

- carrying amounts of intangible assets whose titles are restricted and the carrying amounts of intangible assets pledged as security for liabilities; and
- the number of contractual commitments.

7.12.2 Intangible assets measured after recognition using the revaluation model
If intangible assets are shown at revalued amounts, an entity shall disclose the following:
- By a class of intangible assets:
  - the effective date of revaluation;
  - the carrying amount of revalued intangible assets; and
  - the carrying amount that would have been recognised had the revalued class of intangible assets been measured after recognition using the cost model.
- Revaluation surplus of intangible assets at the beginning and end of the period, indicating the changes during the period and any restrictions on the balance distribution to shareholders.

7.12.3 Research and development
An entity shall disclose the amount of the research and development expenditure recognised during the period.

7.13 SUMMARY
This chapter covered IAS 38 and part of IAS 3 to specify the accounting treatment for intangible assets not covered by another standard. The standards require an entity to recognise an intangible asset only when a criterion is met. The standards also mention how to measure the carrying value of an intangible asset and require certain disclosures regarding intangible assets.

EXERCISES

Exercise 7.1 Sterling Bank
Sterling Bank has purchased information about subscribers from a Vox Telecom company in order to reach its targeted customers via phone, SMS or other advertising medium. Can Sterling Bank recognise the expense incurred to buy this subscriber data as an intangible asset?

The bank expects to generate future economic benefits from the data since it will get new customers using the data, but there is a feeling that the bank does not have sufficient control over the expected economic benefits as it cannot guarantee new sales from the customers.

REQUIRED:
Explain whether the bank should just expense the purchase as a part of the normal advertising activities, or the transaction could be capitalised as an asset.

Exercise 7.2 Akon Lighting Africa
You have been recruited to join Akon Lighting Africa, a project that has been trying to develop solar streetlights and small energy systems and products. You establish that costs amounting to R3 million have been incurred, and paid for, between 2017 and 2020. The auditors tell you that the manner in which costs have been accounted for this project is incorrect, and given the significance of the amounts involved they will have to qualify the report if it is not amended.

Some of the information has been lost, but you are able to ascertain the following details regarding the work done on this project:

2017	
An amount of R400 000 was spent on the project (60% on the scientist and 40% on research). The project was at its initial stage and the company was **establishing** its feasibility.	
2018	
R1 800 000 was spent in laboratories. At this stage, the project was absolutely technically feasible. You are able to ascertain that the recognition criteria had been met. It is evident that the recoverable amount at the end of the financial year was R1 600 000.	

2019	
The project was suspended for January due to financial instability. The budgets were redrafted, and cost projections were performed to ensure that the project was financially and technically viable. R80 000 was incurred for this exercise.	
R720 000 was incurred for the rest of the year (R120 000 for administrative costs) with recognition criteria being met in February. The recoverable amount was calculated to be R2 600 000 at 31 December 2019.	
2020	
The project was implemented for operation on 10 January 2017 and has a useful life of five years, nil residual value and amortisation is calculated on the straight line basis.	

REQUIRED:
Provide all related journal entries in the general journal of Akon Lighting Africa for each of the years ended 31 December 2017 until 2020.

Exercise 7.3 Dell Ltd
Dell Ltd is a South African pharmaceutical company that has embarked on research and development (R&D) of new antibiotic drugs. On 1 March 2017, the company began a project incurring the following costs (paid in cash) evenly over each of the following years:

Period	Cost
1 March 2017–28 February 2018	R270 000
1 March 2018–28 February 2019	R375 000
1 March 2019–28 February 2020	R500 000

The recognition criteria for capitalisation of development costs were met on 1 July 2017.
Since the development asset is an intangible asset not available for use, Dell Ltd is forced to calculate its recoverable amount every year (at a chosen time, but the same time each year) and also to do an indicator review at a reporting date. Dell Ltd decided it would be best to perform the compulsory calculation of its recoverable amount at the same time that it performed its indicator review (ie 28 February).

The recoverable amounts calculated as at 28 February were as follows:

28 February 2018	R195 000
28 February 2019	R530 000
28 February 2020	R1 045 000

At no stage were the variables of amortisation in need of adjustment.

REQUIRED:
Show all journals related to the costs incurred for each of the reporting periods ended 28 February with reference to IAS 38.

Exercise 7.4 Bull Ltd
Bull Ltd is a company manufacturing and retailing food products. The current financial year ends on 30 June 2020. The company owns one brand name, 'Tasty Oats', shown in the statement of financial position at its carrying amount of R600 000.

The right to manufacture (registered trademark No. 00787) under this brand name for a period of 30 years was purchased on 1 July 2016 for R600 000. These rights may be renewed at a cost of R10 000 (an immaterial cost to the company). The brand name is considered to have an indefinite useful life.

Bull Ltd intends not to calculate the recoverable amount of this brand at 30 June 2020 since a detailed calculation of the recoverable amount was done on 30 June 2019, on which date there was an immaterial difference between the recoverable amount and carrying amount and there appears to be no indication of impairment after having performed the indicator review process.

REQUIRED:

Critically analyse the measurement of 'Tasty Oats' in the financial statements of Bull Ltd.

Exercise 7.5 Sneaky Shoes Ltd

Sneakie Shoes Ltd (SS) is a company with a year end of 30 September. A group of fashion designers, facilitated by their accountant, incorporated the company in Cape Town on 15 October 2019, and also on this date opened two stores there. The company retails clothing to fashion-savvy clientele.

1. SS decides to launch its own sneakers line to be sold under the brand Sneaky Shoes. The costs to develop the brand were internally incurred and amounted to R1 750 000. The brand was developed after extensive consumer research was conducted at a cost of R430 000 (this amount is included in the R1 750 000), and it was established that the consumers will most definitely buy the sneakers and cannot wait for the launch of the brand. SS expects the brand to have an indefinite useful life.

2. SS also purchased the SportsLife brand, a premium South Africa sports clothing line. SS is the sole retailer of SportsLife garments for the duration of the contract. The brand has been assessed to have a useful life of five years before the contract will be renegotiated. The brand was purchased for R3 000 000 on 1 October 2019. The market loves the brand and sales are booming.

3. SS started a community development initiative, in which they will provide state-of-the-art training to 15 women from the neighbouring communities around Cape Town. This training will focus in equipping these women to make some of the clothes in the different clothing lines mentioned above. Each of these women will receive a basic salary of R3 500 for the first 18 months (the period of the training provided). These women will have to stay under the employment of SS for a period of two years. Salaries will increase by 25% per year.

   The Western Cape government became aware of this initiative and negotiated with SS to subsidise 75% of these women's salaries, for the duration of the 18-month training period as well as subsidise 40% of their salaries for the two years following their training contracts. The 15 women were all appointed on 1 April 2020. The subsidy was paid over by the Western Cape government at 20 April 2020. All the conditions relating to the subsidy were met from 1 April 2020.

REQUIRED:

1. Discuss in terms of IAS 38 *Intangible assets* whether or not the Sneaky Shoes brand should be recognised as an intangible asset in the records of SS for the year ended 30 September 2020. Assume in your answer that the **definition** of an intangible asset was met; only discuss the **recognition criteria**. Ignore taxation.

2. Discuss in an email to the management of SS how the SportsLife brand (an intangible asset) should be measured in terms of IAS 38 in the financial statements of SS for the year ended 30 September 2020. Ignore taxation.

Exercise 7.6 Adam (Pty) Ltd

The following is an abbreviated statement of financial position of Luvo (Pty) Ltd as at 31 December 2019:

ASSETS	
Land and buildings	240 000
Vehicles	60 000
Current assets	200 000
	500 000
EQUITY AND LIABILITIES	
Share capital	320 000
Reserves	100 000
Current liabilities	80 000
	500 000

On 31 December 2019, Adam (Pty) Ltd acquired all the assets and liabilities of Luvo (Pty) Ltd for R760 000. In settlement, Adam (Pty) Ltd issued 760 000 ordinary shares of R1 each to Luvo (Pty) Ltd.

The value of the assets and liabilities of Luvo (Pty) Ltd are considered to the fair except for land and buildings, which are considered to be worth R360 000.

REQUIRED:
Calculate the amount of goodwill acquired when Adam (Pty) Ltd acquired Luvo (Pty) Ltd.

Exercise 7.7 Mgenge Ltd
The following information relates to Mgenge Ltd:

Mgenge Ltd	
Statement of financial position at 31 December 2019	
ASSETS	
Non-current assets	135 000
Machinery and equipment	110 000
Office furniture	25 000
Current assets	130 000
Consumable material	30 000
Work in progress	5 000
Finished goods	40 000
Receivables	50 000
Bank	5 000
TOTAL ASSETS	265 000
EQUITY AND LIABILITIES	
Equity and reserves	190 000
Share capital (issued at R1,00 per share)	150 000
Reserves	40 000
Non-current liabilities	50 000
Long-term loan	50 000
Current liabilities	25 000
Payables	25 000
TOTAL EQUITY AND LIABILITIES	265 000

On 31 December 2019, Mgenge Ltd took over Elethu (Pty) Ltd as a going concern except for the bank overdraft. The purchase price was agreed at R60 000. Mgenge Ltd issued 28 000 shares at R1,80 per share as payment and paid the balance in cash for which a loan was acquired for any shortfall.

Elethu (Pty) Ltd	
Statement of financial position at 31 December 2019	
ASSETS	
Non-current assets	39 000
Machinery and equipment	34 000
Office furniture	5 000
Current assets	26 000
Consumable material	4 000
Inventory	10 000
Receivables	12 000
TOTAL ASSETS	65 000
EQUITY AND LIABILITIES	
Equity and reserves	47 000
Capital	47 000
Current liabilities	18 000
Payables	15 000
Bank overdraft	3 000
TOTAL EQUITY AND LIABILITIES	65 000

REQUIRED:

1. Calculate the purchased/acquired goodwill when Mgenge Ltd takes over Elethu (Pty) Ltd.

2. Show the new statement of financial position of Mgenge Ltd immediately after the purchase of Elethu (Pty) Ltd.

CHAPTER 8

STATEMENT OF CASH FLOWS (IAS 7)

LEARNING OUTCOMES

After studying this chapter, you should be able to:

- Understand the underlying principles outlined in IAS 7.
- Use those principles to prepare a statement of cash flows, with notes to the financial statements, so as to comply with the requirements of International Financial Reporting Standards (IFRS).
- Analyse the cash flow items from business transactions.

PREAMBLE

Mr Mhlongo (known as Njomane), is worried and has been arguing with his business friend about profitability and cash flow. Njomane comes to your office for professional business advice. He states that as long as his business is making a profit, he does not worry himself with cash flow matters. This is because he believes that profit should solve the cash flow problems. He asks you to explain to him the difference between the two and how to manage his business cash flow.

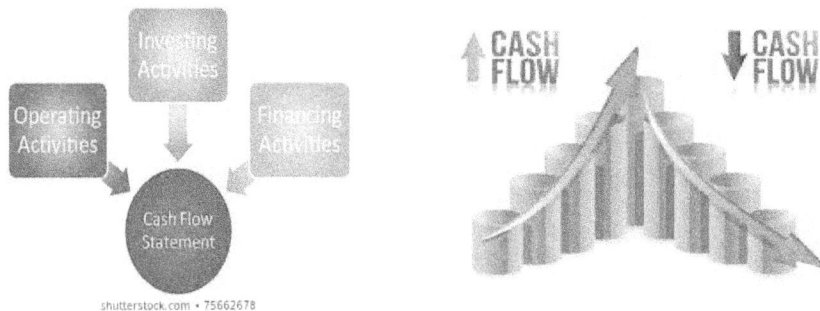

Figure 8.1: Cash flow in a business

8.1 INTRODUCTION

It is very possible to have a profitable business that is experiencing cash flow problems. Think of a business that has most of its sales on credit and has a great turnover, but it is taking too long to collect its receivables. That business could be making huge profits but having cash flow problems because of these cash collection difficulties. The success of any company is dependent on the strategic choices that are made and how the company's funds (resources) are utilised. Cash management in a business entity is one of the most important aspects of ensuring that the company is successful in its endeavours. The statement of cash flows is one of the important tools that most companies employ to achieve the cash management requirement. This statement is useful in forecasting or predicting future cash receipts and payments. It uses the cash basis instead of the accrual basis that is followed when preparing the other elements of the annual financial statements.

8.2 PURPOSE

The main purpose of a statement of cash flows is to provide information about a business entity's cash during an accounting period (money being received and paid out by the entity), in that the statement reports the sources and uses of its cash. This statement is useful as it helps users (both internal and external) to assess a business entity's liquidity, its operating capability, the ability to obtain finance and its risks. Detailed information is provided about a business entity's cash receipts and cash payments over a specific period of time. Cash flows can also be used as a forecasting tool, to make future decisions based on the current information provided.

There are four sections to the statement of cash flows, namely operating activities, investing activities, financing activities, and changes in cash and cash equivalents. There are two methods that can be used when preparing a statement of cash flows, either the direct method or indirect method. It is more common for business entities to use the 'direct method' to prepare the statement of cash flows. Therefore, the direct method will be adopted for our purposes. Using this method, operating cash inflows less operating cash outflows determines the net cash flow from operating activities. A note to the annual financial statements, called a reconciliation of profit before tax and cash generated from operations, is also prepared

8.3 SECTIONS OF THE STATEMENT OF CASH FLOWS

The sections of the statement of cash flows are as follows:

1. **Cash flow from operating activities** (usually associated with the buying and selling of goods and/or providing of services over a specific period of time)

   These will include all amounts received and paid in the ordinary operations of the business, including finance costs and returns on investments which have become normal to incur nowadays. Examples include the following:
   - Amounts received from customers
   - Amounts paid to suppliers and employees
   - Amount of taxation to be paid to the South African Revenue Services
   - Amount to be paid to shareholders for dividends
   - Amount to be received for investments in other business entities
   - Interest to be paid to banks/finance houses

2. **Cash flow from investing activities** (usually associated with the purchases and sale of non-current assets and investments)

   These will include **inflows** from:
   - sale of any property, plant and equipment
   - sale of investments
   - receipts from repayments of long term loans by other entities

   and **outflows** from:
   - purchase of any property, plant and equipment
   - purchase of investments
   - issue of long-term loans to other entities

3. **Cash flow from financing activities** (usually associated with movements in the non-current liabilities and share capital)

   These will include **inflows** from:
   - sale of shares
   - members' or owners' contributions
   - obtaining loans from finance houses
   - issuing of debentures

   and **outflows** from:
   - redemption of preference shares
   - repayment of loans to finance houses
   - redemption of debentures.

4. **Changes in cash and cash equivalents** (usually the difference between the opening and closing balances in the bank account and related accounts of the business entity).

8.4 CALCULATION OF CASH FLOWS

Calculation of cash flows involves a lot of working backwards to arrive at a particular cash flow desired. This requires a strong understanding of the double entry system. The preparer of the statement of cash flows has to consider that most of the information will be taken from the other elements of the financial statements which are prepared on the accrual basis. This statement is prepared on the cash basis and the preparer should therefore be aware of that and be able to sift through the information to arrive at cash amounts received or paid at a given period.

This involves understanding the relationships between different accounts, the use of T-accounts and sometimes pure mathematical calculations. The preparer of the statement of cash flows has to work backwards to adjust for the following in order to arrive at amounts received or paid:

- Non-cash items (eg depreciation, amortisation, impairment loss, credit loss, discounts, etc)
- Non-operating items (profit or loss on sale of assets, etc)
- Disclosable items (finance costs, finance income, investment income, dividends paid, etc)
- Working capital items (inventories, trade receivables, trade payables, accruals, prepayments, etc).

The illustrative examples that follow will explain the calculations involved in the statement of cash flows.

EXAMPLE 8.1 Khawuleza (Pty) Ltd

Khawuleza (Pty) Ltd is a copper mining operation in Emandeni, KwaZulu-Natal. It has prepared the following financial statements for the year ended 31 December 2019:

Khawuleza (Pty) Ltd
Statement of profit or loss and other comprehensive income for the year ended 31 December 2019

	R
Revenue	2 808 000
Cost of sales	(1 560 000)
Gross profit	1 248 000
Interest received	75 000
Other expenses	(648 000)
Profit before tax	675 000
Income tax expense	(210 000)
Profit for the year	465 000
Other comprehensive income	0
Total comprehensive income	465 000

Khawuleza (Pty) Ltd
Statement of financial position as at 31 December 2019

	R 2019	R 2018
ASSETS		
Non-current assets		
Land and buildings	714 000	510 000
Plant at carrying amount	306 000	78 000
Plant at cost	435 000	450 600
Accumulated depreciation: plant	(129 000)	(87 000)
Investments	342 000	324 000
Current assets		
Inventory	264 600	165 000
Accounts receivable	441 000	315 000
Bank	21 000	39 000
	2 088 600	1 431 000
EQUITY AND LIABILITIES		
Equity		
Ordinary share capital of R1 each	615 000	435 000
Asset replacement reserve	123 000	123 000
Retained earnings	537 600	192 600

↳

Non-current liabilities

Long-term loans	630 000	551 400

Current liabilities

Accounts payable	150 000	84 000
Current tax payable	18 000	15 000
Shareholders for dividends	15 000	30 000
	2 088 600	**1 431 000**

Notes to the financial statements for the year ended 31 December 2019:

1. Profit before tax **R**

   Profit before tax is stated after accounting for the following items:
   - – Profit on sale of plant 9 000
   - – Finance costs 51 000
   - – Depreciation 66 000

2. Dividends

   A dividend of R120 000 was declared for the financial year ended 31 December 2019.

Additional information:

1. Plant with a carrying amount of R171 000 (gross carrying amount 1 – R195 000) was sold for R180 000 and replaced at a cost of R300 000.

2. All other non-current assets (land and buildings R204 000; plant 2 – R165 000) were acquired for expansion purposes.

REQUIRED:

Prepare the statement of cash flows and the related notes of Khawuleza (Pty) Ltd for the year ended 31 December 2019 using the direct method in terms of IAS 7.

EXAMPLE 8.1 Solution – Khawuleza (Pty) Ltd
Calculations:

1. The first calculation to embark on will be cash receipts from customers as this will be the first line item on the face of the statement of cash flows, under the operating activities section. The account that could assist with this is the receivables account.

Accounts receivable

Opening balance	315 000	**Cash receipts (balancing figure)**	2 682 000
Revenue from sales	2 808 000	Closing balance	441 000
	3 123 000		**3 123 000**
Balance accounts receivable	441 000		

2. The next line item will be cash paid to suppliers and employees. There are many ways to calculate these figures, but the quickest way is to combine all accounts that have to do with supplying the entity. The suppliers of the business entity will include suppliers of inventory, which is closely related to an expense called cost of sales; employees, who are suppliers of mental and physical efforts, with salaries and wages being related expenses; municipalities, who are suppliers of electricity and water; insurance companies, who render insurance services; telecommunications companies supplying telephone and internet lines, and so on. All of these related accounts can be grouped into one account called 'cash paid to suppliers and employees', which is easier than opening individual accounts, although this can also be done. When considering the statement of profit or loss and other comprehensive income, between revenue and profit before tax all expenses are considered. Therefore, when taking revenue less profit before tax you can be guaranteed that all expenses for the period are covered. You can call the difference **cost of sales and expenses** and then adjust it for or eliminate non-cash items, non-operating items, disclosable items and working capital items. You will be left with cash paid to suppliers and employees.

Statement of profit or loss and other comprehensive income for the year ended 31 December 2019

	R
Revenue	xxxxx
Cost of sales	xxxxx
Gross profit	xxxxx
Interest received	xxxxx
Other expenses	xxxxx
Profit before tax	xxxxx
Income tax expense	xxxxx
Profit for the year	xxxxx
Other comprehensive income	xxxxx
Total comprehensive income	xxxxx

Cash paid to suppliers and employees

Opening inventories	165 000	Opening accounts payable	84 000
Depreciation	66 000	Cost of sales and expenses	2 133 000
Finance costs	51 000	Interest received	75 000
Cash paid (balancing figure)	**2 133 600**	Profit on sale of equipment	9 000
Closing accounts payable	150 000	Closing inventories	264 600
	2 565 600		**2 565 600**
Balance inventories	264 600	Balance accounts payable	150 000

The rest of the calculations depend on the operations of an entity and information given. The T-accounts are always useful in working backwards to arrive at cash received and cash paid during the period. The calculations that follow are relevant for the information supplied.

3. **Taxation payable**

Cash paid (balancing figure)	207 000	Opening balance	15 000
Closing balance	18 000	**SOCI**	210 000
	225 000		**225 000**
		Balance	18 000

4. **Dividends payable**

Cash paid (balancing figure)	135 000	Opening balance	30 000
Closing balance	15 000	**SOCE**	120 000
	150 000		**150 000**
		Balance	15 00

5. **Plant at carrying amount**

Opening balance	78 000	Disposal	171 000
Cash paid – Replacement	300 000	Depreciation	66 000
– Expansion	165 000	Closing balance	306 000
	543 000		**543 000**
Balance	306 000		

6. Land and Buildings at cost

Opening balance	510 000	Closing balance	714 000
Cash paid – Expansion	204 000		
	714 000		**714 000**
Balance	714 000		

Khawuleza (Pty) Ltd
Statement of cash flows for the year ended 31 December 2019

	R
Cash flows from operating activities	**230 400**
Cash receipts from customers	2 682 000
Cash paid to suppliers and employees	(2 133 600)
Cash generated from operations 3	548 400
Finance costs	(51 000)
Taxation paid	(207 000)
Dividends paid	(135 000)
Interest received	75 000
Cash flows from investing activities	**(507 000)**
Replacement of plant	(300 000)
Expansion of plant	(165 000)
Expansion of land and buildings	(204 000)
Proceeds from sale of plant	180 000
Purchase of investments	(18 000)
Cash flows from financing activities	**258 600**
Proceeds from issue of ordinary shares	180 000
Long-term loan raised	78 600
Decrease in cash and cash equivalents	**(18 000)**
Cash and cash equivalents at the beginning of the year	39 000
Cash and cash equivalents at the end of the year	21 000

Khawuleza (Pty) Ltd
Notes to the statement of cash flows for the year ended 31 December 2019

Reconciliation between profit before tax and cash generated from operations

Profit before tax	**R675 000**
Adjustments/reversals of:	
Depreciation on plant	66 000
Profit on sale of plant	(9 000)
Interest received	(75 000)
Finance costs	51 000
Working capital changes:	
Increase in inventories	(99 600)
Decrease in accounts payable	66 000
Increase in accounts receivable	(126 000)
Cash generated from operations	**548 400**

EXAMPLE 8.2 Mafukuzela Steam (Pty) Ltd

The following information was extracted from Mafukuzela Steam (Pty) Ltd's trial balance for the year ended 28 February 2019. The company specialises in airport dry cleaning services and was founded by Thembisile, a young entrepreneur from Umlazi Township in Durban.

	2019	2018
Debits	R	R
Land and buildings	240 000	200 000
Machinery at cost	14 800	52 300
Investments	-	2 400
Inventory	15 000	19 000
Trade and other receivables	18 000	15 400
Cash and cash equivalents	8 000	14 000
	295 800	**303 100**
Credits		
Issued share capital	100 000	100 000
Long-term loan	40 000	50 000
Revaluation of land and buildings	40 000	-
Retained earnings	60 500	107 000
Asset replacement reserve	19 500	15 000
Shareholders for dividends	20 000	10 000
Accumulated depreciation – machinery	3 400	4 800
Allowance for credit loss	1 000	1 200
Trade and other payables	7 400	11 300
Tax payable	4 000	3 800
	295 800	**303 100**

Additional information:

1. Mafukuzela Steam (Pty) Ltd

Statement of comprehensive income for the year ended 29 February 2019

	R
Revenue	**179 500**
Cost of sales	(76 200)
Other income	1 200
Other expenses	91 000
Profit before tax	**13 500**
Income tax expense	(5 500)
Profit for the year	**8 000**
Other comprehensive income	-
Total comprehensive income for the year	**8 000**

2. Other income

Profit on sale of machinery	R1 000
Decrease in allowance for credit loss	R200

3. Other expenses

Among other things, included in **other expenses** were: loss on sale of investments of R400 and depreciation on machinery of R42 600.

4.

Mafukuzela Steam (Pty) Ltd
Statement of changes in equity for the year ended 29 February 2019

	Retained earnings	Asset replacement reserve	Total
Balance as at 28 February 2018	**107 000**	**15 000**	**122 000**
Total comprehensive income	8 000	-	8 000
Dividends declared	(50 000)	-	(50 000)
Transfer to reserve	(4 500)	4 500	-
Balance as at 28 February 2019	**60 500**	**19 500**	**80 000**

5. A new machine was purchased to replace the old machine that was sold. The old machine had a cost of R45 500 and an accumulated depreciation of R44 000.

6. The investments were sold during the year.

REQUIRED:

1. Use the information provided above to prepare a statement of cash flows for Mafukuzela Steam (Pty) Ltd for the year ended 28 February 2019.

2. Prepare a reconciliation of the profit before tax and the cash generated from operations.

EXAMPLE 8.2 Suggested solution – Mafukuzela Steam (Pty) Ltd

1.

Mafukuzela (Pty) Ltd
Statement of cash flow for the year ended 28 February 2019

	R
Cash flow from operating activities	**7 500**
Cash receipts from customers	176 900
Cash paid to suppliers and employees	(124 100)
Cash generated from operations	52 800
Dividends paid (10 000 + 50 000 – 20 000)	(40 000)
Taxation paid (3 800 + 5 500 – 4 000)	(5 300)
Cash flow from investing activities	**(3 500)**
Replacement of machinery	(8 000)
Proceeds from sale of machinery	2 500
Proceeds from sale of investments	2 000
Cash flow from financing activities	**(10 000)**
Long-term loan repaid (50 000 – 40 000)	(10 000)
Net increase/(decrease) in cash and cash equivalents	**(6 000)**
Cash and cash equivalents at beginning of the year	14 000
Cash and cash equivalents at the end of year	8 000

2.

Reconciliation between profit before tax and cash generated from operations

Profit before tax	13 500
Adjust for non-cash and non-operating items	
Profit on sale of machinery	(1 000)
Loss on sale of investments	400
Credit loss/bad debts	(200)
Depreciation	42 600
Operating profit before working capital changes	55 300
Decrease in inventory (19 000 – 15 000)	4 000
Increase in trade and other receivables (15 400 – 18 000)	(2 600)
Decrease in trade payables (11 300 – 7 400)	(3 900)
Cash generated from operations	**52 800**

WORKINGS:

Receivables			
Opening balance	15 400	Bank	176 900
Sales	179 500	Closing balance	18 000
	194 900		**194 900**

Cash paid to suppliers and employees			
Opening balance (inventory)	19 000	Closing balance (inventory)	15 000
Closing balance (trade payables)	7 400	Opening balance (trade payables)	11 300
Loss on sale	400	Profit on sale	1 000
Depreciation	42 600	Decrease in allowance	200
		C.O.S. & expenses (179 500 – 13 500)	166 000
Cash paid (balancing figure)	**124 100**		
	193 500		**193 500**

Machinery (cost)			
Opening balance	52 300	Realisation	45 500
Purchases	8 000	Closing balance	14 800
	60 500		**60 500**

Accumulated depreciation: Machinery			
Realisation	44 000	Opening balance	4 800
Closing balance	3 400	Depreciation	42 600
	47 400		**47 400**

8.5 SUMMARY

This chapter discussed the purpose and the use of the statement of cash flows. The format and the structure of the statement of cash flows were also discussed in detail, with examples to illustrate the principles followed. The direct method was adopted for the purposes of this textbook, as this is the format encouraged by IAS 7.

EXERCISES

Exercise 8.1 Siyandiza Aviation Fuels Ltd

Siyandiza Aviation Fuels Ltd provides Jet Fuel to various flight schools and airplane charter companies operating at four small airports (Lanseria, Grand Central, Rand and Wonderboom) located in Johannesburg and Pretoria.

Below are their financial statements for the year ended 31 March 2019.

Siyandiza Aviation Fuels Ltd
Statement of profit or loss and other comprehensive income for the year ended 31 March 2019

	R
Revenue	10 250 000
Cost of sales	(6 150 000)
Gross profit	**4 100 000**
Interest received	144 000
Dividend income	202 500
Other expenses	(2 609 000)
Finance costs	(115 000)
Profit before tax	**1 722 500**
Income tax expense	(482 300)
Profit for the year	**1 240 200**
Other comprehensive income	0
Total comprehensive income	**1 240 200**

Siyandiza Aviation Fuels Ltd
Statement of financial position as at 31 March 2019

	2019	2018
	R	R
ASSETS		
Non-current assets	**8 350 000**	**6 850 100**
Land and buildings	2 000 000	2 000 000
Fuel storage tanks	1 250 000	750 000
Fuel delivery trucks	4 800 000	3 900 100
Investments	300 000	200 000
Current assets	**5 302 100**	**5 600 500**
Inventory	2 800 800	3 200 300
Accounts receivable	2 000 900	1 800 000
Cash and cash equivalents	500 400	600 200
TOTAL ASSETS	**13 652 100**	**12 450 600**

	2019	2018
	R	R
EQUITY	**8 874 100**	**6 093 600**
Ordinary share capital	5 000 000	3 000 000
Retained earnings	3 874 100	3 093 600
LIABILITIES	**4 778 000**	**6 357 000**
Non-current liabilities	**2 200 000**	**3 600 000**
Long-term loans	2 200 000	3 600 000
Current liabilities	**2 578 000**	**2 757 000**
Accounts payable	2 000 500	2 182 000
SARS tax liability	300 500	255 000
Shareholders for dividends	277 000	320 000
TOTAL EQUITY AND LIABILITIES	**13 652 100**	**12 450 600**

Additional information:

1. Profit before tax includes the following:
   - Depreciation expense   R484 000
     - Tanks   R200 000
     - Trucks   R284 000
   - Profit on sale of fuel delivery trucks   R40 000

2. A dividend of R459 700 was declared for the current financial year.

3. Three fuel delivery trucks with a total cost of R1 800 000 and an accumulated depreciation of R1 070 000 were sold and replaced at a cost of R1 913 900; no other trucks were purchased or sold. Two new fuel storage tanks were purchased to expand the amount of fuel that their depot can hold; no other tanks were purchased or sold.

REQUIRED:

1. Prepare the statement of cash flows for Siyandiza Aviation Fuels Ltd for the year ended 31 March 2019. Clearly show all your workings.

2. Prepare the reconciliation of profit before tax and cash generated from operations note to the financial statements of Siyandiza Aviation Fuels Ltd.

Exercise 8.2 Mbalenhle Catering Services (Pty) Ltd

The following were extracted from the accounting records of Mbalenhle Catering Services (Pty) Ltd:

Mbalenhle Catering Services (Pty) Ltd
Statement of profit or loss and other comprehensive income for the year ended 30 June 2019

	R
Revenue	495 000
Cost of sales	(247 500)
Gross profit	247 500
General expenses	(110 250)
Profit before tax	137 250
Taxation paid	(51 750)
Profit after tax	85 500
Other comprehensive income	0
Total comprehensive income for the year	85 500

Mbalenhle Catering Services (Pty) Ltd
Statement of financial position as at 30 June 2019

	2019	2018
	R	R
ASSETS		
Non-current assets	**922 500**	**778 500**
Land and buildings	571 500	283 500
Equipment at cost	351 000	495 000
Current assets	**151 200**	**131 400**
Inventory	22 500	13 500
Receivables	81 000	67 500
Bank	47 700	50 400
Total assets	**1 073 700**	**909 900**
EQUITY AND LIABILITIES		
Equity	**848 400**	**661 800**
Ordinary share capital	712 650	574 050
Retained earnings	105 750	87 750
Non-distributable reserve	30 000	Nil
Non-current liabilities	**150 000**	**181 500**
Long-term loan	150 000	181 500
Current liabilities	**75 300**	**66 600**
Creditors	43 500	39 000
Dividends payable	30 000	27 000
Taxation payable	1 800	600
Total equity and liabilities	**1 073 700**	**909 900**

Mbalenhle Catering Services (Pty) Ltd
Extract from statement of changes in equity for the year ended 30 June 2019

	Retained earnings
	R
Opening balance	87 750
Profit for the year	85 500
Dividends for the year	(67 500)
Closing balance	105 750

Additional information:

1. Profit before tax included the following:
   Interest paid   R25 200
   Profit on sale of equipment   R9 000
   Depreciation   R???

2. The non-distributable reserve arose from a revaluation of land and buildings during the year. Additions were also made to land and buildings during the year. Land and buildings are not depreciated.

3. During the year, equipment with a carrying amount of R27 000 was sold at a profit of R9 000. There were no further purchases or sales of equipment during the year.

REQUIRED:

Prepare the statement of cash flows of Mbalenhle Catering Services (Pty) Ltd for the year ended 30 June 2019 using the direct method so as to comply with IAS 7. Notes are required. Show all workings.

Exercise 8.3 Zimele Trading

The following set of financial statements of Zimele Trading is made available to you:

Zimele Trading

Statement of comprehensive income for the year ended 31 December 2019

	Additional information	R
Sales		901 500
Operating income before interest		280 923
Interest		(24 750)
Operating income		265 173
Profit before tax		145 773
Income tax expense		(65 598)
Profit for the year		80 175

Zimele Trading

Statement of changes in equity for the year ended 31 December 2019

	Ordinary share capital R	Asset replacement reserve R	Retained earnings R	Total R
Balance at 1 January 2019	300 000	22 500	17 325	339 825
Profit for the year	-	-	80 175	80 175
Transfer to asset replacement	-	7 500	(7 500)	Nil
Ordinary dividends	-	-	(45 000)	(45 000)
Issue of ordinary shares	150 000	-	-	150 000
Balance at 31 December 2019	450 000	30 000	45 000	525 000

Zimele Trading

Statement of financial position as at 31 December 2019

	Additional information	2019 R	2018 R
Non-current assets			
Property, plant and equipment	2	528 000	327 000
Current assets			
Investments		114 960	108 975
Trade and other receivables		80 130	86 985
Cash at bank		47 628	34 812
		770 718	557 772
Equity and reserves			
Ordinary share capital		450 00	300 000
Retained earnings		45 000	17 325
Asset replacement reserve		30 000	22 500
Non-current liabilities			
Long-term loan		180 000	150 000

↪

Current liabilities			
Trade and other payables		36 942	45 819
Shareholders for dividends		22 500	18 000
Taxation payable		6 276	4 128
		770 718	**557 772**

Additional information:

1. Total depreciation for the year amount to R30 000.

2. Property, plant and equipment

At 31 December 2018	Cost price	Accumulated depreciation	Carrying amount
Land and buildings	150 000	Nil	150 000
Vehicles	183 000	(63 000)	120 000
Machinery	102 000	(45 000)	57 000
	435 000	**(108 000)**	**327 000**
At 31 December 2019			
Land and buildings	300 000	Nil	300 000
Vehicles	189 000	(54 000)	135 000
Machinery	129 000	(36 000)	93 000
	618 000	**(90 000)**	**528 000**

3. A vehicle with a carrying amount of R45 000 was sold for R60 000 during the year and replaced with a new model. Depreciation on vehicles during the year amounted to R21 000.

4. Improvements to and land and buildings were completed during the year which resulted in the doubling of the firm's capacity. No depreciation is written off in respect of land and buildings.

5. Machinery with a carrying amount of R24 000 was sold during the year for R18 000, as the machinery became obsolete.

6. The authorised share capital of the firm consists of 600 000 ordinary shares of no-par value shares.

REQUIRED:

1. Prepare the statement of cash flow of Zimele Trading for the financial year ended 31 December 2019, so as to comply with the requirements of IAS 7.

2. Prepare the reconciliation between profit before tax and cash generated from operations note of Zimele Trading for the financial year ended 31 December 2019.

NB: Show all workings.

Exercise 8.4 Phemba Enterprises

The following are the financial statements of Phemba Enterprises for the financial year ended 30 June 2019:

Phemba Enterprises
Statement of profit or loss and other comprehensive income for the year ended 30 June 2019

		R
Revenue		2 415 000
Cost of sales		(1 399 000)
Gross profit		1 016 000
Distribution costs		(195 000)
Other expenses		(280 000)
Audit fees	100 000	
Depreciation: machinery	110 000	
Depreciation: furniture	10 000	
Credit losses	50 000	
Loss on disposal of machinery	10 000	
Other income		280 000
Profit on sale of land	280 000	
Profit from operations		821 000
Finance costs		(10 000)
Profit before tax		811 000
Income tax expense		(200 000)
Profit after tax		**611 000**

Phemba Enterprises
Statement of changes in equity for the year ended 30 June 2019

	Share capital R	Revaluation surplus R	Retained earnings R	Total R
Balance at 1 July 2018	800 000	Nil	350 000	1 150 000
Issue of ordinary shares	1 000 000			1 000 000
Share issue expenses			(50 000)	(50 000)
Revaluation of land		1 000 000		1 000 000
Profit for the year			611 000	611 000
Dividends			(616 000)	(616 000)
Balance at 30 June 2019	1 800 000	1 000 000	295 000	3 095 000

Phemba Enterprises
Statement of financial position as at 30 June 2019

	2019	2018
Property, plant and equipment	2 460 000	1 000 000
Land	2 000 000	620 000
Machinery	400 000	330 000
Cost price	800 000	700 000
Accumulated depreciation	(400 000)	(370 000)
Furniture	60 000	50 000
Cost price	100 000	80 000
Accumulated depreciation	(40 000)	(30 000)
Current assets	4 340 000	3 300 000
Inventories	1 600 000	1 400 000
Trade and other receivables	2 200 000	1 800 000
Cash on deposit	300 000	100 000
Bank	240 000	Nil
	6 800 000	**4 300 000**
Capital and reserves		
Ordinary share capital	1 800 000	800 000
Revaluation surplus	1 000 000	Nil
Retained earnings	295 000	350 000
Non-current liabilities	1 100 000	1 000 000
Current liabilities	2 605 000	2 150 000
Sundry payables	1 400 000	1 600 000
Short-term loan	600 000	100 000
Shareholders for dividends	605 000	400 000
Bank overdraft	Nil	50 000
	6 800 000	**4 300 000**

Additional information:

1. Land with a cost of R270 000 was sold during the year and new land was acquired. This was not done to replace the land that was sold.

2. Machinery with a cost of R200 000 was purchased on 31 October 2018 to replace existing machinery with a carrying amount of R20 000 and was sold on 1 July 2018.

3. Depreciation on furniture and machinery is calculated at 10% per annum and 15% per annum respectively on the straight line method.

4. Furniture with a cost of R20 000 was purchased on 1 July 2018.

REQUIRED:

1. Prepare the statement of cash flows of Phemba Enterprises for the financial year ended 30 June 2019, so as to comply with the requirements of IAS 7.

2. Prepare the reconciliation between profit before tax and cash generated from operations note to the statement of cash flow of Phemba Enterprises for the financial year ended 30 June 2019.

Show all workings.

Exercise 8.5 Fairy Tale (Pty) Ltd

Fairy Tale (Pty) Ltd is a concept company involved in the distribution of goods. The accountant is busy preparing the statement of cash flows for the year ended 28 February 2019 and has asked you to assist with various aspects of the statement of cash flows.

Refer to the following trial balance extracts (brackets are for credit balances):

	2019	2018
	R	R
Bank	?	16 000
Petty cash	2 000	2 000
Inventory	11 000	8 000
Accounts payable	(14 000)	(12 000)
Shareholder for dividends	0	(3000)
South African Revenue Service (Note 4)	30 000	(27 000)
Motor vehicle: cost (Note 2)	1 200 000	0
Motor vehicle: accumulated depreciation (Note 2)	?	0
Loan: Nedbank Capital (Note 4)	(1 736 560)	(486 560)

The following general ledger account balances for 2013 may also be relevant:

Sale of goods	?
Interest paid (correctly calculated)	148 656
Dividends paid	?
Cost of sales	189 962
Salary costs	32 000
Electricity	4 800
Rent	12 000
Depreciation (Note 2)	?
Proceeds on disposal of motor vehicle (Note 3)	280 000
Taxation expense	0

Additional information:

1. All sales are for cash. Goods are marked up by 50% on the cost.

2. The accountant was unsure how to account for the disposal in note 3 below and so has completely ignored it (the depreciation is calculated on the basis that there was no disposal). The company uses the straight line method to calculate depreciation and the **entire** fleet of three motor vehicles was purchased for cash on the 31 August 2012 at R300 000 per motor vehicle. The estimated residual value used in the depreciation calculations is 30% of the original cost of the vehicles and motor vehicles are depreciated at 20% per annum.

3. On the 31st January 2019, one of the vehicles was written off in an accident and the insurance company, Brolly Ltd, paid the company R280 000 in full and final settlement for this vehicle. The accountant allocated the receipt to an account named 'proceeds from insurance company' and has done nothing else. The replacement vehicle, a sparkling new Toyota Double Cap, was acquired for cash on 28 February 2019 and included in the 'cost' account for motor vehicles.

4. Despite making losses, the company made provisional tax payments in the year.

5. The accountant never capitalised interest and instead always paid it monthly. A new loan for R1 250 000 was taken out during the current year as the company needed funds to expand the business. Interest of 10% pa is charged on the loan.

6. As the company's turnover has not reached R1 000 000, the directors have not registered the company for VAT.

REQUIRED:

1. Using the direct method, prepare the statement of cash flows of Fairy Tale (Pty) Ltd for the year ended 28 February 2019. Comparative information is not required.

2. Prepare the reconciliation of profit/loss to cash generated from operations.

CHAPTER 9

THE EFFECTS OF CHANGES IN FOREIGN EXCHANGE RATES (IAS 21)

LEARNING OUTCOMES

After studying this chapter, you should be able to:

- Understand the underlying principles outlined in IAS 21 *The effects of changes in foreign exchange rates*.
- Use these principles to account for transactions that cover buying and selling in foreign currencies.
- Disclose the effects of changes in foreign exchange rates in the financial statements of an entity in compliance with International Financial Reporting Standards (IFRS).

PREAMBLE

Mr Mhlongo (known as Njomane) is planning on importing goods from overseas. He also has some goods that he believes he can export. He has been on several trips to the US, Europe and the Far East, and sees enormous potential for his business there. He is concerned, however, at the number of different currencies with which he will be dealing.

Njomane comes to your offices for professional business advice. He wants to know how he should account for imports and exports in foreign currencies as well as what disclosures will be required in his financial statements.

Before you sit down with him, you study the principles relating to the effects of changes in foreign currencies that are covered in this chapter.

9.1 INTRODUCTION

Not all business in South Africa is conducted in rands. This is because some products are imported from other countries or sold to other countries. These transactions may well take place in Japanese yen, British pounds or American dollars. Similarly, businesses in South Africa may borrow money from overseas organisations or lend money to these same organisations, and the currency could well be anything except rands. However, the financial statements of South African companies are prepared in rands and, sooner or later, the foreign currency element has to be translated into South African currency.

It may also be the case that a South African business has a branch in Kenya. This branch will do business in the local currency, shillings. However, when the South African company prepares its financial statements, it has to incorporate the results of the branch in Kenya. Before it can do this, it has to convert the branch's accounts from shillings to rands.

IAS 21 provides guidelines for the treatment of foreign currency transactions and foreign operations within the functional or presentation currency used by the South African entity. A foreign currency is any currency other than the functional currency, while the functional currency is the currency of the primary economic environment in which the entity operates. In South Africa, this is rands, but this is not the case in absolutely every instance. Take a gold mining company, for example. Gold is sold in dollars, but the cost of mining is all in rands. Gold mines have many international investors and the shares in South African gold mines are traded all over the world. What is the functional currency in this case? You can argue either way and as a result, the financial results are often prepared in both dollars and rands.

The value of currencies fluctuates continuously on a day-to-day basis. You might read in a newspaper that there has been 'a run' on the rand. This means that too many rands were sold, supply exceeded demand and the value of the rand fell. Similarly, you might read a month later that the rand has 'firmed' against the dollar and the value of the rand went up. Minor fluctuations in exchange rates occur every day in all currencies. Currency dealers make a living out of trading foreign currency and it is big business. Exchange rates are often quoted daily in newspapers like *The Daily News* and *The Mercury*. The price of US dollars, for example, may be as follows:

	10 June 2019		11 June 2019	
	Bank selling rate	Bank buying rate	Bank selling rate	Bank buying rate
US dollars ($1 = R)	14,60	14,48	14,65	14,53

The above table shows the rates a bank might sell and buy US dollars at on two different days. The table indicates that one dollar may be purchased from a bank for R14,60 on 10 June. Similarly, one dollar may be sold to the bank for R14,53 the following day. Had you done this, you would have realised a foreign exchange loss. However, had you waited until the rate hit R14,70 at some later stage, you would have realised a foreign exchange gain. Note that in the above table the rand has weakened slightly from 10 to 11 June.

IAS 21 *The effects of changes in foreign exchange rates* encompasses extensive and complicated transactions. Therefore, the scope for the purposes of this book excludes the following:
- Foreign interest-bearing borrowings
- Translation of foreign branches' financial statements
- Hedge accounting – forward exchange contracts
- Gains or losses recognised in other comprehensive income.

9.2 DEFINITIONS
Foreign currency is any currency other than the functional currency.

Functional currency is the currency of the primary economic environment in which the entity operates.

Presentation currency is the currency in which the financial statements are presented.

The **spot rate** is the spot rate for immediate delivery.

The **transaction date** is the date the risks and rewards of ownership transfer / the date on which the transaction first qualifies for recognition in accordance with IFRS.

The **settlement date** is the date upon which the foreign debtor/creditor pays or is paid.

The **reporting date** is the financial year end.

Monetary items are units of currency held and assets and liabilities to be received or paid in a fixed or determinable number of units of currency.

Non-monetary items are those items that do not have a right to receive or an obligation to meet any payments of fixed or determinable number of units of currency.

9.3 UPFRONT GUIDELINES FOR CONVERTING CURRENCIES
Fluctuations in the value of currencies relative to each other occur because of movements in the world markets. We have no control over this.

Care needs to be taken when converting from a foreign currency to a local currency and vice versa. This is because sometimes a rate might be quoted as 1$ = R14 and on other occasions it might be quoted as R1 = $0,0714. If you use the exchange rate incorrectly, you will wind up with a ridiculous answer. If the rate is quoted as 1$ = R14 and you are converting $5 000 into rands, then you need to multiply, giving you an answer of R70 000. If the rate is quoted as R1 = $0,0714 and you are translating $5 000, then you need to divide 5 000 by 0,0714 and you will get the same number, R70 000.

The golden rule is as follows:
When translating from a weaker currency to a stronger currency, you 'divide'.
When translating from a stronger currency to a weaker currency, you 'multipy'.

9.4 FOREIGN CURRENCY TRANSACTIONS
Goods that are imported or exported are shipped by the seller to the buyer according to agreed shipping terms. These terms can influence the date that risks and rewards are transferred from the seller to the buyer. Types of arrangements can include the following:

- **Free on board (FOB):** The seller makes the goods available for collection at a specific port or terminal at a specific price and the buyer pays for any subsequent transportation and insurance.
- **Cost insurance freight (CIF):** The buyer agrees to pay all insurance and transportation costs, with the seller simply making the transportation and insurance arrangements.

In both cases, the risks and rewards that come with ownership are transferred to the buyer when the goods are delivered to the port or terminal. This date of shipment then becomes the transaction date and the spot rate on that day will decide the rate that is used when the transaction is initially measured and recorded.

Another arrangement that needs to be noted is as follows:
- **Delivery at terminal (DAT):** The seller is responsible for arranging transportation and insurance all the way to the buyer's port or terminal for collection. Risks and rewards are transferred from the seller to the buyer only when the goods are unloaded at the buyer's port or terminal.

    Under this arrangement, the date of unloading becomes the transaction date and the spot rate on that day will decide the rate at which the transaction will be measured initially.

There are a number of other arrangements that the seller and the buyer could enter into regarding the shipping of goods which are not discussed in this textbook. The three arrangements above have been chosen to illustrate the accounting treatment for our purposes.

9.5 INITIAL MEASUREMENT
On initial recognition, a foreign currency transaction should be recorded by applying the 'spot rate' at the date of the transaction.

EXAMPLE 9.1
Goods worth $1 000 were delivered to a port of shipment in the US (for onward shipment to Durban) on 1 May 2019 and the spot rate was $1 = R14,50. On 1 May, the transaction would be recorded by the South African entity as follows:

1 May 2019	R	R
Dr Inventory (non-monetary item)	14 500	
Cr Accounts payable (foreign) (monetary item)		14 500

9.6 SUBSEQUENT MEASUREMENT
The subsequent measurement for foreign transactions differs depending on whether the foreign currency item is a monetary or a non-monetary item. Monetary items are units of currency held and assets and liabilities to be received or paid in a fixed or determinable number of units of currency. Monetary items therefore include cash, accounts payable, accounts receivable as well as loans to customers and loans from entities. Non-monetary items include property, plant and equipment, goodwill, intangible assets and inventories.

If a monetary item is settled before the reporting date (year end), the total difference between the amount initially recognised and the amount subsequently paid is accounted for in the profit or loss account as an exchange difference.

EXAMPLE 9.2
Consider the example used above for the goods costing $1 000. The payment was actually made on 15 June 2019 and the spot rate applicable for payment was $1 = R14,60. None of the goods were sold by payment date. Journal entries would be as follows:

15 June 2019	R	R
Dr Accounts payable	14 500	
Dr Foreign exchange loss	100	
Cr Bank		14 600

EXAMPLE 9.3

Now consider how it would have been recorded if the spot rate had been $1 = R14,30 on 15 June 2019:

15 June 2019	R	R
Dr Foreign accounts payable	14 500	
Cr Foreign exchange gain		200
Cr Bank		14 300

What if the company had arranged extended terms and only needed to pay the account after its year end?

EXAMPLE 9.4

Use the information above, ie goods worth $1 000 were delivered to a port of shipment in the US for onward shipment to Durban on 1 May 2019 when the spot rate was 1$ = R14,50. The foreign creditor only needed to be settled on the 31 July 2019, ie a month after year end. All goods were sold by year end. The spot rate at year end was $1 = R14,40 and the spot rate at 31 July 2019 was $1 = R14,70.

The company would have passed the following entries:

15 May 2019	R	R
Dr Inventory	14 500	
Cr Foreign accounts payable		14 500

30 June 2019	R	R
Dr Foreign accounts payable (14,50 – 14,40) × 1 000	100	
Cr Foreign exchange gain		100
Dr Cost of sales		14 500
Cr Inventory		14 500

If the payables account was paid on the 31 July 2019, and the spot rate was $1 = R14,70, then the accounting records would have been as follows:

30 June 2019	R	R
Dr Foreign accounts payable (14 500 – 100)	14 400	
Dr Foreign exchange loss	300	
Cr Bank		14 700

Disclosure

	R
Statement of financial position as at 30 June 2019	
Equity and liabilities	
Liabilities	
Current liabilities	
Accounts payable (14 400 + XXX)	YYY

Statement of profit and loss and other comprehensive income for the year ended 30 June 2019

Cost of sales (14500 + XXX)   YYY

Notes for the year ended 30th June 2019

Profit before tax

Profit before tax is stated after the following:

Income

Foreign exchange gain (100 + XXX)   YYY

Remember that the above disclosure is at year end and therefore cannot include the effects of fluctuations in exchange rates after year end.

EXAMPLE 9.5

Up until now, examples have been on the purchase of goods for resale. However, they could just as easily have been for the purchase of property, plant and equipment. Consider the following:

Khumalo Ltd, a Durban manufacturer, purchased plant from a UK company for £40 000 that was shipped FOB on 15 January 2019 and was invoiced on 31 January 2019. The plant arrived in Durban on 15 February and was available for use on 1 March 2019. The supplier was paid on 30 April 2019. The year end is 31 March 2019.

Khumalo's policy is to depreciate plant at 20% per annum, using the straight line method. The residual value for the plant has been estimated at R20 000.

Key spot rates are as follows:

15 January: £1 = R20,72
31 January: £1 = R20,65
15 February: £1 = R20,75
31 March: £1 = R20,80
30 April: £1 = R20,85

Journal entries to record the above would be as follows:

15 January 2019

	R	R
Dr Plant (non-monetary item) (40 000 × 20,72	828 800	
Cr Accounts payable		828 800

31 March 2019

Dr Foreign exchange loss [(20,80 – 20,72) × 40 000]	3 200	
Cr Foreign accounts payable (monetary item) 3 200		
Dr Depreciation [(828 800 – 20 000) × 20% × 1/12]		13 480
Cr Accumulated depreciation	13 480	

30 April 2019

Dr Foreign accounts payable (828 800 + 3 200)	832 000	
Dr Foreign exchange loss	2 000	
Cr Bank (40 000 × 20,85)		834 000

Disclosure

Khumalo Ltd

Statement of financial position as at 31 March 2019

Assets

Non-current assets

Property, plant and equipment (828 800 – 13 480 + XXX)	YYY	

Equity and liabilities

Current liabilities

Accounts payable (828 800 + 3 200 + XXX)	YYY	

Statement of profit and loss and other comprehensive income for the year ended 31 March 2019

Cost of sales (13 480 + XXX)	YYY	
Other expenses (3 200 + XXX)	YYY	

Notes for the year ended 31 March 2019

Profit before tax

Foreign exchange loss (3 200 + XXX)	YYY	

9.7 SALES TO FOREIGN ENTITIES

The examples so far have all been about importing goods and how to record various transactions.

However, many South African businesses are involved in exporting. The principles that are used in importing apply equally to exporting, both being transactions involving foreign currency receipts.

EXAMPLE 9.6

Consider an example where a South African company, Thulani Ltd, sold goods to a British firm for £20 000. The goods were shipped FOB on 15 May 2019. Applicable exchange rates are as follows:

15 May 2019:   1£ = R20,20
30 June 2019:   1£ = R20,40 (year end)
31 July 2019:   1£ = R20,10 (day payment is due)

The following journal entries are appropriate:

15 May 2019	R	R
Dr Accounts receivable	404 000	
Cr Revenue		404 000
30 June 2019		
Dr Accounts receivable 4 000		
Cr Foreign exchange gain	4 000	
31 July 2019		
Dr Bank 402 000		
Dr Foreign exchange loss [(20,40 – 20,10) × 20 000]	6 000	
Cr Accounts receivable		408 000

Disclosure

	R
Statement of financial position as at 30 June 2019	
Assets	
Current assets	
Accounts receivable (408 000 + XXX)	YYY

Statement of profit and loss and other comprehensive income for the year ended 30 June 2019

Revenue (404 000 + XXX)   YYY

Notes for the year ended 30 June 2019

Profit before tax

Profit before tax is stated after the following:

Income

Foreign exchange gain (4 000 + XXX)   YYY

9.8 SUMMARY

This chapter dealt with key definitions in the accounting for foreign transactions, the basic principles involved when converting from one currency to another as well as the initial and subsequent measurement of foreign currency transactions.

EXERCISES

Exercise 9.1 Ngcobo Ltd

Ngcobo Ltd is an exporter of machinery that it manufactures. The company's year end is 31 December. On 15 October 2018, following a big sale, Ngcobo Ltd shipped off machinery at an agreed price of KES250 000 (Kenyan shillings) to a customer in Nairobi. The cost price of the machinery was R21 000. No forward exchange contract was taken out. The following rates of exchange apply:

15 October 2018:   KES1 = R0,140
31 December 2018:   KES1 = R0,136
15 January 2019:   KES1 = R0,143

Ngcobo Ltd was paid in full on 15 January 2019.

REQUIRED:
Journalise all transactions.

Exercise 9.2 Mkhwanazi Ltd

Mkhwanazi Ltd is a manufacturer with 30 June year end. It entered into an expansion phase and decided to import more plant and machinery to help increase its production capacity. The supplier in Denmark shipped the plant and machinery from Copenhagen on 10 March 2019. The price was agreed at DKK150 000 (Danish krone). No forward exchange contract was taken out. The plant and machinery were put into use on 30 April 2010. Mkhwanazi Ltd paid the supplier on 31 July 2019. The entity depreciates its plant and machinery 20% pa straight line, no residual. The following rates of exchange apply:

10 March 2019:   R1 = DKK0,450
30 April 2019:   R1 = DKK0,448
30 June 2019:   R1 = DKK0,440
31 July 2019:   R1 = DKK0,455

REQUIRED:

1. Journalise all transactions for the 2019 financial year. Make all appropriate disclosures at 30 June 2019.
2. Journalise the payment of the supplier on 31 July 2019.

Exercise 9.3 Mchunu Trading

Mchunu Trading is an organisation that imports goods for resale. Its year end is 31 March. Goods at a price of $15 000 (15 widgets at $1 000 each) were shipped CIF by its supplier in the US from New York on 15 January 2019. The goods landed in Durban on 20 February 2019 and were delivered to Mchunu Ltd's warehouse on 28 February 2019. Mchunu had sold one third of the goods for R20 000 each by 31 March 2019. All goods were paid for on 1 April 2019. No forward exchange contract was taken out. The following rates of exchange apply:

15 January 2019: $1 = R14,20
20 February 2019: $1 = R14,19
28 February 2019: $1 = R14,25
31 March 2019: $1 = R14,32
1 April 2019: $1 = R14,30

REQUIRED:

Journalise all transactions.

CHAPTER 10

PROPERTY, PLANT AND EQUIPMENT (IAS 16)

LEARNING OUTCOMES

After studying this chapter, you should be able to:
- Determine when to recognise an item of property, plant and equipment (PPE) as an asset, in accordance with IAS 16.
- Determine what constitutes the initial cost of the PPE items.
- Calculate the initial cost of the PPE items.
- Understand when to capitalise or expense subsequent expenditure incurred on PPE items.
- Calculate the depreciation and residual values, considering the useful life of an asset.
- Disclose PPE items in the financial statements.

PREAMBLE

Mr Mhlongo (known as Njomane) is struggling to distinguish property, plant and equipment from other assets and to understand what constitutes the cost of property, plant and equipment items as well as the general measurement of property, plant and equipment. He approaches you for some clarification.

10.1 INTRODUCTION

Property, plant and equipment (PPE) is an important section in accounting, as it deals with the measurement of assets of a business (ie tangible assets). Tangible assets are revenue-generating assets that many entities cannot do without. This section will delve into the intricacies of correctly measuring property, plant and equipment items from initial purchase or construction, to subsequent valuation during the life of an asset, up until the asset is alienated from the company records (ie sold or scrapped).

10.2 DEFINITIONS

Property, plant and equipment can be described as tangible assets which are used in the production and/or supply of goods and services, for rental to others or administration purposes, and are expected to be used during more than one period (IAS 16: 6).

Depreciation is defined as the systematic allocation of the depreciable amount over the useful life of an asset.

Depreciable amount is cost price less the residual value of an asset.

Residual value is the amount for which an entity would be able to sell the asset assuming it had already reached the end of its useful life.

Carrying amount is cost price less accumulated depreciation of an asset.

Recoverable amount is the greater of the fair value less costs to sell (net selling price) and the value in use.

10.3 INITIAL MEASUREMENT

Initial cost of an asset is its purchase price PLUS any direct costs and certain future costs (initial estimates of future costs if the entity has obligation to incur theses costs) incurred to bring it to its location and to a working condition, as intended by management of the company.

Purchase price:
- includes all non-refundable taxes and import duties
- less discounts and rebates received
- less taxes that can be claimed back from the tax authorities.

Direct costs include the following:
- Cost of preparing the site
- Initial delivery and handling costs

- Installation and assembly costs
- Employee benefits (salaries, wages, etc) relating directly to the asset's construction or acquisition
- Professional fees
- Cost of testing that the asset is functioning properly.

Ownership of an asset may come with future obligations. These obligations can be, for example, dismantling the asset, removing it from the premises or restoring the site on which the asset is located.

Some assets are made of different components or significant parts. Collectively, these components or significant parts make up the asset. These significant parts are recorded separately in order to account for their depreciation correctly.

There are also conditions attached to the purchase of an asset. Sometimes regular inspections may need to be performed on the asset. These conditions will also form part of the purchase price of the asset. Depreciation will have to be calculated and allocated as normal for such assets. Once the asset has been fully used and the conditions attached to it come to an end, the asset has to be removed from the accounting books. This is called **de-recognition of an asset**. The total depreciation that was accumulated over the period will have to be written off against the asset.

10.4 SUBSEQUENT MEASUREMENT

Depreciation needs to be considered on the asset as soon as it is available for use. The different methods of depreciation, namely the straight line method, reducing balance method and sum of the digits method, are discussed in detail in the first year of university studies. What we would like to emphasise in this chapter is that depreciation must be taken into account as soon as the asset is available for use – not when the entity starts using the asset. In simple terms, depreciation is the loss of value of an asset through usage. As the definition of depreciation clearly states that depreciation is the systematic allocation of the depreciable amount over the useful life of an asset, it is important to accurately allocate this asset reduction cost to an asset to ensure that the asset value is kept at its future economic benefit.

Sometimes after an asset has been bought, there may be other costs incurred, such as the following:
- Repairs and maintenance
- Replacement of parts
- Major inspections.

10.4.1 Repairs and maintenance

Repairing or maintaining an asset means the asset is being brought to its original state. This process does not increase the useful life of an asset and therefore does not extend its ability to generate future economic benefits for the entity. Hence, these costs are expensed and transferred to the profit and loss account.

10.4.2 Replacement of parts

There are times when some property, plant and equipment items need to be replaced on a regular basis (usually as a condition of purchase and/or continued use). There could also be times when a part needs to be replaced due to damage. When a part of an asset is replaced (as per condition of purchase and/or continued use), the carrying amount of the old part must be removed from the asset and accounting records. Profit or loss incurred during the replacement of a part must also be taken into account. The following are possible journal entries:
Dr Accumulated depreciation
Dr or Cr Loss or profit on disposal
Cr Asset

If a certain part of an asset needs to be replaced because of damage, then an impairment test has to be performed before removing the carrying amount of an asset from the accounting records. If the damage has caused the recoverable amount of the part to drop below its carrying amount, then the carrying amount must be reduced to reflect the impairment loss and removed from the accounting records. The following are possible journal entries:
Dr Accumulated depreciation
Dr Accumulated impairment loss
Dr or Cr Profit or loss on disposal
Cr Asset

10.4.3 Major inspections

Sometimes regular inspections are a condition of purchase and/or continued use. If that is the case then the cost of this major inspection must be capitalised as soon as the cost is incurred or an obligation arises, making this inspection an asset.

This 'major inspection' asset is then depreciated over the period until the date of the next inspection. If an asset has been bought and a major inspection has already taken place, and does not need another inspection for a period of time, then the cost must be separated into:
- cost relating to the physical asset
- cost relating to the balance of the previous major inspection purchased.

EXAMPLE 10.1 SASA Ltd (initial cost)

SASA Ltd, an aeronautical company based in South Africa, decided to purchase a spaceship called Space Ship 13 to travel to the moon on 1 July 2018. The spaceship was purchased for cash.

The list below details the costs incurred in purchasing the spaceship:

Details	R
Marked price (including VAT)	34 500 000
Discount (offered to long-standing customers)	1 500 000
Government space rebate	150 000
Cash discount	300 000
Import duties – non-refundable	850 000
Installation costs	1 500 000
Fuel (incurred while transporting the plant to the factory)	300 000
Administration costs	30 000
Staff party to celebrate the acquisition of the spaceship	250 000
Staff training	30 000
Testing to ensure spaceship fully operational	150 000
Initial operating loss	120 000

SASA Ltd qualifies for all the terms and conditions of purchase. SASA Ltd is a registered VAT vendor. VAT is calculated at 15%.

SASA Ltd has a 30 June financial year end.

REQUIRED:

Calculate the initial costs to be capitalised to the asset account. Where necessary, round calculations off to the nearest whole rand.

EXAMPLE 10.1 Solution – SASA Ltd (initial cost)

	R
Marked price (100/115 × R34 500 000)	30 000 000
Discount (offered to long-standing customers)	(1 500 000)
Government space rebate	(150 000)
Cash discount	(300 000)
Import duties (non-refundable)	850 000
Installation costs	1 500 000
Fuel expense (incurred while transporting the plant to the factory)	300 000
Testing to ensure space ship is fully operational	150 000
Costs to be capitalised	**30 850 000**

EXAMPLE 10.2 Zwelibanzi Rescue Services (significant parts and major inspection)

Zwelibanzi Rescue Services purchased a helicopter on 1 October 2017 at a cost of R1 600 000. The company, which has a 30 September year end, identified the following significant components:

Description of component	Cost	Residual value	Useful life
	R	R	
Airframe and interior	900 000	-	10 years
Engine and rotor blades	540 000	40 000	40 000 km
Inspection – 01/10/2017	160 000	-	2 years
Total price paid	**1 600 000**		

In order to maintain the operating licence for the helicopter, inspections are required to be made every two years. The first inspection was done on 1 October 2017 when the helicopter was purchased (see table above). The second inspection was due on 30 September 2019. This was duly performed at a cost of R192 000.

Additional information:

1. The helicopter flew a total of 8 000 km for the year ended 30 September 2018 and 10 000 km for the ended 30 September 2019.

2. Depreciation on the airframe and interior is to be provided on the straight line method.

REQUIRED:

Prepare the journal entries necessary for the financial years ended 30 September 2018 and 30 September 2019. Ignore VAT.

EXAMPLE 10.2 Solution – Zwelibanzi Rescue Services (significant parts and major inspection)

Date	Detail	Dr	Cr
		R	R
1/10/2017	Helicopter: airframe and interior	900 000	
	Helicopter: engine and rotor blades	540 000	
	Helicopter: inspection	160 000	
	Bank		1 600 000
	Purchase of helicopter		
30/9/2018	Depreciation	90 000	
	Accumulated depreciation: airframe and interior		90 000
	Depreciation for the year		
	Depreciation	100 000	
	Accumulated depreciation: engine and rotor blades		100 000
	Depreciation for the year		
	Depreciation	80 000	
	Accumulated depreciation: inspection		80 000
	Depreciation for the year		
30/9/2019	Depreciation	90 000	
	Accumulated depreciation: airframe and interior		90 000
	Depreciation for the year		
	Depreciation	125 000	
	Accumulated depreciation: engine and rotor blades		125 000

↳

	Depreciation for the year		
	Depreciation	80 000	
	Accumulated depreciation: inspection		80 000
	Depreciation for the year		
30/9/2019	Accumulated depreciation: inspection	160 000	
	Helicopter: inspection		160 000
	De-recognition of helicopter inspection costs		
30/9/2019	Helicopter: inspection	192 000	
	Bank		192 000
	Payment of second inspection of helicopter		

10.5 SUMMARY

In this chapter, the definition of property, plant and equipment according to IAS 16 was discussed. The initial and subsequent measurement of property, plant and equipment was also discussed in detail. Examples were provided to deal with different aspects of property, plant and equipment transactions.

EXERCISES

Exercise 10.1 Sibanyoni Ltd

Sibanyoni Ltd operates in the air freight business. The company has a 31 December year end.

On 1 January 2017, the company purchased a helicopter for R1 200 000.

The directors identified the following major components upon initial recognition:
- The motor was valued at R320 000 with an estimated useful life of five years and a residual value of R24 000.
- The body and interior were valued at R720 000 with an estimated useful life of 10 years and a nil residual value.
- The inspection cost was capitalised at R160 000. This was to be performed every three years and was a condition of the purchase.

On 1 January 2020, the second inspection was performed at a cost of R192 000, paid for in cash.
All amounts stated above exclude VAT unless specifically indicated.

REQUIRED:
Prepare the journal entries necessary for Sibanyoni Ltd for the financial year ended 31 December 2020.

Exercise 10.2 Thubeleza City Transport
On 1 July 2017, Thubezela City Transport purchased a bus for R1 260 000 cash for the purpose of carrying commuters to and from the city.

The economic useful life of the bus was estimated to be eight years.

In terms of the current legislation, public transport buses are required to undergo regular major inspections every two years.

The 2017 inspection, which was done on 30 June 2017, cost R60 000 and is included in the purchase price of the bus acquired.

The next inspection was due on 30 June 2019 and was duly performed at a cost of R72 000.

All amounts exclude VAT unless otherwise indicated.

REQUIRED:

Prepare the journal entries to record the above-mentioned transactions in the accounting books of Thubeleza City Transport for the financial years ended 30 June 2018 and 30 June 2019.

Exercise 10.3 Uthukela Ltd

The following balances appear among others in the ledger of Uthukela Ltd at 31 March 2020:

	R
Machinery	900 000
Accumulated depreciation: machinery	400 000

The following occurred during the year ending 31 March 2020:

* On 30 November 2019, one of the old machines, with a cost of R300 000 and included in the figure of R900 000, was traded in on a new machine with a cost of R500 000. On 31 March 2019, the accumulated depreciation of the old machine was R140 000 and an amount of R120 000 was received for it as traded-in value. The outstanding amount for the new machine was paid by cheque.
* An account of R12 500 was received from Thandanani Engineering in respect of work done to repair the old machine.
* Depreciation is written off at 15% per annum on cost.

REQUIRED:

1. Prepare the journal entries in respect of the above transactions for the year ended 31 March 2020.
2. Prepare the following extracts of the notes to the financial statements of Uthukela Ltd for the year ended 31 March 2020:
   a) The accounting policy note for machinery
   b) The property, plant and equipment note relating to machinery.

Note: Ignore VAT and show all workings.

Exercise 10.4 Mamba (Pty) Ltd

The following information relates to Mamba (Pty) Ltd:

	R	R
Balances at 1 January 2019		
Plant and machinery at cost	300 000	
Accumulated depreciation: plant and machinery		120 000

Additional information:

1. According to the assets register, plant and machinery consist of two machines (machine A and machine B) of equal value. Both the machines were purchased and installed on the same date.
2. Depreciation is written off at 20% per annum on the straight line basis to a nil residual value.
3. On 31 May 2019, management decided to increase production capacity and purchased machine C on credit from Fennel Ltd for R180 000.
   Machine A was traded in, reducing the amount owing to Fennel Ltd to R101 000.

4. Other costs incurred and paid in cash in relation to the purchase of machine C are as follows:

Description of cost	R	Transaction date
Delivery and installation	15 000	5 June 2019
Staff training	2 700	16 June 2019
Testing to ensure machine fully operational before start of production	5 000	20 June 2019
Launch party	2 300	25 June 2019

5. Machine C was available for use in production on 1 July 2012, although production only began on 1 August 2019.

REQUIRED:

1. Prepare the journal entries to give effect to the above transactions relating to plant and machinery for the year ended 31 December 2019.

   Disclose the property plant and equipment note in the financial statements of Mamba (Pty) Ltd for the year ended 31 December 2019.

Exercise 10.5 Leisure Bay Ltd

Leisure Bay Ltd owns one item of property, plant and equipment: a ferry boat that was purchased on 2 January 2019 at a cost of R3 million.

The boat is used for doing sightseeing tours of the bay and harbour areas of the city and it also ventures out to the open sea to view the coastline during the day and night.

The purchase price paid for the ferry has been analysed into the cost per each significant component as follows:

Description of component	Cost R	Comments
Hull and fittings	1 800 000	Estimated useful life of eight years with a residual value of R200 000
Engine room	972 000	Estimated useful life of 300 000 nautical miles with a nil residual value
Major inspection (the last inspection had been performed on 4 January 2017 at a cost of R570 000)	228 000	Major inspections, which are done every 2,5 years, are a pre-requisite to the continued use of the ferry. The next major inspection was due and performed on 30 June 2011 at a cost of R680 000 – paid in cash. The following major inspection is due on 31 December 2021 at an expected cost of R800 000.
Total price paid (02/01/2019)	3 000 000	

Depreciation on the hull and fittings is to be provided for on the straight line method. During the financial year, the ferry travelled a total of 36 000 nautical miles.

There were no sales or any other purchases of property, plant and equipment during the year ended 31 December 2019.

All the amounts stated above exclude VAT.

REQUIRED:

Prepare the journal entries necessary for the financial year ended 31 December 2019 in the accounting books of Leisure Bay Ltd.

CHAPTER 11

GOVERNMENT GRANTS (IAS 20)

LEARNING OUTCOMES

After studying this chapter, you should be able to:

- Detail definitions used in the context of this chapter.
- Demonstrate an understanding of the different forms of government grant that may be available to entities.
- Demonstrate how government grants may differ from government assistance.
- Use the information provided to perform calculations necessary for the presentation in the financial statement of an entity, using the accounting policy that may apply.
- Disclose the government grants and government assistance in the financial statements.

PREAMBLE

Mr Mhlongo (known as Njomane) has just applied for National Youth Development Agency (NYDA) financing and it appears that he may be approved. The news about the possible transfer of the funds has left Njomane with mixed emotions. He is overjoyed to hear that he is due to receive such an awesome opportunity to serve his community by assisting in eradicating poverty. However, he is confused about whether the amount should be presented as income or an asset, or perhaps equity. You are requested to assist by explaining to Njomane how the amount should be accounted for in his accounting records.

11.1 INTRODUCTION

The government is one of the key players in the commercial and financial world. One of its major roles is ensuring fair trade by promoting fair competition and preventing monopolies. This role is executed by way of regulations and governance. Anyone wanting to do business within the country and within a specific industry must adhere to these regulations. Governance involves ensuring that the rules that have been set out are in fact adhered to by businesses. An example of governance structures are courts or the competition tribunal, which hands out hefty fines for non-compliance.

In this chapter, our focus is on a rare yet practical role that the government plays in the commercial and financial world, this being the provision of grants. The government may provide companies with grants in different ways, such as providing an asset, reducing an expense or waiving a debt:

The government may provide an asset to an entity so that it may conduct business and make profits.

The government may also provide a subsidy to help reduce certain expenditure so that the end user of the service or product does not have to pay an excessive amount to cover the actual cost of providing it, while the supplier of such goods or services will still be able to make a profit and continue operating.

The government may ask that certain creditors of an entity waive, cancel or transfer a debt owed by the entity, such that the government becomes responsible for the debt, thus relieving the entity from its liability.

This chapter is based on IAS 20, which deals with accounting for government grants and disclosure of government assistance.

11.2 DEFINITIONS

Government refers to government, government agencies and similar bodies, whether local, national or international.

Government assistance is action by government designed to provide an economic benefit specific to an entity or range of entities qualifying under certain criteria.

Government grants are assistance by the government in the form of transfers of resources to an entity in return for past or future compliance with certain conditions relating to the operating activities of the entity.

Grants related to assets are government grants whose primary condition is that the entity qualifying for them should purchase, construct or otherwise acquire long-term assets. Subsidiary conditions may also apply, which restrict the type and location of the assets, or the period during which the assets should be acquired or held.

Grants related to income are government grants other than those related to assets.

Forgivable loans are loans which the lender undertakes to waive repayment of, under certain prescribed conditions.

Fair value is the price that would be received to sell an asset or paid to transfer the liability in an orderly transaction between market participants at the measurement date.

11.3 EXCLUSIONS FROM DEFINITIONS
It is important to note that the following are not included as part of the definition of items defined above:
- In relation to government assistance, benefits provided only indirectly through actions affecting general trading conditions, such as the provision of infrastructure in development areas or the imposition of trading constraints on competitors
- For government grants, those forms of government assistance which cannot reasonably have a value placed upon them and where the transaction with the government cannot be distinguished from the normal trading transactions of the entity.

11.4 IMPORTANCE OF GOVERNMENT GRANTS TO USERS OF FINANCIAL STATEMENTS
Government grants are meant to induce entities to act in a way that is not ordinary for them, such as providing excessive discounts in certain areas that they would not normally provide, with the intention for government to make basic food products accessible to people living in such an area.

Receiving a government grant as an entity is significant for two reasons: (1) if an asset (a resource) has been given to an entity, an appropriate method to account for it must be determined, and (2) it is important to establish the extent to which the entity has benefited from government assistance.

This chapter deals mostly with how to recognise and measure the government grant obtained by an entity. This revolves around the question of whether the asset or expense should be recognised net of the grant received by the entity.

Grants may be referred to by other names, such as subsidy, subvention or premium.

11.5 RECOGNITION
A government grant, including non-monetary grants at fair value, shall not be recognised until the following conditions are both met (IAS 20, par 7):
- There is reasonable assurance that the entity will comply with the conditions attaching to them; and
- There is reasonable assurance that the grants will be received.

Satisfying one condition without the other being met may not lead to the recognition. The government utilises taxpayers' money, and countries' debt, to settle or finance these grants. Whenever a government issues a grant, taxpayers will automatically ask for reasons supporting government actions. Where there are no reasonable grounds, the citizens may deem the expense by the government as wasteful.

Note that the grant is an income on the part of the entity receiving it, but it is in essence an expense on the side of the government. The government has to account for the expense that they have incurred, otherwise the personnel that authorised the expense may lose their jobs or the ruling party at that period may lose on material votes.

It is because of this accountability to its citizenry that government is expected to make a condition when it provides a grant to an entity, to ensure that it enforces operation/conduct by an entity in a manner that it would normally never consider to do.

For these reasons above, all government grants are expected to be linked to a condition. In South Africa, the government is often accused of taking too much time to settle debts that it owes any entity that supplied it with goods or services. For this reason, a government grant shall only be recognised when there are reasonable grounds that it will be received, when an entity has a valid expectation that an amount (or other economic benefit) promised to it (or the group it belongs to) will indeed transfer.

The manner in which the grant is received, whether an asset, income or reduction of debt, should not affect the accounting method adopted.

Whether a non-current asset, an expense, a contingent liability or a financial instrument shall be dealt with using the relevant standards that are applicable in the circumstance. As an example, the government may provide an interest-free loan, or low-interest loan, to persons in a certain region that earn within a specified income range, to induce these persons to buy houses of a certain value. Assuming that these persons prepare financial statements, the loan itself will be accounted for under IFRS 9, while the zero-rate or low-rate interest portion will result in a government grant, the grant being the difference between market value (specifically determined for each group of persons) less the amount payable by the persons. The grant will be accounted for using the guidelines of this chapter.

Government grants shall be recognised in profit or loss, on a systematic basis, over the periods in which the entity recognises as expenses the related costs for which the grants are intended to compensate (IAS 20, par 12).

EXAMPLE 11.1 Lehasa Spaza Shop

Figure 11.1: Qhabanga Spaza Shop
Source: https://mg.co.za/article/2015-01-29-township-politics-fuel-the-attacks-on-outsiders

Lehasa (Pty) Ltd is a spaza shop in the Turfloop township in Polokwane, Limpopo. The spaza shop has been operating for five years and makes lucrative profits. For the year ended 30 September 2019, Lehasa obtained a grant from the local municipality on 1 August 2018 worth R100 000. R80 000 of this was used to improve the interior of the spaza shop, while the remaining R20 000 was used to buy additional stock to make the spaza shop more attractive to the local community, with the intention to induce them to buy more from the shop.

It is expected that the improvement will remain for a maximum of 20 years, while the stock is expected to be consumed in full within the year it was acquired.

Assuming that both the conditions for recognising the government grant are satisfied, determine the amounts that will be recognised in profit and loss in the 30 September 2019 year end.

EXAMPLE 11.1 Suggested solution – Lehasa Spaza Shop

Details	R
Grant recognised in profit and loss shall be determined as follows:	
– Relating to inventory	20 000
– Relating to renovation: 　　1. R80 000/20 　　(*R80 000 is the grant money obtained and 20 is the number of years that the improvement will be depreciated over*)	4 000
Total grant income	**24 000**
The above amounts will be netted off by the expenses to which they relate. Whether the amounts should be recognised separately or netted against the expense, brings us to the next topic (see section 11.6).	

11.6 DIFFERING SCHOOLS OF THOUGHT

There are differing opinions about the treatment of government grants. The first (*presentation difference*) is in relation to whether and why the grant should be recognised in profit or loss, while the second (*measurement difference*) is whether the amount should be recognised separately as a gross amount or whether it should be used to net off the expense(s) to which it related.

The presentation difference gives rise to the following two methods of presentation, referred to as the capital approach and the income approach:

1. Under the **capital approach**, the government grant is not recognised in profit or loss. The arguments in favour of this approach are as follows:
   - Government grants are a financing device. Thus, they should be recognised in the statement of financial position as either equity or a liability. However, the liability component would be phased out by the fact that the amount need not be repaid, thus there is no obligation to pass economic resources.
   - It is inappropriate to recognise the amount in profit or loss, as it was not earned. The argument is that the amount is an incentive without a related cost.

2. Under the **income approach**, the grant is recognised in profit or loss, systematically over the period that the cost incurred by the entity will be recognised as an expense in the statement of profit or loss. The arguments in favour of this approach are as follows:
   - Government grants are receipts from a source other than shareholders. Recognising them in equity would give an impression that they are sharing in the residual interest that remains after all financiers of the entities operation have been paid off.
   - Government grants are rarely gratuitous. They always come with a condition that most of the time requires the entity to act in a manner in which it would not normally operate. For this reason, the supporters of this approach believe that there is a cost attached to grants, meaning that they are earned.
   - Income taxes are recognised in profit or loss, so it is logical that government grants will also be recorded there, as they are an extension of fiscal policy.

The preferred method is the **income approach.**

When it comes to the measurement differences, there are two approaches that may be followed, namely gross measurement and net measurement:

1. Under **gross measurement**, the government grant is recognised as a total figure and presented in the statement of financial position as a separate item. The gross amount is recognised as deferred income and released in profit or loss as the expense relating to the cost is incurred. Supporters of this approach argue as follows:
   - It is inappropriate to net off the income and the expense.
   - Separation of the grant from the expense allows comparison with entities that do not obtain similar grants and with prior year financials of the same entity, to assess how the grant has benefitted the entity.

2. Under **net measurement**, the government grant is used to reduce the amount relating to the expense and the amount that is recognised in the financial statement is the net amount. It is argued that the expense would not have been incurred had the grant not been obtained, thus without offsetting the two amounts the presentation would be misleading.

Both methods are acceptable. However, we would like to recommend the gross measurement, as it shows users the full lengths of the expense and the help provided. Consider, for example, a state-owned company got into financial difficulties and the government provided R5 million as a bail-out. If they acquired an asset worth R6 million with the help of the grant, but on the financial statements, when comparing the current year and previous year, there is an asset worth R1 000 000 added to the current year with no financing attached to the acquisition, it would be very confusing. The financial statement would not be depicting both the grant and the full expense incurred in acquiring the asset, nor would it illustrate to users the expected future economic benefits that will arise in using the asset.

11.7 ACCOUNTING FOR TRANSACTIONS THAT WILL NOT TOUCH PROFIT OR LOSS IN FUTURE

Two transactions are possible that would not touch profit or loss in future, for which a government grant may be obtained.

The first such is a transaction that has already occurred, and the government is providing a grant as a subsidy to reduce the burden on the part of the entity. With relation to such transaction, the grant is recognised fully in profit or loss.

The second transaction is an acquisition of a non-depreciable asset, such as land, which is recognised in the statement of financial position and will not touch the profit or loss. The expectation is that the government will only grant land if the obligation on the business is for it to build a factory or another kind of business that will increase the level of employed citizens. In dealing with this kind of transaction, the entity will recognise the grant as it recognises the depreciation of the building, using the systematic allocation applied on the depreciable amount to recognise the grant amount in profit or loss.

EXAMPLE 11.2 King Foil (Pty) Ltd

King Foil (Pty) Ltd ('KF') is an entity in Phuthaditjhaba, Free State, South Africa established in 2007 that specialises in creating different forms of foil, used in private kitchens, restaurants and other commercial enterprises. It is estimated that each factory employs about 50 000 people, including the support staff involved in security, transporting, packaging, testing, etc.

On 1 January 2019, the municipality of Mafikeng in North West approached KF with a request for KF to build a factory there. The municipality anticipated a reduction in the unemployment rate. KF spent R85 000 surveying land, researching the market, speaking to business personnel and communicating with the municipality. The expense was incurred over three month ending 31 March 2019.

On 1 April 2019, the municipality awarded KF with a five-hectare site, valued at R2 000 000, and reimbursed the R85 000 that KF had spent, on the condition that KF moved its major business to Mafikeng and that the Mafikeng factory became the largest, thus employing double the amount of employees KF normally employs. On 1 April 2019, KF started erecting a building, depreciable over 25 years according to KF policy, and the total cost for the building was R7 500 000. The building was available for use on 1 July 2019, at which point KF started with interviews and the recruitment process. Operation commenced on 1 August 2019.

REQUIRED:

Using the information provided, prepare an extract of the statement of financial position and an extract of the statement of comprehensive income (profit or loss, only) for King Foil (Pty) Ltd for the financial year ending 30 September 2019.

EXAMPLE 11.2 Suggested solution – King Foil (Pty) Ltd

Details	R
Extract of the statement of financial position	
Non-current assets	
PPE	2 000 000
Land	7 425 000
Building = 7 500 000* – (7 500 000/25 × 3/12)^	(1 980 000)
Deferred grant income	**7 445 000**
Land = 2 000 000* – (2 000 000/25 × 3/12) ^	
Total non-current assets	
*Cost/total deferred income	
^Accumulated depreciation (or accumulated unwinding of deferred income)	

↳

Extract of the statement of comprehensive income (profit or loss)	
Deferred income	105 000
Current expenses (already incurred) = 85 000	
Land (2 000 000/25 × 3/12) = 20 000	
Total	
Expenses	
Current expenses incurred	(85 000)
Depreciation on building (7 500 000/25 × 3/12)	(75 000)
Extract profit/loss before taxation	**(55 000)**

EXAMPLE 11.3 Look At Dots CC

Look At Dots CC 'LAD' is a beauty and appearance company established in 2014 and based in Qunu, a small village in Eastern Cape, South Africa. LAD specialises in using different forms of soil to make special face creams for African woman. The effect is an 80% reduction in blemishes, smaller pore size, and smooth and radiant skin within just three weeks of use.

Research had shown that about 30% of South Africans suffered from skin problems, leading to low self-esteem, depression and other psychological issues, especially among the youth. This had become a concern for the South African government. Because of this, on 1 February 2019, the government awarded LAD with an 800 m^2 site in Port Elizabeth, valued at R800 000 and including a building valued at R1,2 million. The government continued to provide LAD R1 500 000 in cash to perform its duties, 80% of which was used for research and development, all capitalised as it met the requirements for capitalisation. The remaining 20% was reserved for settling daily expenses such as salaries, testing of prototypes and assessment of market strategies.

LAD estimates that it will use the building in Port Elizabeth for 15 years and the research and development will be useful for approximately 10 years before competitors emerge.

REQUIRED:
Prepare journal entries to account for all transactions to be recognised in the Look At Dots CC accounting records for the financial year ending on 31 December 2019.

EXAMPLE 11.3 Suggested solution – Look At Dots CC

Detail	Dr	Cr
	R	R
Land (SOFP)	800 000	
Building (SOFP) Deferred grant income (SOFP)	1 200 000	2 000 000
Received a grant from government on 1 February 2019		
Bank (SOFP)	1 500 000	
Deferred grant income (SOFP)		1 500 000
Received a grant from government on 1 February 2019		
Depreciation (P/L)	73 333	
Accumulated depreciation (SOFP)		73 333
Depreciation for the 2019 year (1 200 000/15 year × 11/12)		
Deferred grant income (SOFP)	1 222 222	
Grant income (P/L)		1 222 222
Deferred income realised in P/L for the 2019 year (2 000 000/15 year × 11/12)		
Daily expenses (P/L)	300 000	
Bank (P/L)		300 000
Recognising expenditure for the year		

↪

Deferred grant income (SOFP)	300 000	
Grant income (P/L)		300 000
Deferred income realised in P/L for the 2020 year (2 billion/20 year × 3/12)		
Amortisation (P/L)	110 000	
Accumulated depreciation (SOFP)		110 000
Amortisation for the 2019 year (1 500 000 × 80%/10 year × 11/12)		
Deferred grant income (SOFP)	110 000	
Grant income (P/L)		110 000
Deferred income realised in P/L for the 2019 year (1 200 000/10 year × 11/12)		

11.8 SUMMARY

This chapter dealt with the definitions and different forms of government grant, and how to account for them. It considered two different schools of thought, namely the capital approach and the income approach. It also discussed the two approaches that may be followed for measurement, which are gross measurement and net measurement. The chapter ended with accounting for transactions that will not touch profit or loss in future.

EXERCISES

Exercise 11.1 Awesome Expectations Inc

Awesome Expectations Inc ('AE') is a study partner for accounting students in Gauteng, with presence in the Free State and KwaZulu-Natal, tutoring students from Grade 11 to undergraduate level at both colleges and universities. The company helps students better their marks and achieve their academic goals. The entity has a success rate of over 97%.

The Limpopo government would like AE to have a presence in the rural areas of the province, with aim to improve the matric success rate. To facilitate this, the provincial municipality has had to improve roads and pavements, to make rural Limpopo more easily accessible for students and AE representatives as well as suppliers and other business people.

REQUIRED:

Explain whether the expenses incurred by the local municipality will be considered as a government grant received by Awesome Expectations Inc.

Exercise 11.2 Mghodoyi (Pty) Ltd

On 30 April 2019, Mghodoyi (Pty) Ltd ('Mghodoyi') obtained a contract to breed cross-Africanis (a South African breed) and kelpie (an Australian breed) puppies. Mghodoyi had been a successful breeder in Ntuzuma since March 2010.

The eThekwini municipality was impressed by Mghodoyi and its display at an animal care exhibition in December 2018. For this reason, the municipality awarded Mghodoyi with a 10-year grant, covering all expenses from animal storage, feeding, importing, etc. Under the contract, R7 000 000 would be used in constructing once-off infrastructure, such as a new building. An additional R1 000 000 would be deposited annually to manage the day-to-day running. The first payment, made on 1 May 2019, was R8 000 000 and the next payment would be made on 1 May 2020.

REQUIRED:

Explain whether the amount obtained on 1 May 2019 would be classified as a government grant.

Exercise 11.3 Vus' uMzi Ltd

Vus' uMzi Ltd is a construction company formed in Qonce, Eastern Cape. The company was established by three engineering graduates and has made a good name for itself. Since 2004, the Eastern Cape provincial government has been building houses for the local community. Vus' uMzi Ltd scored a tender for three municipalities and is paid R9 500 000 per year for constructing 120 houses.

REQUIRED:

Explain whether the amount paid to Vus' uMzi Ltd may be regarded as a government grant and provide reasons to support your answer.

Exercise 11.4 Keen Cashiers CC

Keen Cashiers CC ('KC') is an entity that provides retail cashiers with better skills to improve their marketability. KC has helped train about 25 000 cashiers across South Africa, many of whom have gone on to become assistant managers, managers, regional managers and other support professionals.

On 1 February 2019, the South African government, being well impressed by the work performed by KC, requested that there be branches throughout South Africa to facilitate improving employability of more people. This project saw KC receiving a once-off R2 billion fee towards its expansion on 30 April 2019. The infrastructure built by KC was completed on 30 November 2019 and it is expected to last for 20 years.

REQUIRED:

Prepare journal entries to account for all the transactions experienced by Keen Cashiers CC in the year ending 28 February 2020.

Exercise 11.5 Luh (Pty) Ltd

Luh (Pty) Ltd is a book distributing company which buys and sells A4, 72-page, feint and margin books to local residents in KwaMashu. The eThekwini municipality received only 80% of the books they had ordered from their usual supplier on 7 January 2019. As schools were opening the following week, the municipality concluded an acquisition contract to buy the remaining 20% needed from Luh (Pty) Ltd. A total of six million books were bought by the local municipality and Luh (Pty) Ltd was paid R18 million for this project. Luh (Pty) Ltd delivered all the required books on 15 January 2019.

REQUIRED:

Assess whether Luh (Pty) Ltd should treat the R18 million received from the eThekwini municipality as a government grant in their books for the year ended 30 April 2019.

CHAPTER 12

IMPAIRMENT OF ASSETS (IAS 36)

LEARNING OUTCOMES

After studying this chapter, you should be able to:

- Identify the overall objective and scope of the standard on impairment of assets (IAS 36).
- Identify and define the elements of impairment loss.
- Disclose the elements of an impairment loss.
- Identify if an asset may be impaired.
- Calculate the recoverable amount through the use of net selling price, value in use estimating cash flows, and discount rate.
- Measure and recognise the impairment loss in the accounting records.
- Recognise a reversal of a previous impairment loss.
- Understand and be able to use the cost model and the revaluation model (net replacement) in the measurement of impairment loss.
- Disclose impairment loss in the financial statements.

PREAMBLE

Mr Mhlongo (known as Njomane) has been arguing with his son, who is an accounting student at university and helps him in his business with accounting-related duties. The argument was sparked when they were reviewing the financial statements produced by their accountant. Njomane was not happy that the business's assets were reduced twice, by the depreciation figure and an impairment loss figure. He said this amounted to double dipping and refused to sign the financial statements until he got a proper explanation. He was now doubting the capabilities of his accountant. The son suggested that they come to you for some clarification and an explanation of impairment of assets.

12.1 INTRODUCTION

This chapter builds upon the foundation that has already been laid in Chapter 10 on property, plant and equipment (PPE) (IAS 16). Chapter 10 dealt extensively with the cost of PPE items and depreciation, which was defined as the systematic allocation of the depreciable amount over the useful life of an asset. Depreciation can also be summarised as the loss of value of an asset through usage. **Impairment of assets**, on the other hand, can be defined as the loss of value through damage. This can be physical damage (eg a conveyor belt gets jammed and cannot operate as it should) or obsolescence (eg the demand for the products that the machinery makes has decreased drastically).

Assets are stated at their carrying amount in the accounting records. When their values are measured, however, it may be that the carrying amount is overstated in terms of the real value of the asset. Such assets are said to be impaired and the value of the carrying amount needs to be adjusted as assets are always supposed to be reflected at their future economic benefits. The impairment loss incurred needs to be taken into consideration to adjust the value of the asset to its real value. Another way of describing the 'real value' of the asset would be to call it the recoverable amount. The impairment loss is therefore the difference between the carrying amount and the recoverable amount.

IAS 36, a standard governing the measurement and disclosure of impairment of assets, sets out the requirements to account for and report impairment of most non-financial assets. The standard specifies when an entity needs to perform an impairment test, how to perform it, the recognition of any impairment losses and the related disclosures. IAS 36 specifically excludes accounting for impairment of assets such as inventory as these are covered by IAS 2.

12.2 DEFINITIONS

Property, plant and equipment can be described as tangible assets which are used in production and/or supply of goods and services or for rental to others or administration purposes and are expected to be used during more than one period (IAS 16: 6).

Recoverable amount is defined as the *higher* of the asset's fair value less costs of disposal and its value in use.

Fair value of an asset is the price that would be received or paid as a result of an arm's length transaction between market participants.

Value in use of an asset is the present value of an estimated future cash flow expected to be derived from the asset.

Depreciation is defined as the systematic allocation of the depreciable amount over the useful life of an asset.

Depreciable amount is the cost price less the residual value of an asset.

Residual value is the amount for which an entity would be able to sell the asset, assuming it had already reached the end of its useful life.

Carrying amount is the cost price less accumulated depreciation.

An impairment loss is an amount by which the carrying amount of an asset or cash-generating unit (CGU) exceeds the recoverable amount of an asset.

A **cash-generating unit** is the smallest identifiable group of assets that generates combined cash inflows as a whole that cannot be attached to any one identifiable individual asset.

12.3 OBJECTIVE OF IMPAIRMENT TESTING

The objective of IAS 36 *Impairment of assets* is to ensure that the entity's assets are not overstated. If the asset's carrying amount exceeds its recoverable amount, the carrying amount will not represent the future economic benefits to be derived from the asset and the asset is described as impaired. In such cases, the standard requires the entity to make provision for impairment loss.

12.4 IDENTIFYING IMPAIRMENT

An indicator review needs to be performed to ascertain if there is any indication that an asset might be impaired. An entity needs to perform a test at the end of each reporting period whether or not there is an indication that any of its assets or CGU are impaired and if there is an indication, the entity should estimate the recoverable amount for that asset at the reporting date. Note that some assets are tested for impairment whether there is an indication of impairment or not, such as intangible assets with indefinite useful lives and intangible assets not yet available for use. These types of assets have to be tested for impairment annually irrespective of whether or not there is indication of impairment. Indications of impairment could come from internal or external sources.

12.4.1 Internal sources
- Evidence indicating that the asset is obsolete or physically damaged, for example the machine is belching smoke or has been struck by lightning.
- Plans are in place to limit the production levels that the machine is operating at or the machine is already idle most of the time.
- Production output reports indicate that the machine's usage is reducing or it has become redundant.

12.4.2 External sources
- There are observable indications that the asset's value has declined.
- Technological, economic or legal changes have taken place that will have an adverse effect on the value of the asset. There could also have been changes in the market environment (eg changes to the laws regulating the sale of tobacco).
- Changes in interest rates may indicate impairment.

Please note that the above lists are not exhaustive.

12.5 MEASUREMENT OF THE RECOVERABLE AMOUNT

An asset is impaired if its carrying amount exceeds its recoverable amount. The recoverable amount is defined as the **higher** of:

- the asset's fair value less costs of disposal; and
- its value in use.

This implies that an asset is **not** impaired if its carrying amount does not exceed either its fair value less costs to sell or its value in use.

EXAMPLE 12.1

An asset has a carrying amount of R200 000. Its fair value is R210 000 and costs of disposal are R5 000. Its value in use cannot be determined.

REQUIRED:
Calculate the impairment loss.

EXAMPLE 12.1 Solution

There is no impairment loss as its carrying amount of R200 000 is less than its fair value less costs of disposal, which amounts to R205 000 (R210 000 – R5 000). There is no point in wasting time and money trying to calculate the value in use in these circumstances.

However, if it is not possible to determine the fair value less costs of disposal, then value in use can be used.

12.5.1 Fair value less costs of disposal

The fair value less costs of disposal of an asset is the price that would be received as a result of an arm's length transaction between market participants at the measurable date less any costs relating to the disposal. Such costs cannot include finance charges or income tax. Examples of costs of disposal are sales commissions, auctioneer's fees, legal costs, costs of removing the asset, etc.

EXAMPLE 12.2

An asset is likely to sell at a public auction for R90 000. Auctioneer's fees are currently at 5% of sale price and the cost of removing the asset amounts to R8 000.

REQUIRED:
Calculate fair value less costs of disposal.

EXAMPLE 12.2 Solution

Fair value less costs of disposal = R90 000 – [(R90 000 × 5%) + R8 000] = R77 500

12.5.2 Value in use

The value in use of an asset is the present value of an estimated future cash flow expected to be derived from the asset. If the asset can be sold after being used within the entity, the residual value must be added to the value in use figure to arrive at the total value in use of the asset.

EXAMPLE 12.3

At 30 June 2019, significant developments in technology by competitors led management of an entity to assess the recoverable amount of the machinery. The fair value less cost of disposal was R550 000. The value in use calculated by an independent actuary was measured at R540 000, but the asset can be sold for R30 000 after being used by the entity.

REQUIRED:
Calculate the recoverable amount.

EXAMPLE 12.3 Solution

The recoverable amount will be R570 000 (value in use of R540 000 + R30 000), which is higher than the fair value less cost of disposal of R550 000.

Recognition and measurement of an impairment loss for an individual asset

In instances where the recoverable amount of an asset is less than its carrying amount, the carrying amount should be reduced to the recoverable amount. This reduction is called an impairment loss. This is done to ensure that the asset is always reflected at its future economic benefit.

EXAMPLE 12.4

Plant has a carrying amount of R580 000, a fair value less costs of disposal of R440 000 and a value in use of R550 000. The recoverable amount will be the higher of R440 000 and R550 000. The asset is thus impaired because the recoverable amount is less than the carrying amount and an impairment loss of R50 000 (R300 000 – R250 000) should be recognised. The journal entry for this is as follows:

	R	R
Dr Impairment loss (SOCI)	30 000	
Cr Accumulated depreciation and impairment losses (SOFP)		30 000
Provision for the impairment loss on plant		

An impairment loss has therefore been recognised immediately as an expense in the profit or loss section as can be seen from the above journal entry.

However, if an asset is carried at a revalued amount, the impairment loss should be accounted for as a revaluation decrease. This means that the impairment loss should be recognised in other comprehensive income (as a reduction in the revaluation surplus), to the extent that the loss does not exceed the revaluation surplus relating to that specific asset. If there is an excess, it should be recognised in the profit or loss section.

EXAMPLE 12.5

Machine Z, a revalued asset, has a historical carrying amount of R100 000 and an actual carrying amount R110 000, a fair value less costs of disposal of R85 000 and a value in use of R95 000. The revaluation surplus applicable to machine B amounts to R10 000.

REQUIRED:

Prepare the appropriate journal entries. You may ignore any tax implications.

EXAMPLE 12.5 Solution

Firstly, the recoverable amount needs to be calculated. In this case, it is the higher of the R70 000 and R75 000, which is the fair value less costs of disposal. The carrying amount is R100 000 and the recoverable amount is R75 000, indicating a write down of R25 000 in total as follows:

	R	R
Dr Impairment loss/revaluation expense (SOCI)	5 000	
Dr Revaluation surplus (OCI)	10 000	
Cr Accumulated depreciation and impairment losses/machine Z – SOFP		15 000
Provision for impairment on machine Z as well as the reduction of the revaluation surplus		

Note that once an impairment loss has been recognised and the value of the asset reduced, future depreciation will be affected because the asset's revised carrying amount will be allocated systematically over its remaining life. At this point, it is always advisable to convert the depreciation percentage to number of years to arrive at a correct depreciation figure (eg 20% = 5 years; 12,5% = 8 years; 25% = 4 years, etc.)

12.6 REVERSAL OF AN IMPAIRMENT LOSS PREVIOUSLY WRITTEN OFF

An entity needs to assess at each reporting date whether there is any indication that an impairment loss recognised in prior years no longer exists or has decreased. If there is any such indication, the entity should re-estimate the recoverable amount. The internal and external indications of impairment listed earlier in this chapter can be of use here, except that the indications will be reversed, for example technological developments may well have given rise to the need for an impairment write-off in the past but, in the same way, some new technological development could well lead to the reversal of previous impairment losses or perhaps their partial reversal as these developments could have made the asset more viable.

EXAMPLE 12.6

Machine C was purchased on 1 January 2018 for R250 000 cash and was brought into use immediately. Costs of moving the machine from the supplier to the factory amounted to R4 000, also paid in cash. Machine C was expected to have an estimated useful life of 10 years with no residual value. At the end of 2018, the directors determined that there could be an impairment problem. They discovered that the fair value of machine C was R200 000 and that costs of disposal would amount to R5 000. They also discovered that the value in use was R197 000.

At the end of 2019, the directors decided to check machine C for impairment. Calculations were done and the recoverable amount for machine C was found to be R190 000.

REQUIRED:

1. Prepare all the necessary journal entries for the year ended 31 December 2018. You may ignore any taxation implications.

2. Prepare all the necessary journal entries for the year ended 31 December 2019.

EXAMPLE 12.6 Solution

1.

1 January 2018	R	R
Dr Plant (250 000 + 4 000) – SOFP	254 000	
Cr Bank		254 000
Being purchase of machine C		
31 December 2018		
Dr Depreciation (10% on R254 000) – SOCI	25 400	
Cr Accumulated depreciation – SOFP		25 400
Being depreciation at 10% with no residual value		
31 December 2018		
Dr Impairment loss (SOCI)	31 600	
Cr Accumulated depreciation and impairment losses – SOFP		31 600
Being impairment loss on machine C [(254 000 – 25 400) – 197 000]		

2.

31 December 2019	R	R
Dr Depreciation – SOCI	21 889	
Cr Accumulated depreciation and impairment losses – SOFP		21 889
Being depreciation on machine C for 2011 [(254 000 – 25 400 – 31 600)/9 remaining years]		
31 December 2019		
Dr Accumulated depreciation and impairment losses – SOFP	14 889	
Cr Impairment loss reversal – SOCI		14 889
Impairment reversal on machine C [190 000 – (254 000 – 25 400 – 31 600 – 21 889) = 190 000 – 175 111]		

Note that when reversing an impairment loss for an individual asset, there is a limit on the amount that may be reversed (ie cost model, to be explained later). The increased carrying amount of the asset after reversal should not exceed the historical carrying amount of the asset that would have been determined (net of depreciation) had no impairment loss been recognised at all. In machine C's case, the impairment reversal could not have exceeded R28 089 {[(254 000 – 25 400 – 25 400) – 175 111] = 203 200 – 175 111 = 28 089}. Any increase above this amount is seen as a revaluation and may only be recognised if the asset is accounted for by means of the revaluation model – this implies that should an entity wish to recognise above this limit, the normal requirements for a revaluation would have to be followed, for example all the assets of that class of PPE would have to be revalued at that date.

12.7 CASH GENERATING UNITS

Sometimes an asset does not generate its own cash flows so its value in use cannot be determined. That same asset may also not have a fair value that is easy to assess because the asset is typically not sold on its own. This does not necessarily make the asset impaired. Testing for the asset's impairment is, however, a problem. To get around this, the CGU has to be considered as a whole. An asset's CGU is the smallest identifiable group of assets that includes the asset and that generates cash inflow. The assets belonging to the CGU can be tested for impairment as a whole as the fair value and value in use can now be determined. If the CGU as a whole is found not to be impaired (the carrying amount of the CGU is less than the recoverable amount of the CGU), then the individual assets within the CGU are also not considered to be impaired. If the carrying amount exceeds the recoverable amount, then an impairment loss needs to be provided for the CGU as a whole.

12.8 COST MODEL AND REVALUATION MODEL

Every entity needs to consider and choose an accounting policy for subsequent measurement of each class of property, plant and equipment. This accounting policy may either be the cost model or the revaluation model. While either model can be chosen, an entity has to use the same model for a similar class of assets and may choose another model for a different class of assets. For example, an entity that owns a fleet of vehicles may not use the cost model for one vehicle and the revaluation model for another vehicle. All vehicles have to be measured using the same model. This is because the vehicles belong to the same class of assets. However, if the entity had another class of asset such as computer equipment, for example, all vehicles could be measured using the revaluation model and all items of computer equipment could be measured using the cost model.

12.8.1 The cost model

Under this model, property, plant and equipment is measured at **cost less accumulated depreciation and accumulated impairment losses**.

In this model, the carrying amount can never be increased above its **historical carrying amount**, but can be increased or decreased below the historical carrying amount. A decrease in the asset is recorded in the impairment loss account. Should the conditions in the market change such that the asset's carrying amount has to be increased, an increase is recorded in the reversal of impairment account, limited to the historical carrying amount. Tracking the historical carrying amount becomes important for impairment loss measurement as the historical carrying amount becomes an important benchmark.

NO TRANSACTION ALLOWED (ABOVE)

Decrease (–) Revaluation surplus   Increase (+) Revaluation surplus

HISTORICAL CARRYING AMOUNT (HCA)

TRANSACTION (BELOW)

Decrease (–) Impairment loss   Increase (+) Impairment loss reversal

Figure 12.1: Cost model (graphical presentation)

EXAMPLE 12.7 Brass Brothers (Pty) Ltd

Brass Brothers (Pty) Ltd is a small company making brass components for the motor industry. The accounting policy relating to machinery owned by the company is as follows: *Machinery is carried at cost less accumulated depreciation and accumulated impairment losses. Depreciation is provided at 20% per annum on the straight line basis.*

The following details relate to the machinery:

Details	R
Cost of machinery	950 000
Date of purchase	01-07-2017
Useful life	5 years

The residual value of the machinery was estimated at nil and there has been no change since acquisition. The useful life has remained unchanged throughout the period.

At 30 June 2018, significant developments in technology by competitors led management to assess the recoverable amount of the machinery. The fair value less cost of disposal was R580 000. The value in use calculated by an independent actuary was measured at R540 000.

At 30 June 2019, it became apparent that the competitors' technology developed in 2018 was not commercially viable. The fair value less cost of disposal amounted to R600 000. The value in use of the machinery calculated by an independent actuary was measured at R520 000.

REQUIRED:

1. Prepare the journal entries for the above transactions for the financial years ended 30 June 2018 and 30 June 2019.

2. Prepare the following notes to the annual financial statements for the year ended 30 June 2019 in accordance with IFRS:
   a) Property plant and equipment note
   b) Profit before tax.

Note: Show all workings.

EXAMPLE 12.7 Suggested solution – Brass Brothers (Pty) Ltd

1. Journal entries

		R	R
01/07/2017	Dr Machinery: cost	950 000	
	Cr Bank/payables		950 000
	Purchase of plant		
30/06/2018	Dr Depreciation (950 000 – 0)/5	190 000	
	Cr Machinery: acc depreciation and impairment loss		190 000
	Depreciation for the year to 30-06-10		
30/06/2018	Dr Impairment loss (carrying amount of 760 000 – fair value of 580 000 = 180 000)	180 000	
	Cr Machinery: acc depreciation and impairment loss		180 000
	Impairment to fair value (760 000 – 580 000 = 180 000)		
30/06/2019	Dr Depreciation (580 000 – 0)/4	145 000	
	Cr Machinery: acc depreciation and impairment loss		145 000
	Depreciation for the year to 30-06-19		
	Dr Machinery: acc depreciation and impairment loss	135 000	
	Cr Impairment loss reversed (profit & loss account)		135 000
	Reversal of impairment up to HCA (current carrying amount of 435 000 – historical carrying amount of 570 000)		

2.

Brass Brothers (Pty) Ltd
Notes to the annual financial statements for the year ended 30 June 2019

Property, plant and equipment

	Machinery	R	
	Net carrying amount: 1 July 2018	**580 000**	
	Gross carrying amount	950 000	
	Accumulated depreciation and impairment losses	(370 000)	
	(2018: dep – 190 000 + imp loss 180 000)		
	Depreciation (580 000/4)	(145 000)	
	Reversal of impairment	135 000	
	Net carrying amount: 30 June 2019	**570 000**	
	Gross carrying amount	950 000	
	Accumulated depreciation and impairment losses	(380 000)	
	(2019: dep – 190 000 + imp loss 180 000) + (2012: dep 145 000 – imp rev 135 000)		
	PROFIT BEFORE TAX		
	Profit before tax is stated after taking into account the following:		
	Depreciation	(145 000)	
	Reversal of impairment	135 000	

Workings: Plant [HCA: historical carrying amount; ACA: actual carrying amount]

		HCA (R)	ACA (R)
01/07/2017	Cost	950 000	950 000
30/06/2018	Depreciation: year to 30/06/2018 (950 000/5)	(190 000)	(190 000)
	Balance	760 000	760 000
30/07/2018	Impairment loss		(180 000)
01/07/2018	**HCA/fair value – 30/07/2018**	760 000	**580 000**
30/06/2019	Depreciation (760 000/5)	(190 000)	
30/06/2019	(580 000/4)		(145 000)
	Balance	570 000	435 000
30/06/2019	Fair value = **R600 000** – Reversal of previous Impairment (reversal of 165 000 limited to 135 000 to bring it to HCA of 570 000)		135 000
30/06/2019	**HCA/fair value – 30/06/2019**	570 000.00	570 000

12.8.2 The revaluation model

Under this model, property, plant and equipment is measured at **fair value at the date of revaluation less any subsequent accumulated depreciation and any subsequent accumulated impairment losses**.

In order to be able to use the revaluation model, the determination of the fair value of the asset must be reliably measurable. Also, an asset must be able to be singled out and revalued on its own. There must be a market for the asset. The entire class (such as land and buildings or machinery or ships) relating to that asset needs to be revalued to prevent selective revaluation and also to prevent a mixture of cost and fair value. Revaluations need to be done with sufficient regularity to ensure that the value of the class indeed reflects fair value. This will depend on the volatility of the fair value for the assets concerned. If fair value changes regularly and significantly, then annual revaluations will be required.

Assets are revalued to their fair value, BOTH above or below the historical carrying amount.

> Carrying amount = Fair value less SUBSEQUENT accumulated depreciation and SUBSEQUENT accumulated impairment loss

If the asset's carrying amount is increased ABOVE its historical carrying amount, then the increase is reflected in a revaluation surplus account (shown as other comprehensive income). This is because the asset would have gained value that has not been earned. As the asset is being used and a year has elapsed, a certain portion of the revaluation surplus will be earned and will be transferred to retained earnings, according to the company policy. The increase below historical carrying amount will be recorded in an income account (profit and loss account) called revaluation income for our purposes.

If the asset's carrying amount is decreased to BELOW its historical carrying amount, then the amount will be taken off the balance in the revaluation surplus; and if the decreased amount is still not covered by the revaluation surplus, then the difference will be impairment loss, which can also be called revaluation expense for our purposes.

TRANSACTION (ABOVE)

Decrease (–) Revaluation surplus   Increase (+) Revaluation surplus

HISTORICAL CARRYING AMOUNT (HCA)

TRANSACTION (BELOW)

Decrease (–) Impairment loss/revaluation expense   Increase (+) Impairment loss reversed / revaluation income

Figure 12.2 Revaluation model (graphical presentation)

There are two methods of revaluation used:

1. The gross replacement value method (GRVM).
2. The net replacement value method (NRVM).

Note: Only the net replacement value method will be used for our purposes.

When the net replacement value method (NRVM) is being used, it means previously accumulated depreciation must be written off against the asset every time before the revaluation is performed, in the specific year in which revaluation is performed. If there was no revaluation for the past three years and at the beginning of the fourth year suddenly there is a revaluation, then the total accumulated depreciation for the past three years must be transferred to the asset before performing the revaluation.

12.9 SUBSEQUENT REVALUATIONS OR DEVALUATIONS

A revaluation is recognised outside of the profit or loss section, in other comprehensive income (provided there was no impairment to reverse first). Similarly, if there is a subsequent devaluation of a revalued asset, then the amount of the decrease should be recognised outside of the profit or loss section, in other comprehensive income first, and any excess adjusted in the profit or loss section.

12.10 REALISATION OF REVALUATION RESERVE

An entity may choose to leave the balance on the revaluation reserve intact for capital maintenance purposes or it may choose to transfer the realised portion of the revaluation reserve to the retained earnings account. There are two main ways of accounting for this realisation. The first way is to wait until the asset has been sold and then transfer the balance (or the portion that relates to the asset) to retained earnings via the statement of changes in equity. The second way is to make transfers annually from the revaluation reserve to retained earnings (in the statement of changes in equity). The company has to decide how revaluation surplus would be transferred to retained earnings and include it in its policies pertaining to impairment of assets.

EXAMPLE 12.8 Vukuzenzele Sisters

Vukuzenzele Sisters owned a plant that had a cost of R100 000 and a useful life of eight years (no residual value) and was acquired on 1 January 2014. The plant is revalued every two years and the revaluation surplus will be regarded as realised only when the asset is sold. The business has a December financial year end.

The plant was revalued as follows:
Beginning of 2016: R80 000
Beginning of 2018: R47 500
Beginning of 2020: R25 000

REQUIRED:

1. Prepare the journal entries for the above transactions.

2. Prepare the following notes to the annual financial statements for the year ended 31 December 2018 in accordance with IFRS:
   a) Property plant and equipment note
   b) Profit before tax.

Note: Show all workings.

EXAMPLE 12.8 Suggested solution – Vukuzenzele Sisters

The revaluation increases/decreases will be accounted for (ignoring any tax implications) as follows.

1. Journal entries

		R	R
01/01/2014	Dr Plant: cost	100 000	
	Cr Bank/payables		100 000
	Purchase of plant		
31/12/2014	Dr Depreciation [(100 000 – 0)/8]	12 500	
	Cr Plant: accumulated depreciation		12 500
	Depreciation for the year to 31-12-2014		
31/12/2015	Dr Depreciation [(100 000 – 0)/8]	12 500	
	Cr Plant: accumulated depreciation		12 500
	Depreciation for the year to 31-12-2015		
01/01/2016	Dr Plant: accumulated depreciation	25 000	
	Cr Plant		25 000
	Net replacement value method journal entry		

↵

01/01/2016	Dr Plant	5 000	
	Cr Revaluation surplus		5 000
	Revaluation of plant on 1/1/2016		
31/12/2016	Dr Depreciation [(80 000 – 0)/6]	13 333	
	Cr Plant: accumulated depreciation		13 333
	Depreciation for the year to 31-12-2016		
31/12/2017	Dr Depreciation [(80 000 – 0)/5]	13 333	
	Cr Plant: accumulated depreciation		13 333
	Depreciation for the year to 31-12-2017		
01/01/2018	Dr Plant: accumulated depreciation	26 666	
	Cr Plant		26 666
	Net replacement value method journal entry		
01/01/2018	Dr Revaluation surplus	3 334	
	Dr Revaluation expense	2 500	
	Cr Plant		5 834
	Revaluation of plant on 1/1/2018		
31/12/2018	Dr Depreciation [(47 500 – 0)/4]	11 875	
	Cr Plant: accumulated depreciation		11 875
	Depreciation for the year to 31-12-2018		
31/12/2019	Dr Depreciation [(35 625 – 0)/3]	11 875	
	Cr Plant: accumulated depreciation		11 875
	Depreciation for the year to 31-12-2019		
01/01/2020	Dr Plant: accumulated depreciation	23 750	
	Cr Plant		23 750
	Net replacement value method journal entry		
01/01/2020	Dr Plant	1 250	
	Cr Revaluation income		1 250
	Revaluation of plant on 1/1/2020		

2.

Vukuzenzele Sisters		
Notes to the annual financial statements for the year ended 31 December 2018		
Property, plant and equipment		
Plant	**R**	
	Net carrying amount: 1 January 2018	**53 334**
	Gross carrying amount	53 334
	Accumulated depreciation and impairment losses	(0)
	Revaluation surplus decrease/devaluation	(3 334)
	Revaluation expense	(2 500)
	Depreciation (47 500/4)	(11 875)
	Net carrying amount: 31 December 2018	**35 625**
	Gross carrying amount	53 334
	Accumulated depreciation and impairment losses	(17 709)
	(2018: dep – 11 875 + reval exp 2 500 + reval surplus 3 334)	
	PROFIT BEFORE TAX	
	Profit before tax is stated after taking into the following:	
	Depreciation	11 875
	Revaluation surplus/devaluation	3 334
	Revaluation expense	2 500

Workings: Plant [HCA: historical carrying amount; ACA: actual carrying amount]

		HCA (R)	ACA (R)
01/01/2014	Cost	100 000	100 000
31/12/2014	Depreciation: year to 31/12/2014 (100 000/8)	(12 500)	(12 500)
	Balance	87 500	87 500
31/12/2015	Depreciation: year to 31/12/2015 (100 000/8)	(12 500)	(12 500)
	Balance	75 000	75 000
01/01/2016	Revaluation surplus	-	5 000
	Balance	75 000	80 000
31/12/2016	Depreciation: year to 31/12/2016 (80 000/6)	(12 500)	(13 333)
	Balance	62 500	66 667
31/12/2017	Depreciation: year to 31/12/2017 (66 667/5)	(12 500)	(13 333)
	Balance	50 000	53 334
01/01/2018	Revaluation surplus	-	(3 334)
	Revaluation expense	-	(2 500)
	Balance	50 000	47 500
31/12/2018	Depreciation: year to 31/12/2018 (47 500/4)	(12 500)	(11 875)
	Balance	37 500	35 625
31/12/2019	Depreciation: year to 31/12/2019 (35 625/3)	(12 500)	(11 875)
		25 000	23 750
01/01/2020	Revaluation income	-	1 250
		25 000	25 000

EXAMPLE 12.9 Abathungi Co-operative Society

Abathungi Co-Operative Society purchased a weaving machine for R200 000 cash on 1 January 2016. The machine will be depreciated at 20% straight line with no estimated residual value.

The machine was revalued to the following values:
31 December 2017:   R150 000
31 December 2019:   R37 000
The entity's policy is to realise the revaluation surplus as the asset is used.

Note: NRVM is used.

REQUIRED:

Show the related journal entries for the above information until 31 December 2020 and the effect on the statement of comprehensive income and the statement of financial position.

EXAMPLE 12.9 Suggested solution – Abathungi Co-operative Society

Workings: Machine [HCA: historical carrying amount; ACA: actual carrying amount]

		HCA (R)	ACA (R)
01/01/2016	Cost	200 000	200 000
31/12/2016	Depreciation: year to 31/12/2016 (200 000/5)	(40 000)	(40 000)
	Balance	160 000	160 00
31/12/2017	Depreciation: year to 31/12/2017(160 000/4)	(40 000)	(40 000)
	Balance	120 000	120 000
31/12/2017	Revaluation surplus	-	30 000
	Balance	120 000	150 000
31/12/2018	Depreciation: year to 31/12/2018 (150 000/3)	(40 000)	(50 000)
	Balance	80 000	100 000
31/12/2019	Depreciation: year to 31/12/2019 (100 000/2)	(40 000)	(50 000)
	Balance	40 000	50 000
31/12/2019	Revaluation surplus	-	(10 000)
	Revaluation expense	-	(3 000)
	Balance	40 000	37 000
31/12/2020	Depreciation: year to 31/12/2020 (37 000/1)	(40 000)	(37 000)
	Balance	Nil	Nil

The journal entries to record the above (ignoring any tax implications) are as follows:

	R	R
1 January 2016		
Dr Property, plant and equipment at cost – SOFP	200 000	
Cr Bank – SOFP		200 000
Being purchase of asset		
31 December 2016		
Dr Depreciation (200 000/5) – SOCI	40 000	
Cr Accumulated depreciation – SOFP		40 000
Being depreciation for 2016		
31 December 2017		
Dr Depreciation – SOCI	40 000	
Cr Accumulated depreciation – SOFP		40 000
Being depreciation for 2017		
Dr Accumulated depreciation (40 000 + 40 000) – SOFP	80 000	
Cr Property plant and equipment at cost – SOFP		80 000
Being reversal of accumulated depreciation		
Dr Property, plant and equipment at net replacement cost – SOFP	30 000	
Cr Revaluation surplus – OCI and SOCE		30 000
Being revaluation surplus for machine J [150 000 – (200 000 – 80 000)]		
31 December 2018		
Dr Depreciation (150 000/3 years remaining life) – SOCI	50 000	
Cr Accumulated depreciation – SOFP		50 000
Being depreciation for 2018		
Dr Revaluation Surplus (30 000/3 remaining years) – OCI and SOCE	10 000	
Cr Retained earnings – OCI and SOCE		10 000
Being realisation of one-third of the revaluation surplus		
31 December 2019		
Dr Depreciation – SOCI	50 000	
Cr Accumulated depreciation – SOFP		50 000
Being depreciation for 2019		
Dr Revaluation surplus – OCI and SOCE	5 000	
Cr Retained earnings – OCI and SOCE		5 000
Being realisation of the 2019 portion of the retained surplus		
Dr Accumulated depreciation – SOFP	100 000	
Cr Property, plant and equipment – SOFP		100 000
Being reversal of accumulated depreciation (50 000 + 50 000)		
Dr Revaluation surplus (entire balance) – OCI and SOCE	10 000	
Cr Property, plant and equipment – SOFP		10 000
Being revaluation of machine		
Dr Revaluation expense – SOCI	3 000	
Cr Property, plant and equipment – SOFP		3 000
Being revaluation of machine (50 000 – 10 000 – 37 000)		

↪

31 December 2020		
Dr Depreciation (37 000/one remaining year) – SOCI	37 000	
Cr Accumulated depreciation – SOFP		37 000
Being depreciation for 2020		

The following extracts show the effect of the above information on the statement of profit and loss and other comprehensive income and the statement of financial position:

Statement of profit or loss and other comprehensive income for the years ended 2016 to 2020

	2016	2017	2018	2019	2020
	R	R	R	R	R
Revenue	xxx	xxx	xxx	xxx	xxx
Cost of sales – depreciation included here					
Gross profit	xxx	xxx	xxx	xxx	xxx
Other expenses – Depreciation – Revaluation expense	40 000	40 000	50 000	50 000 3 000	37 000
Profit before tax	xxx	xxx	xxx	xxx	xxx
Other comprehensive income					
Revaluation surplus on machinery	-	30 000	-	-	-
Portion of revaluation surplus transferred to retained earnings	-	-	(10 000)	(5 000)	-
Reversal of revaluations surplus	-	-	-	(10 000)	-
Total comprehensive income for the year	xxx	xxx	xxx	xxx	xxx

Statement of financial position as at 2016 to 2020

	2016	2017	2018	2019	2020
	R	R	R	R	R
Assets					
Non-current assets					
Property, plant and equipment	160 000	150 000	100 000	37 000	-
Equity and liabilities					
Equity					
Share capital	xxx	xxx	xxx	xxx	xxx
Retained earnings	xxx	xxx	xxx	xxx	xxx
Revaluation reserve	-	30 000	20 000	5 000	-

12.11 SUMMARY

This chapter dealt with IAS 36, a standard governing the measurement and disclosure of impairment of assets. The definitions relating to the elements impairment of assets were supplied. The chapter further dealt with the intricacies of the calculations involved in the measurement and the disclosure of impairment of property, plant and equipment items.

EXERCISES

Exercise 12.1 Khabazela Ltd

The following information was extracted from the records of Khabazela Ltd in respect of machinery owned by the company for the year ended 28 February 2019:

Cost of machinery at 01 March 2018 amounted to R600 000.

Machinery is depreciated at 20% pa on the straight line method over a useful life of five years with a nil residual value.

While preparing the annual financial statements for the year ended 28 February 2019, management were of the opinion that the equipment might be impaired. There is an active market for this type of machinery and it is estimated that the machinery can be sold for a net value of R440 000. Value in use at this date was determined by management to be R417 000.

REQUIRED:

1. Calculate whether the machinery is impaired at 28 February 2019.
2. Prepare the journal entries to record the information above for the year ended 28 February 2019.
3. Prepare the profit before tax note for the year ended 28 February 2019 showing the disclosure relating to machinery.

Exercise 12.2 Amazizi Co-Operative Society

Amazizi Co-Operative Society uses the revaluation model and has a policy of revaluing their assets to fair values on an annual basis using the net replacement value method. The company has a 28 February year end.

Plant was purchased on 1 March 2017 at a cost of R700 000. It has a useful life of five years with no residual value. Depreciation is provided on the straight line method over the plant's estimated useful life. At 28 February 2018, in terms of the company's policy, the plant was revalued by an independent valuer who determined the fair value to be R680 000.

The fair value determined at 28 February 2019 amounted to R400 000.

There is no change in the expected useful life or residual value of the plant. The revaluation surplus is transferred to retained earnings over the remaining estimated useful life of the asset.

REQUIRED:

Prepare all the journal entries for the above transactions for the financial years ended 28 February 2018 and 28 February 2019.

Exercise 12.3 Mason Ltd

Mason Ltd is a manufacturing company which uses the revaluation model to measure its property, plant and equipment. The company, which has a 28 February year end, revalues its assets to fair value on an annual basis using the net replacement value method.

On 1 March 2016, the company purchased machinery at a cost of R600 000.

The machinery is depreciated on a straight line basis over five years to a nil residual value.

An independent valuer determined the following fair values:
   29 February 2017: R430 000
   28 February 2018: R385 000

The useful life and residual value of the machinery have remained unchanged since acquisition.

REQUIRED:

1. Prepare the journal entries relating to machinery for the financial years ended 29 February 2017 and 28 February 2018.

2. Prepare the following notes to the annual financial statements for the year ended 28 February 2018 in accordance with IFRS:
   a) Accounting policy relating to machinery
   b) Property, plant and equipment.

Note: Show all workings.

Exercise 12.4 Walala Ltd

Walala Wasala Ltd is a manufacturing company with a year end at 31 December. The company purchased an item of plant, machine N, on 1 January 2017 for R450 000 and paid cash. It was available for use immediately. Management believes machine N has a useful life of four years but will have no residual value.

Walala adopted the revaluation model some time ago for the measurement of property, plant and machinery. Walala has a policy of revaluing its machinery annually due to the volatility of the market. The net replacement value method is used. The company transfers the revaluation surplus to retained earnings as the asset is used.

The fair value of machine N was calculated by Mr Slammer, a sworn appraiser, as follows:

Date	Fair value – R
31 December 2017	412 500
31 December 2018	200 000

REQUIRED:

Prepare the journal entries for the above transactions for the financial years ended 31 December 2017 and 31 December 2018.

Exercise 12.5 Brazo Ltd

The following information is applicable in respect of plant owned by Brazo Ltd:

Cost price of plant – 1 March 2014	R1 760 000
Estimated residual value at date of acquisition	R160 000

The company provides for depreciation at 20% per annum on the straight line method.

While preparing the annual financial statements for the year ended 28 February 2016, management was of the opinion that the plant might be impaired. There is an active market for the plant and it is estimated that it can be sold for R990 000. The cost of disposal of the plant was estimated at R30 000. Value in use at this date was determined by management to be R928 000.

The company uses the cost model to measure its property, plant and equipment.

REQUIRED:

1. Calculate whether the plant is impaired at 28 February 2016.

2. Assuming that your calculation above indicates the plant is impaired, draft the journal entry to process the impairment loss.

3. Explain the purpose of testing assets for impairment.

Exercise 12.6 4IR Ltd

4IR Ltd has a 31 December financial year end and applies the cost model for measurement of its assets.

The company uses specialised robotic machines which are used as a CGU and were purchased at a cost of R4 million cash on 1 January 2018. The robotics have a useful life of four years and the residual value over the years was assessed to be nil. Depreciation of 25% is provided using the straight line method over its useful life.

Details of the machinery's estimated recoverable amount are as follows:

	R
31 December 2018	3 300 000
31 December 2019	1 800 000

REQUIRED:

1. Prepare the journal entries for the above transactions for the financial years ended 31 December 2018 and 31 December 2019.

2. Prepare the following notes to the annual financial statements for the year ended 31 December 2019 in accordance with IFRS:
   a) Accounting policy note relating to machinery
   b) Property plant and equipment note.

Note: Show all workings.

Exercise 12.7 Full Steam (Pty) Ltd

Full Steam (Pty) Ltd is specialising in locomotives. The company has a 31 December financial year end and applies the cost model for measurement of its assets.

The company purchased a bus to transport passengers around the train station for R2 000 000 on credit on 1 January 2017. The bus has a useful life of four years and the residual value over the years was assessed to be nil. Depreciation of 25% is provided using the straight line method over its useful life.

Details of the machinery's estimated recoverable amount are as follows:

	R
31 December 2017	1 800 000
31 December 2018	700 000
31 December 2019	650 000

REQUIRED:
Prepare the relevant journal entries for the above transactions.

CHAPTER 13

ANALYSIS AND INTERPRETATION OF FINANCIAL STATEMENTS

LEARNING OUTCOMES

After studying this chapter, you should be able to:

- Discuss the nature, scope and objectives of financial statement analysis.
- Explain the need for financial statement analysis.
- Define, calculate and interpret the following ratios:
  - Return on equity
  - Return on total assets
  - Gross profit percentage
  - Profit margin
  - Financial leverage and leverage effect
  - Current ratio
  - Acid test ratio
  - Trade receivables collection period
  - Trade payables settlement period
  - Inventory turnover rate
  - Inventory holding period
  - Debt-equity ratio
  - Times interest earned ratio
- Discuss the limitations of financial statement analysis.

PREAMBLE

Mr Mhlongo (commonly known as Njomane) is concerned and has been debating with his business friend about a proper assessment of his business performance and financial condition. This is because in many instances his business associates have found it difficult to understand what is presented in the financial statements of his business. Njomane comes to you for professional advice on how to interpret information contained in the financial statements. He mentions that, up until now, as long as his business was making a profit, he has not worried too much about analysis and interpretation of what is contained in the financial statements because he believes that profit is king. He asks you to enlighten him about the importance of financial statement analysis.

13.1 INTRODUCTION

Financial statement analysis is typically associated with ratio analysis, defined as the analysis of relationships between various financial statement items both at a point in time and over time. It uses the financial statements in a unique manner to provide a different viewpoint about the business entity.

To complete a ratio analysis, the financial statements are used to calculate a set of ratios. Each ratio emphasises a particular aspect of the statement of financial position and/or statement of profit or loss and other comprehensive income. The calculated set of ratios are then compared to industry averages or historical standards to assess the financial performance and position of the business entity. The general rule is that ratios deviating largely on either side from industry standards may necessitate an enquiry on the aspects affecting that particular ratio.

Ratios for any one year can be misleading because they are high or low for some temporary reason. Therefore, it is also important to analyse trends in the ratios to assess changes in the business entity's performance over time. A trend analysis involves graphs of the various ratios, where each graph consists of a particular ratio plotted against time, usually expressed in years. Thread analysis of the ratios adds depth to the study because it looks at several years and assists in distinguishing between isolated instances of suspicious ratios and the pervasive deterioration of ratios that indicates trouble.

Time trends in a business entity's ratios are useful, but it is often more useful to compare the entity trends with industry trends. This comparison illustrates how well an entity has been doing over time relative to its competitors and may assist to explain trends in the entity's ratios. If the entity's profit margin is declining over time, for example, the user of the analysis would like to know whether this decline is mainly because of declining industry profit margins or whether the entity is not competitive when compared with other entities operating in the same industry.

There are three groups of financial ratios that are commonly used to assess the entity's financial performance and financial position: profitability, liquidity and solvency. A fourth category, market ratios, is also useful in assessing the entity but falls outside the scope of this book.

13.2 PROFITABILITY RATIOS

Profitability ratios measure the profits of the entity relative to sales, assets or equity. It is important to emphasise that profitability ratios describe an entity's past profitability. Investors are continually bombarded with statements to the effect that a business earned a certain percentage of profit on equity during the previous year and therefore should earn the same or higher percentage during the current year. However, because there is little evidence that past profitability results foretell future profitability, it is important that the reader of such information avoid attaching too much importance to these numbers as they are historical. They certainly tell a story about where the business entity has been, but not necessarily where it is going. However, a lower profitability ratio when compared with the previous years' or industry ratios is not desirable as it may indicate lack of profitability.

The **gross profit margin** shows what percentage of every sales 'rand' the business entity was able to convert into gross profit. The gross profit percentage is the first level of profitability of an entity indicating how well management is able to control costs relating to sales when the entity is compared with its competitors. The gross profit percentage is an important yardstick as it indicates the percentage of profit that is left from sales to meet other operating expenses after deducting the cost of sales. Without a good cushion of gross profit, a business entity will struggle to pay for its operating expenses.

The gross profit percentage is calculated as follows:

$$\text{Gross profit percentage} = \frac{\text{Gross profit}}{\text{Sales}} \times 100$$

The **profit margin** expresses the percentage of every sales 'rand' a business entity was able to convert into net income. The profit margin ratio shows profit before tax for the year as a percentage of sales. Flowing from gross profit, the profit margin is one of the important measures of the overall results of a business entity, showing management's ability to operate an entity profitably by recovering the costs relating to sales, other expenses relating to operating a business, and the interest payable on borrowed funds. This is also an important measure of good management stewardship in containing the operating expenses to ensure that a reasonable amount of profit is available to the owners as compensation for investing in the entity.

The profit margin is calculated as follows:

$$\text{Profit margin} = \frac{\text{Profit before tax}}{\text{Sales}} \times 100$$

The **return on assets (ROA)** ratio relates net income to total assets, ie it measures how profitably the business entity has used its assets. The ratio reflects the profitability of the entity as a whole in that it compares the profit for the year before interest and tax with the total assets, ie total funds employed in the business. The importance of this ratio lies in the fact that it is an indicator of how effectively the entity's total assets are being used to generate profits.

The return on assets ratio is calculated as follows:

$$\text{Return on total assets} = \frac{\text{Profit before interest and tax}}{\text{Total assets}} \times 100$$

The **return on equity (ROE)** ratio indicates the rate of the return earned on the funds attributable to the owners of a business entity. The ROE ratio measures how successful an entity is in using equity to attain its key financial objectives, ie remaining viable in the long run and increasing the wealth of its owners. From the owners' point of view, the return on equity is deemed to be a crucial calculation as it measures the return on their investment.

The return on equity ratio is calculated as follows:

$$\text{Return on equity} = \frac{\text{Profit before tax}}{\text{Total equity}} \times 100$$

The **financial leverage ratio** is an assessment of how a business entity is using borrowed funds. It measures whether a business is generating positive returns on the borrowed funds, ie returns that are higher than the cost thereof.

The financial leverage ratio is calculated as follows:

$$\text{Financial leverage} = \frac{\text{Return on equity}}{\text{Return on assets}}$$

The result of the calculated ratio above will indicate whether an entity is benefiting from the use of borrowed funds or not. A financial leverage ratio of one is generally regarded as an acceptable standard as that is a break-even point between the cost on borrowed funds (interest) and the benefits (return) of using borrowed funds. A leverage ratio that exceeds one indicates that an entity is generating higher returns on the borrowed funds than the cost thereof. Conversely, a leverage ratio of less than one indicates that the cost on borrowed funds exceeds the return thereon.

The exact impact of the profitability of borrowed funds on the entity can be measured by calculating the **financial leverage effect**. The financial leverage effect is expressed as the difference between the return on equity and return on assets. The analysis of the leverage effect is important to equity investors as it provides an indication of the return that is attributable to them from the use of borrowed funds.

The financial leverage effect ratio is calculated as follows:

$$\text{Leverage effect} = \text{Return on equity} - \text{Return on total assets}$$

A positive result on the calculation of the leverage effect is desirable as it will indicate that borrowed funds are being used profitably to increase the wealth of the equity investors (owners) of the business.

13.3 LIQUIDITY RATIOS

For an entity to continue with its business endeavours, it must be able to pay its debts as they come due. Liquidity ratios measure the extent to which a business can service its immediate obligations, in effect assessing the entity's ability to meet short-term financial contingencies. The liquidity of an entity is of interest to short-term credit providers, especially suppliers of goods and services, banks and other institutions that provide short-term unsecured loans. Long-term providers of credit also assess the liquidity position of an entity because liquidity has a direct influence on the ability of an entity to make interest payments on long-term borrowings. The following are liquidity ratios that are commonly used:

- Current ratio
- Acid test ratio or quick ratio
- Inventory turnover rate
- Trade receivables collection period
- Trade payables settlement period.

The **current ratio** relates current assets to current liabilities. Current assets include cash, bank balances, financial instruments held for trading, trade and other receivables, and inventory. Current liabilities include trade and other payables, bank overdraft, current portion of long-term borrowings, current taxes payable, and other accrued expenses.

The current ratio is calculated as follows:

$$\text{Current ratio} = \frac{\text{Current assets}}{\text{Current liabilities}}$$

Relatively high current ratios are interpreted as an indication that a business entity is liquid and in a good position to meet its current obligations; low current rations indicate the opposite. The current ratio supposedly measures liquidity because it relates the business entity's pending need for cash to the entity's present cash and near cash position. Near cash in this case is represented by financial instruments held for trading, trade and other receivables, and inventory. One shortcoming of the current ratio as a measure of liquidity, however, is that it does not differentiate between the various liquidities of the near cash assets. For example, the current ratio implicitly assumes that inventory is as liquid as financial instruments held for trading, whereas in actual case it is not. The acid test ratio attempts to correct for this.

The **acid test ratio**, otherwise known as the quick ratio, is the same as the current ratio except that the numerator does not include inventory. Inventory is typically the least liquid component of the current assets.

The acid test ratio is calculated as follows:

$$\text{Acid test ratio} = \frac{\text{Current assets} - \text{Inventory}}{\text{Current liabilities}}$$

Like the current ratio, the acid test ratio is meant to reflect the entity's ability to pay its short-term obligations, and the higher the acid test ratio, the more liquid the entity's position. There are two dangers that the entity may face if its liquidity position is too low, namely (1) the entity may be unable to pay its obligations as they come due, and (2) the short-term lenders may perceive the entity as being unable to meet its obligations and be unwilling to advance new credit to the entity.

While such ratios provide an assessment of the entity's liquidity position, it is important to note that they do not assess the amount or timing of the entity's cash flows. To assess cash flows, additional ratios may be required to be computed.

The **activity ratios** fall under the umbrella of liquidity ratios. Activity ratios indicate how well the entity manages its assets by relating important asset accounts to operating results. These ratios are called turnover ratios because they show how rapidly assets are being converted (turned over) into sales. Although generalisation of these ratios can be misleading, high turnover ratios are usually associated with good asset management and low turnover ratios with bad asset management. Activity ratios that fall within the scope of this book involve accounts receivable, accounts payable, sales and inventory.

The **inventory turnover ratio** is one of the yardsticks that are used to gauge the efficiency the entity's inventory is being managed. It is a rough measure of how many times per year the inventory level is replaced (turned over).

The inventory turnover ratio is calculated as follows:

$$\text{Inventory turnover rate} = \frac{\text{Cost of sales}}{\text{Average inventory}}$$

Generally, higher than average inventory turnovers are suggestive of good inventory management. Low turnovers may result from excessive inventory levels. On the other hand, abnormally high inventory turnovers may indicate inventory levels so low that shortages of inventory will occur, and future sales opportunities may be jeopardised.

The **trade receivables collection period** indicates the efficiency of the entity's collection policy by showing how long it takes for accounts receivable to be cleared. The collection period is the time period between the date of the credit sales and receipt of payment from trade debtors for the credit sales. The significance of this ratio as a liquidity ratio is that it gives an indication of the time an entity must wait before receiving cash from trade debtors.

The trade receivables collection period is calculated as follows:

$$\text{Trade receivables collection period} = \frac{\text{Average trade receivables}}{\text{Credit sales}} \times 365$$

The significance of the trade receivables collection period figure is that it answers this question: assuming all sales are made on credit, how many days' worth of sales are tied up in receivables? The collection period supposedly measures the quality of the entity's receivables: the shorter the collection period, the better that quality of the receivables because a short collection period means that the entity's customers are prompt payers.

Long collection periods may indicate that the entity's receivables policy is not very effective. An important standard associated with the collections period is the terms stating within what period payment is due by the entity's customers. If the collection period is substantially longer than the stated credit terms, receivables are not being managed well in relation to the entity's credit policy.

On the contrary, collection periods shorter than the industry average are usually viewed as an indication that the receivables policy is effective. A collection period that is too low in relation to the industry standards may mean that the entity's credit policy is too restrictive. If the entity were to relax its credit policy by extending credit to customers now on a cash basis, it might increase its sales and profits significantly. The trade receivables collection period will possess more meaning if compared with the trade payables settlement period.

The **trade payables settlement period** indicates the time it takes an entity to settle its trade creditors. An ideal situation will be that an entity will push to extend this payables settlement period to longer than the receivables collection period. This is because the cash that is received from trade debtors is often used to settle trade creditors. The longer the payment period, the more time is available for an entity to generate cash to settle its trade creditors.

The trade payables settlement period is calculated as follows:

$$\text{Trade payables settlement period} = \frac{\text{Average trade payables}}{\text{Credit purchases}} \times 365$$

The implication of the trade payables settlement period figure is that if all purchases are made on credit, how many days does it take the entity to settle its debts with its creditors? A cautious interpretation of a longer payables settlement period is necessary as it may be (1) due to favourable credit terms accorded by creditors to the entity; or (2) a sign of cash flow problems and hence a worsening financial condition. On the other hand, a shorter payables settlement period must also be read with circumspection as it may indicate (1) the entity is paying its suppliers more promptly, seeking to take advantage of early payment discounts or actively working to improve its credit rating and (2) the entity's creditors are demanding to be paid quickly.

Contrasted with the trade receivables collection period, a lower trade receivables collection period compared with a higher trade payables payment period is desirable. The implication of this is that the entity will receive amounts owing by debtors long before the settlement of entity's creditors accounts.

13.4 SOLVENCY RATIOS

Solvency ratios are also called debt or leverage ratios and indicate the extent to which a business entity has financed its investment by borrowing. These ratios focus on the entity's financial structure, ie the way the entity's existence is financed. The issues are the amount of debt an entity is using and the entity's ability to service this debt. Debt financing can in some instances increase the risk of bankruptcy, so the more extensive the use of debt, the larger the entity's solvency ratios and the more risk present in the entity.

The **debt–equity ratio** is the ratio of the total debt in a business entity, both long term and short term, to equity, where equity is the sum of all funds attributable to the owners of the business.

The debt–equity ratio is calculated as follows:

$$\text{Debt–equity ratio} = \frac{\text{Total debt}}{\text{Total equity}} \times 100$$

The debt–equity ratio reflects the financial structure of an entity by showing the entity's financial risk position, of primary interest to investors. The higher the percentage of financing provided by creditors, the higher the financial risk in the business entity.

The **times interest earned ratio** measures the ability of an entity to meet its interest obligations.

The times interest earned ratio is calculated as follows:

$$\text{Times interest earned ratio} = \frac{\text{Profit before interest and tax}}{\text{Finance costs}}$$

Times interest earned is deemed to be one of several debt service ratios as it describes the ability of an entity to pay its interest obligations as they come due. Times interest earned is a kind of interest coverage ratio that shows how many times the interest payments are covered by funds that are normally available to pay interest expenses. This does not include other financial resources that could be available to meet interest expenses. The higher this ratio, the better for the entity, as it means that interest obligations of the entity are well covered by profits.

13.5 LIMITATIONS OF FINANCIAL STATEMENT ANALYSIS

Financial statement analysis is widely used by the entity's management, its creditors and potential investors. It is an important technique, and anyone wishing to have a complete understanding of managerial finance must have a good grasp of it. Nevertheless, financial analysis has limitations and potential problems, including the following:

- Financial statements are prepared following the accrual basis of accounting and are historical in nature. The figures presented on the current financial statements may not be closely related to cash flows.
- Because of alternative accounting treatments, comparisons among entities, within the same industries, may be difficult. Furthermore, one entity's accounting procedures may change over time, making trend analysis less reliable.
- Large entities have multiple divisions operating in multiple industries. Compilation of the industry averages may therefore be difficult, and the benchmarking can be inaccurate.
- Inflationary periods can significantly distort an entity's recorded values relative to the actual market values. Inventory costs and depreciation charges may affect the calculation of profits. Inflation can distort the comparison of ratios for several entities, or one entity's ratios over time.
- Financial ratios can be used to assess whether the performance of an entity is satisfactory by comparing it with other entities operating in the same industry, and by comparing current period results with those achieved in the previous accounting periods. However, ratios do not always provide explanations for observed changes, and further inquiry is sometimes needed. Therefore, the interpretation of calculated ratios requires a certain level of knowledge about the entity and the industry in which the entity operates to arrive at an informed decision.

The above limitations do not reduce the ratio analysis usefulness but rather highlight problems that analysts should be aware of when interpreting the ratios. Ratio analysis conducted in a blunt manner can be dangerous, but if used carefully can provide useful insight into an entity's performance and financial position.

EXAMPLE 13.1 Uthungulu Ltd

Uthungulu Ltd is an incorporated company operating in KwaZulu-Natal. The following information is extracted from the financial statement of the company as at 28 February 2019, the end of the financial period.

Abstract from the financial statements of Uthungulu Ltd as at
28 February 2019

	2019	2018
	R	R
Share capital	300 000	300 000
Retained earnings	48 000	15 000
Other components of equity	75 000	75 000
Long-term borrowings	70 000	100 000
Property, plant and equipment	374 000	418 000
Unlisted share investments	35 000	50 000
Inventory – 28 February	25 000	21 000
Trade and other receivables (trade receivables)	36 000	37 000
Cash and cash equivalents	47 000	–
Trade and other payables (trade payables)	24 000	34 000
Bank overdraft	–	2 000
Revenue (sales)	234 000	179 800
Purchases	74 500	57 400
Administrative expenses	27 500	19 250
Interest on long-term borrowing	8 400	12 000
Profit before tax	123 600	91 150

Industry averages as at 28 February 2019:

Return on equity	18,30%
Return on total assets	15,80%
Gross profit percentage	53,55%
Profit margin	53,69%
Financial leverage	1,16
Current ratio	2,53:1
Acid test ratio	1,96:1
Trade receivables collection period	80,04 days
Trade payables settlement period	85,11 days
Inventory turnover rate	6,01 times
Inventory holding period	105,20 days
Debt–equity ratio	57%
Times interest earned ratio	13,24 times

Additional information:

1. All sales and purchases are on credit. The trade debtors and trade creditors, at the beginning of the 2019 financial year, amounted to R27 500 and R29 000 respectively.

2. Inventory at the beginning of the 2019 financial year amounted to R15 000.

3. The unlisted share investment is designated as at fair value through profit or loss.

REQUIRED:

Calculate the following ratios and interpret the calculated ratios for Uthungulu Ltd in relation to the industry averages. Assume 365 days in a year.

1. Profitability ratios

2. Liquidity ratios

3. Solvency ratios.

EXAMPLE 13.1 Suggested solution – Uthungulu Ltd

1. Profitability ratios

Gross profit percentage:

	2019	**2018**

$$\text{Gross profit percentage} = \frac{\text{Gross profit}}{\text{Sales}} \times 100 = \frac{\text{R163 500}②}{\text{R234 000}} \times 100 : \frac{\text{R128 400}②}{\text{R179 800}} \times 100$$

$$= 69,87\% \qquad : = 71,41\%$$

When compared to 2018, the gross profit percentage deteriorated by 1,54% (71,41 – 69,87). The gross profit of 69,87% for 2019 it is still higher than the industry average of 53,55%. It is possible that the company achieved a better gross profit percentage than the industry because of a higher mark-up on inventory, or that inventory was obtained at a lower cost, or a combination of both.

Profit margin:

	2019	**2018**

$$\text{Profit margin} = \frac{\text{Profit before tax}}{\text{Sales}} \times 100 = \frac{\text{R123 600}}{\text{R234 000}} \times 100 : \frac{\text{R91 150}}{\text{R179 800}} \times 100$$

$$= 52,82\% \qquad : = 50,70\%$$

Uthungulu Ltd recorded a lower profit margin than the industry average of 53,69%. It slightly increased from 2018 to 2019. The deviation from the industry average can possibly be attributed to higher distribution, administrative and general expenses.

Return on assets (ROA):

	2019	2018

$$\text{Return on total assets} = \frac{\text{Profit before interest}}{\text{Total assets}} \times 100 = \frac{\text{R132 000}①}{\text{R517 000}⑥} \times 100 : \frac{\text{R103 150}①}{\text{R526 000}⑥} \times 100$$

$$= 25{,}53\% \qquad : = 19{,}61\%$$

Uthungulu Ltd recorded an improvement in the return on total assets in 2019 when compared with 2018. The return on assets is also relatively higher than the industry average of 15,80%, which is an indication of good management skills in the use of assets by the company.

Return on equity (ROE)

	2019	2018

$$\text{Return on equity} = \frac{\text{Profit before tax}}{\text{Total equity}} \times 100 = \frac{\text{R123 600}}{\text{R423 000}③} \times 100 : \frac{\text{R91 150}}{\text{R390 000}③} \times 100$$

$$= 29{,}22\% \qquad : = 23{,}37\%$$

The return attributed to shareholders of the company improved in 2019 when compared with 2018. When compared to the industry average of 18,30%, the shareholders are earning above average returns on their invested funds.

Financial leverage:

	2019	2018

$$\text{Financial leverage} = \frac{\text{Return on equity}}{\text{Return on assets}} = \frac{29{,}22\%}{25{,}53\%} : \frac{23{,}37\%}{19{,}61\%}$$

$$= 1{,}14 \qquad : = 1{,}19$$

The financial leverage for Uthungulu Ltd deteriorated in 2019 when compared with 2018. The financial leverage of the company is also slightly below the industry average of 1,16. However the company's financial leverage still exceeds one, which indicates that the entity is generating positive returns on borrowed funds.

Leverage effect:

		2019		2018
Leverage effect =	Return on equity	29,22%	:	23,37%
	Less: Return on total assets	(25,53%)		(19,61%)
		3,69%	:	3,76%

The effect of financial leverage gives an indication of the surplus amount of profit that is attributable to the company from the use of borrowed funds. Despite a decline in the leverage effect, the company is still generating positive returns from the use of borrowed funds.

2. Liquidity ratios
Current ratio:

	2019	2018

$$\text{Current ratio} = \frac{\text{Current assets}}{\text{Current liabilities}} = \frac{\text{R108 000}⑤}{\text{R24 000}⑧} : \frac{\text{R58 000}⑤}{\text{R36 000}⑧}$$

$$= 4{,}50{:}1 \qquad : = 1{,}61{:}1$$

Uthungulu Ltd recorded a significant improvement of the current ratio in 2019 when compared with 2018. In comparison with the industry average of 2,53:1, the entity seems to be more liquid than other entities in the same industry.

Acid test ratio:

	2019	**2018**

$$\text{Acid test ratio} = \frac{\text{Current assets } less \text{ inventory}}{\text{Current liabilities}} = \frac{\text{R}(108\,000 - 25\,000)}{\text{R}24\,000} : \frac{\text{R}(58\,000 - 21\,000)}{\text{R}36\,000}$$

$$= 3,46:1 \qquad : = 1,03:1$$

The acid test ratio also improved significantly since the previous year and compared favourably to the industry average of 1,96:1. This is an indication that Uthungulu Ltd is managing its liquid assets better than other entities in the industry.

Trade receivables collection period

	2019	**2018**

$$\text{Trade receivables collection period} = \frac{\text{Average trade receivables}}{\text{Credit sales}} \times 365 = \frac{\text{R}36\,500*}{\text{R}234\,000} \times 365 : \frac{\text{R}32\,250**}{\text{R}179\,800} \times 365$$

$$= 56,93 \text{ days} \qquad : = 65,47 \text{ days}$$

* R(36 000 + 37 000) ÷ 2 = R36 500
** R(37 000 + 27 500) ÷ 2 = R32 250

Uthungulu Ltd recorded an improvement in the collection of debt during 2019 when compared with 2018. The entity's collection period is even better than that of the industry (80,04 days), which implies that the collection strategy of the entity is more effective than that of the industry.

Trade payables settlement period:

	2019	**2018**

$$\text{Trade payables settlement period} = \frac{\text{Average trade payables}}{\text{Credit purchases}} \times 365 = \frac{\text{R}29\,000*}{\text{R}74\,500} \times 365 : \frac{\text{R}31\,500**}{\text{R}57\,400} \times 365$$

$$= 142,08 \text{ days} \quad : = 200,30 \text{ days}$$

* R(24 000 + 34 000) ÷ 2 = R29 000
** R(34 000 + 29 000) ÷ 2 = R31 500

The trade payables settlement period of 142,08 days for 2019 is favourable when compared with the industry average of 85,11 days. Though there has been a deterioration in the payment period in 2019, the entity is still in a favourable position when the receivables collection period is taken into consideration. Creditors are paid 85,15 (142,08 – 56,93) days after debtors are collected.

Inventory turnover rate:

	2019	**2018**

$$\text{Inventory turnover rate} = \frac{\text{Cost of sales}}{\text{Average inventory}} = \frac{\text{R}70\,500②}{\text{R}23\,000*} : \frac{\text{R}51\,400②}{\text{R}18\,000**}$$

$$= 3,07 \text{ times} \quad : = 2,86 \text{ times}$$

* R(21 000 + 25 000) ÷ 2 = R23 000
** R(15 000 + 21 000) ÷ 2 = R18 000

The inventory turnover rate for Uthungulu Ltd improved slightly in 2019 when compared with 2018. However, in comparison with the industry average of 6,01 times, the entity's inventory turnover rate is slower.

3. Solvency ratios
Debt–equity ratio:

	2019	**2018**

$$Debt\text{--}equity\ ratio = \frac{Total\ debt}{Total\ equity} \times 100 = \frac{R94\ 000\text{⑨}}{R423\ 000\text{③}} \times 100 : \frac{R136\ 000\text{⑨}}{R390\ 000\text{③}} \times 100$$

$$= 22{,}22\% \qquad : = 34{,}87\%$$

The debt–equity ratio of Uthungulu Ltd improved significantly in 2019 when compared with 2018. The company's ratio is, however, significantly lower than that of the industry in which it operates. This indicates that Uthungulu Ltd has a lower financial risk than the industry in general, as a smaller percentage of its assets are financed by borrowed funds.

Times interest earned ratio:

	2019	**2018**

$$Times\ interest\ earned\ ratio = \frac{Profit\ before\ interest}{Interest\ expense} = \frac{R132\ 000\text{①}}{R8\ 400} : \frac{R103\ 150\text{①}}{R12\ 000}$$

$$= 15{,}71\ times\ : = 8{,}60\ times$$

The times interest earned ratio is slightly better than that of the industry average of 13,24. It also improved during 2019 when compared with 2018.

Calculations:
- **Profit for the year before interest**

	2019	2018
	R	R
Profit for the year	123 600	91 150
Interest on long-term borrowings	8 400	12 000
	132 000	103 150

- **Cost of sales and gross profit**

	R	R
Sales	234 000	179 800
Cost of sales	(70 500)	(51 400)
Opening inventory	21 000	15 000
Purchases	74 500	57 400
Closing inventory	(25 000)	(21 000)
Gross profit	163 500	128 400

- **Equity**

	R	R
Share capital	300 000	300 000
Retained earnings	48 000	15 000
Other components of equity	75 000	75 000
	423 000	390 000

- **Non-current assets**

	R	R
Property, plant and equipment R(240 000 + 177 000 – 43 000)	374 000	
R(276 000 + 191 000 – 49 000)		418 000
Unlisted share investment at fair value through profit or loss	35 000	50 000
	409 000	468 000

- **Current assets**

	R	R
Inventories	25 000	21 000
Trade receivables	36 000	37 000
Cash and cash equivalents	47 000	–
	108 000	58 000

- **Total assets**

	R	R
Non-current assets	409 000	468 000
Current assets	108 000	58 000
	517 000	526 000

- **Non-current liabilities**

	R	R
Long-term borrowing	70 000	100 000
	70 000	100 000

- **Current liabilities**

	R	R
Trade payables	24 000	34 000
Bank overdraft	–	2 000
	24 000	36 000

- **Total liabilities (debt)**

	R	R
Non-current liabilities	70 000	100 000
Current liabilities	24 000	36 000
	94 000	136 000

EXAMPLE 13.2 KwaMuhle Ltd

The following information appeared in the accounting records of KwaMuhle Ltd:

KwaMuhle Ltd
Balances as at 28 February 2019

	2019	2018
	R	R
Share capital	100 000	100 000
Retained earnings	30 000	10 000
Long-term loan: Zulu National Bank	100 000	100 000
Furniture and fittings (at carrying amount)	120 000	140 000
Inventories	100 000	100 000
Trade payables control	110 000	99 000
Trade receivables control	88 000	66 000
Bank	33 000	25 000
Income tax payable	1 000	2 000
Sales	400 000	360 000
Purchases	320 000	290 000
Administrative expenses	50 000	45 000
Interest on long-term loan	10 000	10 000
Ordinary dividend paid	5 000	2 000

Additional information:

1. The opening inventories for the years ending 2019 and 2018 amounted to R80 000 and R75 000 respectively.

2. The income tax expense for the year ending 2018 amounted to R8 000 and the income tax expense for the current year is yet to be determined.

REQUIRED:

1. Calculate all the profitability and liquidity ratios, for both years, of KwaMuhle Ltd and comment on the financial position and results of the company's activities.

2. Briefly discuss the implications of a higher debt–equity ratio.

3. Calculate and comment briefly on the solvency position of KwaMuhle Ltd for the years ended 2019 and 2018.

EXAMPLE 13.2 Suggested solution – KwaMuhle Ltd

1. PROFITABILITY RATIOS:

Gross profit percentage:

$$\text{Gross profit percentage} = \frac{\text{Gross profit}}{\text{Sales}} \times 100$$

	2019	**2018**
	$= \frac{\text{R100 000①}}{\text{R400 000}} \times 100$	$: \frac{\text{R75 000①}}{\text{R360 000}} \times 100$
	$= 25{,}00\%$	$: 20{,}83\%$

The 2019 gross profit percentage has improved when compared with 2018. Any change in the gross profit percentage must be traced back to the elements which affect the gross profit, ie mark-up, sales mix, inventory levels, different forms of discounts.

Profit margin:

$$\text{Profit margin} = \frac{\text{Profit before tax}}{\text{Sales}} \times 100$$

	2019	**2018**
	$= \frac{\text{R40 000②}}{\text{R400 000}} \times 100$	$: \frac{\text{R20 000②}}{\text{R360 000}} \times 100$
	$= 10{,}00\%$	$: = 5{,}56\%$

An improvement in the net profit margin is recorded in 2019. Fluctuations in the net profit margin can be attributed to changes in gross profit percentage and changes in the administrative and selling expenses relative to the level of sales, ie expenses expressed as a percentage of sales.

Return on assets (ROA):

$$\text{Return on total assets} = \frac{\text{Profit before interest}}{\text{Total assets}} \times 100$$

	2019	**2018**
	$= \frac{\text{R50 000②}}{\text{R341 000③}} \times 100$	$: \frac{\text{R30 000②}}{\text{R311 000③}} \times 100$
	$14{,}66\%$	$: = 9{,}65\%$

The return on assets has clearly improved in the year 2019. This indicates that the entity was more profitable in 2019 when compared with 2018. This can be traced to the efficient use of assets to generate more revenue and reduced operating expenses by the entity.

Return on equity (ROE):

$$\text{Return on equity} = \frac{\text{Profit before tax}}{\text{Total equity}} \times 100$$

	2019	**2018**
	$= \frac{\text{R40 000②}}{\text{R130 000④}} \times 100$	$: \frac{\text{R20 000②}}{\text{R110 000④}} \times 100$
	$= 30{,}77\%$	$: = 18{,}18\%$

A significant increase in the return on equity of the entity is recorded in year 2019. Generally, increases in the return on equity ratio are attributed to decreases in expenses, increases in profit mark-ups and decreases in equity. The increase in this ratio can be linked to an increase in profit.

Financial leverage:

			2019		2018
Financial leverage	$=$	$\dfrac{\text{Return on equity}}{\text{Return on assets}}$ $=$	$\dfrac{30{,}77\%}{14{,}66\%}$	$:$	$\dfrac{18{,}18\%}{9{,}65\%}$
		$=$	2,10	$:$	= 1,88

The company's financial leverage improved in 2019 when compared with 2018.

Leverage effect:

			2019		2018
Leverage effect	$=$	$\dfrac{\text{Return on equity}}{\textit{Less}:\text{ Return on total assets}}$	$\dfrac{30{,}77\%}{(14{,}66\%)}$	$:$	$\dfrac{18{,}18\%}{(9{,}65\%)}$
			16,11%	$:$	8,53%

The leverage effect of KwaMuhle Ltd indicates that the owners, shareholders, received more on their investment than they would have if they had financed everything themselves.

LIQUIDITY RATIOS

Current ratio:

			2019		2018
Current ratio	$=$	$\dfrac{\text{Current assets}}{\text{Current liabilities}}$ $=$	$\dfrac{\text{R221 000}③}{\text{R111 000}⑤}$	$:$	$\dfrac{\text{R171 000}③}{\text{R101 000}⑤}$
		$=$	1,99:1	$:$	= 1,69 : 1

The company's current ratio increased by 17,75% over the year, which is an ideal result for the company. This means that each R1 of the current liabilities is covered by R1,99 of current assets or a margin of 99%.

Acid test ratio:

			2019		2018
Acid test ratio	$=$	$\dfrac{\text{Current assets } \textit{less inventory}}{\text{Current liabilities}}$ $=$	$\dfrac{\text{R(221 000 – 100 000)}}{\text{R111 000}⑤}$	$:$	$\dfrac{\text{R(171 000 – 80 000)}}{\text{R101 000}⑤}$
		$=$	1,09: 1	$: =$	0,9 : 1

The company's acid test ratio improved by more than 100% which is a good coverage of current liabilities. It means that each R1 of current liabilities is covered by R1,09 of 'quick' assets. This also indicates that the cash flow position of the company is favourable.

Trade receivables collection period:

		2019		2018
Trade receivables collection period $= \dfrac{\text{Average trade receivables}}{\text{Credit sales}} \times 365 =$		$\dfrac{\text{R70 000*}}{\text{R400 000}} \times 365$	$:$	$\dfrac{\text{R60 000**}}{\text{R360 000}} \times 365$
		= 64 days	$: =$	61 days

* R(80 000 + 60 000) ÷ 2 = R70 000
** R60 000 (In the absence of prior year amount)

The company's credit control weakened as debtors' amounts were outstanding for a longer period in 2019 that in 2018. KwaMuhle Ltd decreased its collection period by 4,92% which was accompanied by an 11,11% increase in sales. This means that the company extended credit terms to boost sales.

Trade payables settlement period:

$$\text{Trade payables settlement period} = \frac{\text{Average trade payables}}{\text{Credit purchases}} \times 365$$

	2019	2018
	$\frac{\text{R95 000*}}{\text{R320 000}} \times 365$	$\frac{\text{R90 000**}}{\text{R290 000}} \times 365$
	= 108 days	: = 113 days

* R(100 000 + 90 000) ÷ 2 = R95 000
** R90 000 (In the absence of prior year amount)

KwaMuhle Ltd paid its creditors sooner in 2019 than in 2018. When compared with trade receivables collection period, the trade payables settlement period is still favourable to the company's cash flow. The company will receive payments from its debtors sooner that it would be required to settle it creditors accounts.

Inventory turnover rate:

$$\text{Inventory turnover rate} = \frac{\text{Cost of sales}}{\text{Average inventory}}$$

	2019	2018
	$\frac{\text{R300 000②}}{\text{R90 000*}}$	$\frac{\text{R285 000②}}{\text{R77 500**}}$
=	3,3 times	: = 3,7 times

* R(100 000 + 80 000) ÷ 2 = R90 000
** R(80 000 + 75 000) ÷ 2 = R77 500

The inventory moved a bit slower in 2019 when compared with 2018. Lower inventory turnover ratio is considered a negative indicator of ineffective inventory management. However, a lower inventory turnover ratio will not always mean bad inventory management performance. It may in some instances indicate adequate inventory levels, which may result in increase in sales.

2. Implications of a higher debt–equity ratio:

The debt–equity ratio is the ratio of total debt (liabilities) to total equity. This ratio indicates the extent that debt is covered by owner's equity. A higher debt–equity ratio indicates excessive financial risk. While a higher debt–equity ratio may be unattractive because of the high level of risk, a very low ratio would also be unattractive because it may indicate forgone opportunity to earn higher returns from borrowed funds.

3. SOLVENCY POSITION:

Debt–equity ratio:

$$\text{Debt–equity ratio} = \frac{\text{Total debt}}{\text{Total equity}} \times 100$$

	2019	2018
	$\frac{\text{R211 000⑥}}{\text{R130 000④}} \times 100$	$\frac{\text{R201 000⑥}}{\text{R110 000④}} \times 100$
	= 162,31%	: = 182,73%

Times interest earned ratio:

$$\text{Times interest earned ratio} = \frac{\text{Profit before interest}}{\text{Interest expense}}$$

	2019	2018
	$\frac{\text{R50 000②}}{\text{R10 000}}$	$\frac{\text{R30 000②}}{\text{R10 000}}$
	= 5 times	: = 3 times

The extent of debt financing is too high. This indicates that KwaMuhle Ltd uses higher levels of debt to finance its growth. This points to the direction that the company's assets are largely funded through debt financing. While the level of debt is astronomically high, the company is however able to generate good returns for the owners (shareholders) as indicated by the leverage effect. The company is also able to generate adequate profits to settle the interest payments.

Calculations:

- **Gross profit:**

	2019	2018
	R	R
Sales	400 000	360 000
Cost of sales	(300 000)	(285 000)
Opening inventory	80 000	15 000
Purchases	320 000	57 400
Closing inventory	(100 000)	(21 000)
Gross profit	100 000	75 000

- **Profit for the year before interest and tax:**

	R	R
Gross profit	100 000	75 000
Administrative expenses	(50 000)	(45 000)
Profit before interest	**50 000**	**30 000**
Interest expense	(10 000)	(10 000)
Profit before tax	**40 000**	**20 000**

- **Total assets**

	R	R
Non-current assets	120 000	140 000
Furniture and fittings	120 000	140 000
Current assets	221 000	171 000
Inventories	100 000	80 000
Trade receivables	88 000	66 000
Bank	33 000	25 000
Total assets	341 000	311 000

- **Equity**

	R	R
Share capital	100 000	100 000
Retained earnings	30 000	10 000
	130 000	110 000

- **Current liabilities**

	R	R
Trade payables	110 000	99 000
Bank overdraft	1 000	2 000
Current liabilities	111 000	101 000

- **Total debt**

	R	R
Long-term loan	100 000	100 000
Trade payables	110 000	99 000
Income tax payable	1 000	2 000
	211 000	201 000

13.6 SUMMARY

Financial statements analysis involves the study of financial statements in order to learn more about a business entity. It is often associated with ratio analysis, which examines the relationships between various financial statement items, both at a point in time and over time.

Financial ratios have been divided into three categories: profitability, liquidity and solvency. Ratios must be compared with a standard, normally industry averages, to get any meaning. Trend analysis, which looks at the ratios over time, are also useful in the financial statement analysis process.

Like any other analytical tool, ratios have limitations, including the standard used for comparison, differences in accounting methods, the impact of inflation and the impact of accounting policies.

EXERCISES

Exercise 13. 1 Amanzi CC

Amanzi CC is a water-processing business entity operating near Umngeni River in Durban. The CC has applied for a loan from a bank to finance the purchase of a water filtration equipment. The bank manager has requested certain financial ratios as part of the information required to determine whether Amanzi CC is eligible for a loan.

Mr Mkhize, the only member of the CC, requested you to assist him in calculating these ratios. He supplied you with the following information that pertains to Amanzi CC:

Statement of financial position information as at 31 August 2018

	R
Member's contribution	185 000
Retained earnings (1 September 2017)	29 600
Long-term loan: Third National Bank	72 000
Fixed deposit	43 000
Property, plant and equipment	249 300
Inventory	24 000
Trade receivables	36 500
Prepayments	3 200
Trade and other payables	21 700
Bank overdraft	2 700

Selected information from the statement of profit or loss and other comprehensive income statement for the year ended 31 August 2018:

	R
Sales	214 040
Interest on long-term loan	6 000
Gross profit	160 760
Profit before tax	63 380
Profit for the period	45 000
Income tax expense	18 380

Additional information:

1. On 31 August 2018, a profit distribution of R30 000 was made to the member.
2. The balance of the inventory account at 1 September 2017 was R26 000.
3. Some of the ratios that were calculated for the 2017 financial year are as follows:
   - Inventory turnover rate   2,5 times
   - Current ratio   2,17:1
   - Debt–equity ratio   48,7%
4. Industry standards as at 31 August 2018:
   - Current ratio   2:1
   - Acid test ratio   1:1

REQUIRED:

1. Calculate the following ratios on 31 August 2018:
   a) Return on equity
   b) Profit margin.
2. Calculate the inventory turnover rate on 31 August 2018 and interpret the ratio in relation to the previous year's ratio.
3. Calculate the current ratio on 31 August 2018 and interpret the ratio in relation to the previous year's ratio and industry standard.

Exercice 13.2 Lerato Ltd

The following information was extracted from the accounting records of Lerato Ltd for the financial year ended 31 December 2018.

Selected income and expense items for the year ended 31 December 2018:

	R
Sales	1 000 000
Gross profit	250 000
Total expenses	120 000
Total comprehensive income for the year	66 000

Statement of financial position information as at 31 December 2018

	2018	2017
	R	R
Property, plant and equipment	900 000	1 000 000
Fixed deposit	100 000	–
Inventories	95 000	80 000
Trade receivables	80 000	65 000
Cash and cash equivalents	25 000	–
	1 200 000	1 145 000
Share capital	160 000	160 000
Retained earnings	620 000	535 000
Long-term borrowings	300 000	300 000
Trade and other payables	110 000	100 000
Current tax payable	10 000	15 000
Bank overdraft	–	35 000
	1 200 000	1 145 000

Additional information:

1. Finance costs and income tax expenses for the 2018 year amounted to R20 000 and R44 000 respectively.

2. Some of the ratios that were calculated for the 2017 financial year are as follows:
   - Gross profit percentage   30%
   - Return on total assets   8%

3. Industry standards as at 31 December 2018:
   - Gross profit percentage   25%
   - Return on total assets   12%

REQUIRED:

1. Calculate the following ratios on 31 December 2018:
   a) Gross profit percentage
   b) Return on total assets.

2. Explain, in relation to entity's previous year and industry standards, the result of the ratios calculated above.

3. In your own words, explain the importance of the calculation of the acid test ratio in contrast to current ratio.

CHAPTER 14

INCOME TAXES (IAS 12)

LEARNING OUTCOMES

After studying this chapter, you should be able to:
- Detail definitions used in the context of the subject matter.
- Illustrate an understanding of the definitions by explaining them and applying information provided in a simple scenario.
- Demonstrate the ability to calculate income tax expense, using information provided.
- Demonstrate the ability to calculate deferred tax asset or liability, using information provided.
- Demonstrate the ability to present and disclose the information pertaining to income tax and deferred tax in a set of financial statements.

PREAMBLE

Mr Mhlongo (known as Njomane) has seen his business grow from strength to strength. Profits are great and the business is doing well. His only worry is understanding the differences in accounting treatment and tax treatment of transactions determining tax liability. He completely understands the concept of different users of financial statements, how each user's needs differ; he also understands that preparing the information that is useful requires different thinking premises. However, it seems he cannot quite grasp the concept of income tax expense and how it is formulated. You have been contacted by Njomane to explain.

14.1 INTRODUCTION

This chapter is based on IAS 12, which deals with accounting for income taxes. Income taxes may be split into two sections, being current tax and deferred tax (an accounting view of taxes, calculated to provide information that is relevant to users for making informed economic decisions).

What may be understood from the above statements is that income tax expense is not necessarily an immediately discharged (or paid out) expense and for purposes of accounting, calculations are performed to ensure that proper planning and decision making includes this additional future expenditure, given the information that is available at hand, at year end. Deferred tax, in a nutshell, arises as a result of the differences in treatment of an item between accounting and taxation. However, there are limitations to these differences, as we will note later on in the chapter.

14.2 DEFINITIONS

Accounting profit is the profit calculated (using accounting principles) before deducting tax expense.

Taxable profit (or tax loss) is the profit (or loss) for a period, determined in accordance with the rules established by the tax authorities (SARS), upon which income taxes are payable (or recoverable).

Tax expense (or tax income) is the aggregate amount included in the determination of profit or loss for the period in respect of current tax and deferred tax.

Current tax is the amount of income tax payable (recoverable) in respect of taxable profit (or tax loss) for a period.

Deferred tax liabilities are the amounts of income tax payable in future periods in respect of taxable temporary differences.

Deferred tax assets are the amounts of income taxes recoverable in future periods in respect of:
- deductible temporary differences
- the carry forward of unused tax losses, and
- the carry forward of unused tax credits.

Temporary differences are differences between the carrying amount of an asset or liability in the statement of financial position and its tax base. Temporary differences may be either:

- **taxable temporary differences**, which are temporary differences that will result in *taxable amounts* in determining taxable profit (or tax loss) of **future periods** when the *carrying amount* of the asset or liability is recovered or settled, or
- **deductible temporary differences**, which are temporary differences that will result in *deductible amounts* in determining taxable profit (or tax loss) of **future periods** when the *carrying amount* of the asset or liability is recovered or settled.

The tax base (of an asset or liability) is the amount attributed to that asset or liability for tax purposes.

14.3 EXPLANATION OF DEFINITIONS

The difference between accounting and taxable profit is a matter of principle versus rules, respectively. Accounting is a principle/substance-driven subject, which seeks to provide financial information that is relevant to users to make informed economic decisions. Thus, it is embedded on the notion that all users' information needs must be considered. Taxation, on the other hand, is a rule-driven subject, formed by the authorities and utilising financial information to finance the state's administration and the provision of benefits to its citizen.

For example, in a transaction involving the acquisition of a table, accounting would be more flexible and say 'I can explain what this is', while tax would be more assertive and say 'it is what it is'. Accounting looks at the table and asks the business, 'what do you use this table for?' and if you sleep on it, says 'it is a bed', but if you sleep under it, says 'it is a shelter', while taxation says plainly, 'this is a table'. This is, of course, a simplification.

The term 'tax expense' includes both current and deferred taxes. As aforementioned, current tax calculates the amount of taxes that are due to the tax authorities in the current period as a result of using the tax legislation to calculate the tax liability. Deferred tax calculates amounts deductible or taxable in future. Both of these amounts are included in determining tax expenses.

Also, note the similarity and difference in the two definitions, the first being carrying amount and the second being tax base. The starting point in determining both amounts is the same: they both start with cost (*over-simplifying the concept*). From there, accounting deducts accumulated depreciation and accumulated impairment from cost in order to arrive at the carrying amount. Taxation deducts (*tax computed*) allowances from the cost to arrive at the tax base. In other words, accounting deducts an aggregate of accounting depreciation and tax deducts an aggregate of tax-based depreciation. Both are calculating the same amount, using different terminology.

Looking at the term **'permanent difference'**, 'perceived' is used deliberately as the term is not explicitly defined. The standard only defines differences that are temporary, but there tends to be an assumption that there are permanent differences between accounting and taxation. Although not explicitly defined, it is understood that there are differences that will go on indefinitely between accounting and taxation (eg dividends received). For accounting, such an amount will form part of income, however for purposes of taxation, the amount is included in gross income and later exempted from income (*over-simplifying the concept*), thus not forming part of income for tax purposes. This does not illustrate amounts that are either taxable or deductible in future, thus the amount is regarded as a permanent difference.

EXAMPLE 14.1 Qhabanga (Pty) Ltd

Figure 14.1: Qhabanga Spaza Shop
Source: https://mg.co.za/article/2015-01-29-township-politics-fuel-the-attacks-on-outsiders

Qhabanga (Pty) Ltd ('Qhabanga') is a spaza shop that is owned by a sole person, in the neighbourhood of Kwa-Mashu. The spaza shop has been operating for over five years and makes lucrative profits. For the year ended on 31 July 2019, Qhabanga made an accounting profit before tax worth R100 000, however for tax purposes there was R20 000's worth of expenses that was not allowed as a deduction, such as fines and other taxes.

REQUIRED:
Given the South African corporate tax rate is set at 28%, calculate the amount of income tax payable and provide an explanation for the difference.

EXAMPLE 14.1 Suggested solution – Qhabanga (Pty) Ltd

Income tax expense will be calculated as follows:
–   Accounting profit   R100 000
–   Add back: disallowed expenses   R20 000
     Tax profit   R120 000
     Tax expense = R120 000 × 28% = R33 600

The difference between user expected information and the actual information can be illustrated as follows:
–   Users will see an accounting profit of R100 000 in the statement of comprehensive income and multiply this by 28% (R100 000 × 28% = R28 000), while the actual tax expense is R33 600.
–   The difference between the two amounts is R5 600 (R33 600 – R28 000).

To calculate this amount, we utilise the disallowed deductions, if they create a permanent difference, then multiply this by the tax rate applicable: R20 000 × 28% = R5 600

Note that when the term 'deferred tax' is used, we are essentially informing users of financial statements of a difference in treatment of an item(s) between accounting and taxation.

EXAMPLE 14.2 Makhadzikhazi (Pty) Ltd
Makhadzikhazi (Pty) Ltd is a couture and culture entity in Thohoyandou, Venda. The business has existed since mid-1999 and it has managed to make a highly esteemed name for itself. The company focuses on dress making, cultural celebrations, and relationship management between modern and traditional leaders. It paves the way for an easy transition between being cultural and being sophisticated.

The owners have contacted you with a request for clarification on how to record the following information:

1. On 15 January 2019, Makhadzikhazi (Pty) Ltd acquired 500 shares (*for cash*) in Thonjani Ltd, a traditional (sorghum) beer-making business from Mpumalanga. The shares cost R25 per share.

2. Salaries amounting to R1 200 000 were paid in the 2019 year of assessment.

3. Thonjani Ltd paid a dividend of 120 cents per share on 30 November 2019.

4. On 10 December 2019, Makhadzikhazi (Pty) Ltd paid a total of R90 000 in municipal rates, covering the nine months from December 2019 to August 2020 (*this amount is deductible in full for tax purposes*).

5. On 20 December 2019, Makhadzikhazi sold 50% of the shares they held in Thonjani Ltd at R28 per share.

REQUIRED:
Using the information above, provide journal entries for Makhadzikhazi (Pty) Ltd for the year ended 31 December 2019. Clearly show the income tax expense treatment in your journals.

EXAMPLE 14.2 Suggested solution – Makhadzikhazi (Pty) Ltd

Detail	Debit R	Credit R
Investment in shares (SOFP)	12 500	
Bank (SOFP)		12 500
Makhadzikhazi acquired 500 shares, there is no income tax effect, as the transaction affects neither tax nor accounting profits (500 x25)		
Salary expense (P/L)	1 200 000	
Income tax expense (P/L)		336 000
Bank (SOFP)		864 000
Settled salary payments for the year		
(Makhadzikhadzi paid R1 200 000 worth of salaries and later will be allowed to claim back R336 000 as a deduction from the tax expense. In essence, this means that 28% of the expense to trade are paid for by the government.)		
Bank (SOFP)	600	
Dividends income (P/L)		600
Dividends received, no income tax implications as dividends are exempt from tax (500 × 1,20)		
Municipal expenses (P/L)	90 000	
Income tax expense (P/L)		25 200
Bank (SOFP)		64 800
Recognising the expense relating to municipal rates, as it is paid off		
[Similar to the salaries transaction, Makhadzikhadzi paid R90 000 and later it will be allowed to claim back R25 200 as a deduction from the tax expense (90 000 × 28%)]		
Prepaid expenses (SOFP)	80 000	
Municipal expenses (P/L)		80 000
Recognising the effect of the prepaid expense for accounting purposes (R90 000/9 months × 8 months falling in 2020, as the expense is not yet incurred)		
(The amount is prepaid for accounting purposes and is moved to SOFP, as a receivable, thus it will be deductible in the year to which it relates. However, a similar adjustment is not performed for taxation, as the amount is allowed as a deduction in full in the year it is either paid or incurred. Thus, there is a temporary difference.)		
Bank (SOFP)	7 000	7 000
Investment in shares (SOFP)		
Recognising the sale of shares (500 × 50% × R28). There is no income tax effect as the transaction affects neither accounting nor taxable profits.		

14.4 CURRENT TAX

Current tax is calculated in the current period using the rules (regulations) stipulated by the tax authorities, which in South Africa is the South African Revenue Services (SARS). For the position of businesses, this calculation often comes at the end of the year, once the financial statements have been completed by the accounting officer (or accountant) of the entity. For this reason, our starting point will be the accounting profit, which is sometimes referred to as the operating income, or other names as the accounting standards may allow.

As our starting point is the accounting profit, it is necessary for us to perform adjustments to our profits to ensure that we end up with the correct taxable profit. In order to determine the taxable profit, we will go through the statement of comprehensive income and the statement of financial position to identify items that may be included or deducted for accounting purposes, in determining the accounting profit, but may not necessarily be included or deducted for taxation purposes in determining the taxable profit.

Examples of income that may be included in the accounting profit which may not necessarily be included as part of determining the taxable profit are amounts arising as a result of a dividend received. In conjunction, accounting tends to reduce the accounting profit with amounts received in advance. As these amounts create an obligation to transfer economic resources in future, there will be a liability on the part of accounting, which will in equal lengths create an expense, reducing the accounting profit. For taxation purposes, gross income is defined to include amounts accrued and received by a person. The fact that there is an obligation to transfer economic benefits does not have an impact for taxation purposes, and such an amount will have to be included. In accounting, this amount will be included, say in revenue, as it is received, then deducted to show a balance in the statement of financial position. This is the reason why it is necessary to consider both the statement of comprehensive income and the statement of financial position.

Similar to income, some expenses may be deductible for accounting purposes in determining the accounting profit but are not allowable for taxation in calculating taxable profits. An example of such an amount would be a commission payable when acquiring shares, as the amount is an actual expenditure and is deductible for determining accounting profits (*unless otherwise capitalised*). For purposes of taxation, in determining taxable profit the expense incurred would be regarded as 'not in the production of income' as it is incurred to produce dividends, which are exempt from calculating taxable profit and thus do not form part of income.

On the other hand, an entity may incur an expense that is not presented on the face of the statement of comprehensive income, thus not included in calculating accounting profits, while taxation may regard such an expense to be fully deductible in the year of assessment. An example of such an expense may be certain development costs which accounting may capitalise and deduct over a period of years, while taxation seeks the amount to be fully deducted for purposes of determining taxable profits.

Not all differences between accounting and tax account for the full treatment of an amount; some may be partial differences. An example is with the treatment of depreciation on certain assets. Accounting may allow the entity to deduct the depreciation of a period of use (ie *useful life*), which would entail that should the entity plan to utilise the asset for three years (*period of intended usage*), while it has economic life of five years (*period that the asset could operate without permanent disruption*), depreciation will only be calculated over three years. For taxation purposes, the allowance may still be granted for five years. The difference between the two treatments is partial as in fact, both accounting and taxation allow a deduction; the difference is in the number of years that the entity will claim each set of allowance, being three years for accounting versus five years for taxation.

EXAMPLE 14.3 MaRadebe (Pty) Ltd

Figure 14.2 Mrs MaRadebe started a brick-making company
Source: https://www.vukuzenzele.gov.za/using-bricks-rebuild-lives

MaRadebe (Pty) Ltd ('MaRadebe') is an entity in eMonti that started in 1999. Mrs MaRadebe was infuriated by being constantly disturbed by her noisy neighbours, so she decided to make bricks to build a wall between them. Community residents were so impressed that they wanted to buy bricks from her, and before she knew it she was selling bricks to the entire country.

The following transactions relate to the year of assessment ending 30 June 2019. You may assume that an accounting profit of R450 000 was recorded before making the following changes:

1. MaRadebe owns 30% of shares in a small business within the community (Mzimvubu (Pty) Ltd) which sells cement and sand. This business declared a dividend of R100 000 on 15 March 2019.

2. A bonus was approved for all employees on 20 June 2019, totalling R200 000.

3. An accounting depreciation was deducted on all assets, totalling R300 000. SARS allows a deduction of R400 000 on these assets.

4. On 1 February 2019, MaRadebe sold a delivery van for R100 000 that was acquired three years ago, for R350 000. This delivery van had a carrying amount and a tax value of R50 000 and R120 000 respectively.

REQUIRED:
Using the information provided, calculate the current tax payable (*use a 28% tax rate*) by MaRadebe (Pty) Ltd in the 2019 year of assessment, starting with the accounting profit.

EXAMPLE 14.3 Suggested solution (statement of comprehensive income method)

Details	Amount (R)
Accounting profit	450 000
Dividends accrued (exempt income)	100 000
Bonus expense	200 000
Accounting depreciation	300 000
Tax allowances	(400 000)
Accounting profit on sale of delivery van (100 000 – 50 000)	(50 000)
Tax scrapping allowance [s11(o)] (120 000 – 100 000)	(20 000)
Taxable profit	**580 000**

The current tax payable would be R162 400 (R580 000 × 28%).

14.5 DEFERRED TAX

Deferred tax accounts for all amounts that are not deductible or taxable in the current taxable period. These amounts may either be taxable or deductible in future (*temporary differences*) or they may not be taxable or deductible in future (*permanent differences*).

To calculate net profit, both current tax and deferred tax are deducted (or added) in a line item referred to as 'tax expense' (or tax income). This provides users of financial statements with relevant and reliable information as they would like to analyse the value to be obtained from the entity using available assets and how this may transcend into returns on their investment, either as a loan financier or as an equity financier.

Financiers make an estimate of future economic benefits (returns) that they expect to realise from an entity by assessing how the assets (resources) recorded in the statement of financial position will convert into future returns, using current available information. Under this assessment, financiers should not assess future returns by comparing them only to current taxes as they would have forgone an ability to make a correct match between what they expect to receive and what they will in fact receive in future. As this is the case, deferred taxes assess the amount that will not be available for distribution, due to taxes payable in future.

EXAMPLE 14.4 MaRadebe
MaRadebe (Pty) Ltd ('MaRadebe') is an entity in eMonti that started in 1999 and sells bricks countrywide.

The following information was available as it relates to the financial statement of MaRadebe for the year ended 30 June 2019:

1. MaRadebe owns a piece of land in Kwamhlanga, Mpumalanga, South Africa worth R500 000, recorded at the municipality on 1 July 2017 as stand number 3035.

2. Construction was started on a manufacturing building on this stand (stand 3035) on 1 July 2017. The building cost a total of R2 million to construct and was completed on 1 October 2018. It was brought into use for manufacturing on the same day. MaRadebe plans to operate in the building over 10 years, then move to bigger towns like Johannesburg, Cape Town and Durban. SARS allows a 5% deduction on such buildings.

3. Machinery acquired for R250 000 has been used since 1 January 2018, the day it was available for use. The machinery is expected to be used over a period of five years. SARS allows entities to deduct 40% in the year brought into use and 20% in the following years, to a maximum of five years.

4. A bank loan with a fair value of R14 million was obtained from Quiz Bank, being 10% of the financing amount (debt to equity). The loan was obtained on 1 January 2015.

REQUIRED:

Calculate the deferred tax amount to indicate tax payable or refundable in future (*use a 28% tax rate*) by MaRadebe (Pty) Ltd in the 2019 year of assessment.

EXAMPLE 14.4 Suggested solution (statement of financial position method)

Details	Carrying amount	Tax base	Temporary difference	Deferred tax	Asset/liability
1. Land	500 000	500 000	-	-	-
2. Building	a)1 850 000	b)1 900 000	50 000	14 000	Asset
3. Machine	c)175 000	d)100 000	75 000	21 000	Liability
4. Loan	14 000 000	14 000 000	-	-	-
Deferred tax	-	-	-	**7 000**	**Liability**

The R7 000 represents an amount that will be payable in future, as a deferred tax.

1. Carrying amount of building =

    cost (R2 000 000) − Accumulated depreciation (R2 000 000 × 10% × 9/12) = R1 850 000

2. Tax base of the building =

    Cost (R2 000 000) − Total allowances (R2 000 000 × 5%, not apportioned) = R1 900 000

3. Carrying amount of machinery =

    cost (R250 000) − Accumulated depreciation (R250 000 × 40% × 18/24) = R175 000

4. Tax base of the machinery =

    Cost (R250 000) − Total allowances (R250 000 × 60%, not apportioned) = R100 000

14.6 TAX EXPENSE

If we assume that this is all the information that is necessary for our tax expense calculation, MaRadebe would then calculate its tax expense by adding the amount in Example 14.3 with the information in Example 14.4. Our total tax expense would amount to R162 400 plus R7 000, thus R169 400.

14.7 PRESENTATION AND DISCLOSURE

The total amount as it has been shown in section 14.6 is presented in the face of the statement of comprehensive income. Taxation applies the 'truck and trailer' principle, which means that the tax amount should be presented in the statement in which the amount itself is presented. For example, taxation for amounts that are presented in the profit or loss portion of the statement of comprehensive income will be presented in the profit or loss portion, whereas those relating to other comprehensive income will be accounted for in the statement of comprehensive income portion.

Deferred taxes, on the other hand, may either be assets or liabilities. As such, just like any other asset or liability, the deferred tax amount will be recognised in the statement of financial position.

In the notes to the financial statements, we provide users with information that makes it easy for them to understand what makes up the amount presented in the statement of comprehensive income and the statement of financial position. We do so by providing users of financial statements with three sets of notes:

1. Notes to the income tax calculation as they appear in the statement of comprehensive income, sometimes referred to as the net income tax note (*providing summarised information on how the taxable amount payable in the current year is calculated*)

   Deferred tax note (*indicating the set(s) of assets and liabilities making up the amount of tax payable in future, and amounts not levied tax at all*)

   Tax rate reconciliation note (*calculating the effective tax rate and illustrating to users why there is a difference between the actual tax amount and the expected tax amount, as a result of difference in treatment between accounting and taxation*).

EXAMPLE 14.5 Comprehensive example

Monada Enterprises (Pty) Ltd ('Monada') is an entity in Polokwane that was established in 2014 and specialises in marketing, song recording, presenting, image creation and other facets of entertainment.

The following information relates to the financial statement of Monada for the year ended 31 March 2019:

1. Since inception, Monada has operated a three-storey, medium-sized, fully outfitted studio in the busy town of Polokwane. The building is wholly owned and cost Monada R7,5 million to soundproof and equip.

2. Revenue of R15 million was realised for the year.

3. The microphones and other sound equipment are replaced every three years to ensure that Monada is in line with international standards, most recently on 1 April 2017 at a cost of R750 000.

4. Two artists signed with the entity had gold-selling albums and to win their good favour and market them further, Monada bought them A45 OMG Messi Dez's, branded 'Monada Entertainers', at a cost of R850 000 each. Both were acquired on 1 April 2018.

5. The accountant (Mr Marothi) advised Mr Monada that entertainment is a fickle business and profits could fluctuate, so they should diversify. An investment in the JSE Top 40 Index portfolio was subsequently made, costing R1,5 million on 1 March 2018. By 15 November 2018, a dividend worth R315 000 was declared by the portfolio.

6. A music manager was caught using the studio at night to record Blue Rider, a new sensation, without running it through the books. The manager was fired and offered a settlement of R2 million. The deal included a five-year ban from working in the music industry in South Africa, a non-disclosure agreement and the handing over of all work he had done in the studio. He agreed to avoid formal prosecution.

7. In the first half of 2018, Mr Monada and King KG collaborated on a song. Production costs amounted to R500 000 and a music video costing R2,5 million was also made. They contributed equally towards these costs. Shortly after the song's release in June 2018, a local DJ, DJ Hira, accused them of anti-competitive acts and applied for a court order to ban the song. On 15 February 2019, the competition tribunal ruled against Monada & KG. R300 000's worth of legal fees was incurred in the lawsuit. The court also declared that Monada and KG should jointly and severally refund DJ Hira his lawyer's fees worth R800 000.

8. On 31 March 2019, Monada declared a bonus totalling R4 million to be shared by all employees.

9. On their way to a marketing and entertainment event on 15 November 2018, Mr Monada, his PA (Miss Tau) and Mr Marothi were involved in a car accident. The company financed their medical bills totalling R124 800. SARS disallowed the deduction as the driver was drunk and it was considered negligence.

Additional information:

1. Buildings at Monada are depreciated over 12 years (SARS allows a 5% unapportioned rate).

2. SARS allows five-year write-down on microphones and other sound equipment.

3. The two motor vehicles are depreciated over three years; each carries a residual value of 40% on gross value. SARS allows the vehicles over a period of four years.

REQUIRED:

Using the information provided, prepare the notes on tax expense (tax income), tax rate reconciliation and the deferred tax note to be disclosed in the financial statements of Monada Enterprises (Pty) Ltd (*use a 28% tax rate*) for the period ending 31 March 2019. Assume all amounts are exclusive of VAT and start your computation with the R7 800 000 accounting profit, an amount provided by Mr Marothi.

EXAMPLE 14.5 Suggested solution
Calculations

Details (*income statement method*)	Amount (R)
Accounting profit	**7 800 000**
Permanent differences	*3 909 800*
– Dividends	(315 000)
– Anti-competitive acts (accounting)	
(2 500 000 + 500 000 + 300 000 + 800 000)	4 100 000
– Medical/accident expense (accounting)	124 800
Temporary differences	*6 077 500*
– Revenue (*no difference, already included in accounting profit*)	Nil
– Depreciation	
– Building (7 500 000/12)	625 000
– Microphones and recording equipment (750 00/3)	250 000
– Vehicles [(850 000*2*60%)/3]	340 000
– Tax allowances	
– Building (7 500 000 × 5%)	(375 000)
– Microphones and recording equipment (750 000/5)	(150 000)
– Vehicles (850 000/4)	(212 500)
– Restraint of trade (accounting)	2 000 000
– Restraint of trade (taxation)	
The lowest of:	(400 000)
– 2 000 000/5 years = 400 000	
– 2 000 000/3 = 666 666	
– Annual bonus	4 000 000
Taxable profit	**17 787 300**

Current tax = 4 980 444 (*17 787 300 × 28%*)

Deferred tax = –1 701 700 (*6 077 500 × 28%*)

Tax expense = 3 278 744

Statement of financial position method – 2018

Details	Carrying amount	Tax base	Temporary difference	Deferred tax	Asset/liability
1. Building	a) 5 000 000	c) 6 000 000	(1 000 000)	280 000	Liability
2. Microphones	e) 500 000	g) 600 000	(100 000)	28 000	Liability
3. Vehicles	-	-	-	-	-
Deferred tax	-	-	-	**308 000**	**Liability**

Statement of financial position method – 2019

Details	Carrying amount	Tax base	Temporary difference	Deferred tax	Asset/liability
1. Building	b)4 375 000	d)5 625 000	(1 250 000)	350 000	Liability
2. Microphones	f)250 000	h)450 000	(200 000)	56 000	Liability
3. Vehicles	i)1 360 000	j)1 275 000	85 000	(23 800)	Asset
Deferred tax	-	-	-	**382 200**	**Liability**

a) 7 500 000 – [(7 500 000/12) × 4] = 5 000 000

b) 7 500 000 – [(7 500 000/12) × 5] = 4 375 000

c) 7 500 000 – [(7 500 000 × 5%) × 4] = 6 000 000

d) 7 500 000 – [(7 500 000 × 5%) × 5] = 5 625 000

e) 750 000 – [(750 000/3) × 1] = 500 000

f) 750 000 – [(750 000/3) × 2] = 250 000

g) 750 000 – [(750 000/5) × 1] = 600 000

h) 750 000 – [(750 000/5) × 2] = 450 000

i) (850 000 × 2) – [(850 000 × 2 × 60%)/3] = 1 360 000

j) (850 000 × 2) – [1 700 000/4] = 1 275 000

Deferred tax expenses = 382 200 – 382 000 = 74 200 expense

Notes:

1. Tax expenses note for the period ending 31 March 2019
    - Tax expenses comprise the following:
    - Current tax   4 980 444
    - Deferred tax   – 1 701 700

    Total tax expense   **3 278 744**

    Effective tax rate = 3 278 744/7 800 000 = 42%

2. Tax rate reconciliation
    - Profit before tax (at the 28% tax rate)   2 184 000
    - Dividends (315 500 × 28%)   (88,200)
    - Anti-competitive acts (4 100 000 × 28%)   1 148 000
    - Medical expense (124 800 × 28%)   34 944
    - Tax expense   **3 278 744**

3. Deferred tax is made up of the following
    - Permanent differences (3 909 800 × 28%)   1 094 744
    - Building (350 000 – 280 000)   70 000
    - Microphones (56 000 – 28 000)   28 000
    - Vehicles (23 800 – nil)   (23 800)

14.8 SUMMARY

In this chapter, tax calculations were broken down to make it easier to comprehend the method in which tax expense is calculated. However, in an assessment, information will provided in a comprehensive manner and students will need to decipher the information to make it meaningful for themselves so they can calculate the tax expense (income) that should be presented.

EXERCISES

Exercise 14.1 Diropo CC

Diropo CC ('Diropo') is a retail shop in Vaal, Gauteng, supplying the community with multipurpose ropes for, among others, building, towing and animal taming. For the year ending 30 September 2019, Diropo made sales totalling R2 400 000 and 60% of the sales were on credit and not paid by year end. The total amount was included in the profit before tax which amounted to R840 000.

REQUIRED:
Explain how Diropo should account for its sales in determining the taxable profit for the year of assessment ending on 30 September 2019.

Exercise 14.2 Elliot (Pty) Ltd

On 1 April 2019, Elliot (Pty) Ltd ('Elliot') was established following a resurrection scandal in a church in South Africa. The infamous name and the notorious story worked well for this coffin-making business started by four friends from Mtubatuba, KwaZulu-Natal.

Making coffins is regarded as a process of manufacture by the commissioner of SARS. Elliot decided to have a 31 December year end, even though they commenced trading on 1 April 2019. The first manufacturing machine was acquired and brought into use on 1 April 2019, costing R420 000. This machine is being depreciated over five years. For tax purposes, this machine qualifies for the accelerated allowance.

REQUIRED:
Explain what the impact of the machine will be in determining the taxable profit of Elliot for the year ending 31 December 2019. Elliot made an accounting profit of R1 400 000 in its first year of operating.

Exercise 14.3 Nolitha Ltd

Nolitha Ltd ('Nolitha') is a transportation business from Matatiele, Eastern Cape. The company transports passengers by road from cities in the Eastern Cape to cities in KwaZulu-Natal and Gauteng.

On 1 June 2019, Nolitha received a contract from three major companies, including a bank, for a reduced fair for their employees when travelling using their bus service. These companies expect 2 000 trips to be made in total by their employees over the coming six months. Nolitha received a prepayment for the 2 000 trips amounting to R850 000. A 15% discount was negotiated by the three companies, which is non-refundable in the instance that the workers do not use the service.

REQUIRED:
Discuss what the impact of the prepayment will be on Nolitha for its year ending on 30 June 2019.

Exercise 14.4 Jantjie Inc

Jantjie Inc is a company that was established in Khayelitsha, Western Cape, after the notorious fake sign-language interpretation incident involving Thamsanqa Jantjie at Nelson Mandela's funeral. The business inspires local businesses and youngsters to ensure highly exceptional performance, whether at work, sports or any other event.

On 15 August 2019, Jantjie Inc hosted a sign language interpretation event to help ordinary people in the street learn at least five basic signs: 'hello', 'thank you', 'please', 'no' and 'I am happy'. One of the attendees, whose brother was deaf, noticed the instructor mixed up the sign for 'please' with that used to signal for 'cops'. The instructor was investigated and found to be bogus. Jantjie Inc was fined R200 000 (not tax deductible) for misrepresentation. The fine was enforced by the courts.

REQUIRED:
Discuss how the R200 000 will impact the Taxable Profit calculation of Jantjie Inc. for their 30 September 2019 year-end, from the accounting profits of R2,400,000 made by Jantjie.

Exercise 14.5 Sery Us (Pty) Ltd

Sery Us Ltd ('Su') is a fresh fruit crushing entity in Port Edward, KwaZulu-Natal. On 28 February 2019, Su acquired a new fruit crushing machine for R850 000 (SARS allows a four-year allowance on the machine). Su operates in a building that was erected on 1 June 2014 for a cost of R2,2 million (SARS does not allow deductions for this building).

REQUIRED:

Prepare a balance sheet method deferred tax calculation for the 31 May 2019 year end in respect of the above two assets, bearing in mind that Sery Us (Pty) Ltd depreciates the machine and the building for five and 20 years respectively.

Exercise 14.6 Khuli Mchana (Pty) Ltd

Khuliso Makana started a carpentry business in Vhembe District of Limpopo on 1 October 2019 with his nephew, Thabiso Makana. They decided to call it Khuli Mchana (Pty) Ltd ('Khuli Mchana'), a combination of their two names. Khuli Mchana has a September year end.

You have recently been employed in the technical accounting division as a junior consultant. Your main task is to record deferred tax calculations only.

The carpentry business is not regarded as a process of manufacture, nor is it a similar process. The following transactions were provided to you for the financial year ending 30 September 2020:

1. To start the business, a workshop office space in Thohoyandou was located. The office space belongs to the municipality and Khuli Mchana pays a fixed monthly rental of R6 500, renewable annually. The first rental was paid on 1 October 2019. On 15 September 2020, after concluding a renewal contract, Khuli Mchana paid rent for the period starting from 1 October 2020 to 31 July 2021.

2. Equipment was acquired and ready for use from 1 October 2019. It was fitted in the workshop on the same day. It took Khuli Mchana three months to perform staff employment, thus the workshop was not occupied until 31 December 2019. On 1 January 2020, all the equipment, which cost R600 000, was brought into use.

3. Two delivery vans were acquired on 1 October 2019 and they were available for use immediately. Each van cost R150 000. There were no deliveries, whether from suppliers or to clients, until 1 April 2020, thus the delivery vans were only brought into use on 1 April 2020.

4. Sales worth R2 800 000 were made in the 2020 year, from 1 January 2020. This is expected to increase as this was the first year of operation.

5. Salaries of R450 000 were paid in total and there were no bonuses, due to this being the first year of operation.

6. Khuli Mchana used pine wood on a project where a client had specifically requested plywood. The client became aware of the difference three months after accepting delivery, on 1 February 2020. The client took this directly to the small claims court without consulting with Khuli Mchana. Khuli Mchana incurred expenses worth R20 000 in investigating the claim and R30 000 for lawyers' fees during the first phase of the court proceedings, from 1 May 2020 to 31 July 2020.

7. On 16 August 2020, the court found Khuli Mchana negligent in their actions and imposed a fine of R80 000, taking into account that it was a first time offence, the size of the business and that the error was common. The case was regarded as protecting the brand name of Khuli Mchana, thus it was capital in nature.

8. On 10 September 2020, one of the employees of Khuli Mchana tested positive for COVID-19 and was found to have acted negligently. Khuli Mchana continued to pay the employee's salary of R6 000 for the month of September. This amount is already included in the salary amount in transaction 5.

Additional information:

1. Equipment is depreciated over four years. SARS allows a four-year wear-and-tear write-off period in terms of section 11(e), Binding General Ruling No 7.

2. Vehicles are depreciated over four years according to Khuli Mchana's policy. SARS allows a five-year wear-and-tear write-off period in terms of section 11(e), Binding General Ruling No 7.

REQUIRED:

Using the information provided, prepare the notes on tax expense (tax income), the tax rate reconciliation and the deferred tax note to be disclosed in the financial statements of Khuli Mchana (Pty) Ltd (*use a 28% tax rate*) for the period ending 30 September 2020. Assume all amounts are exclusive of VAT and start your computation with the R800 000 accounting profit, an amount provided by Mr Khuliso Makana.

CHAPTER 15

EVENTS AFTER REPORTING PERIOD (IAS 10)

LEARNING OUTCOMES

After studying this chapter, you should be able to:

- Understand the underlying principles outlined in IAS 10 *Events after the reporting period*.
- Use these principles to account for and disclose, where necessary, events after the reporting period in the financial statements, to comply with the requirements of IFRS.

PREAMBLE

Mr Mhlongo (known as Njomane) had a productive and enlightening discussion with his son, who is studying accounting at university, about events that occur after the reporting period. He comes to your offices to confirm and get more clarification regarding these kinds of transactions.

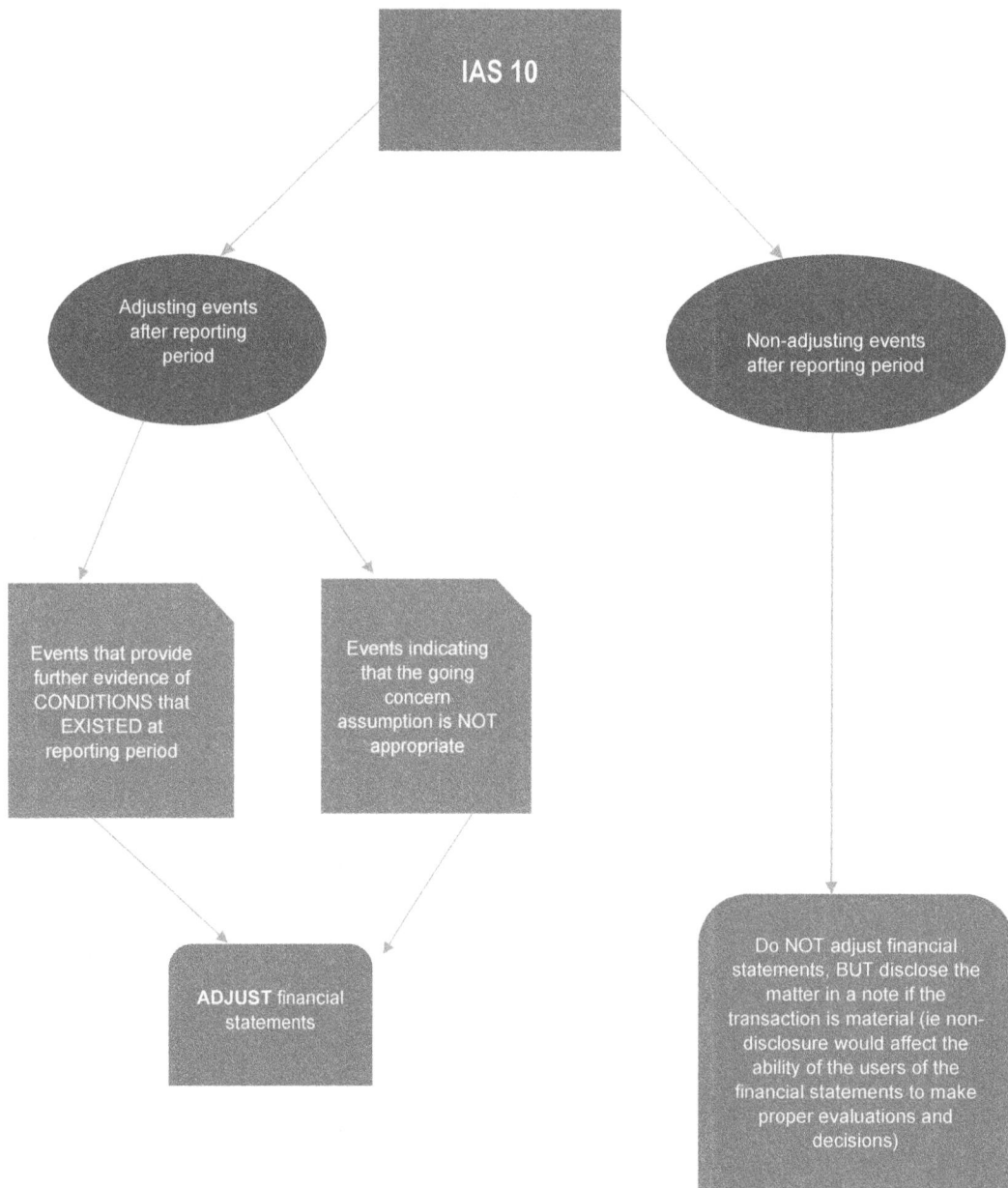

```
                              ┌──────────────┐
                              │    IAS 10    │
                              └──────────────┘
              ┌──────────────────┐        ┌──────────────────┐
              │ Adjusting events │        │ Non-adjusting    │
              │ after reporting  │        │ events after     │
              │ period           │        │ reporting period │
              └──────────────────┘        └──────────────────┘

  ┌──────────────────┐  ┌──────────────────┐
  │ Events that      │  │ Events indicating│
  │ provide further  │  │ that the going   │
  │ evidence of      │  │ concern          │
  │ CONDITIONS that  │  │ assumption is NOT│
  │ EXISTED at       │  │ appropriate      │
  │ reporting period │  │                  │
  └──────────────────┘  └──────────────────┘

        ┌──────────────────┐          ┌──────────────────────┐
        │ ADJUST financial │          │ Do NOT adjust        │
        │ statements       │          │ financial statements,│
        └──────────────────┘          │ BUT disclose the     │
                                       │ matter in a note if  │
                                       │ the transaction is   │
                                       │ material (ie non-    │
                                       │ disclosure would     │
                                       │ affect the ability of│
                                       │ the users of the     │
                                       │ financial statements │
                                       │ to make proper       │
                                       │ evaluations and      │
                                       │ decisions)           │
                                       └──────────────────────┘
```

Figure 15.1: Graphical presentation of IAS 10

15.1 INTRODUCTION

Up until this stage, we have learnt that transactions that occur after the financial year end do not affect the current financial statements. While this is mostly true, it is not always the case. There are transactions that take place in an entity which affect the current financial statements although they come to the knowledge of the entity after year end. These transactions are referred to as 'events after reporting period'. The events which fall into this category are those that come to the knowledge of the entity after year end but before financial statement are authorised for issue.

15.2 DEFINITIONS

Events after reporting period are defined as those events that occur between the end of the reporting period and the date before the financial statements are authorised for issue. These events can be favourable or unfavourable. IAS 10 identifies two types of events after reporting period, namely:

- Adjusting events after reporting period
- Non-adjusting events after reporting period

Adjusting events after reporting period are defined as those events that provide additional evidence of conditions that existed before year end.

Non-adjusting events after reporting period are defined as those events that are indicative of conditions arising after the reporting period.

15.3 RECOGNITION AND MEASUREMENT

Adjusting events after reporting period: An entity shall adjust the amounts in its financial statements to reflect adjusting events after the reporting period.

EXAMPLE 15.1 Hot Steel (Pty) Ltd

Hot Steel (Pty) Ltd was notified by Mutrisolve Liquidators on 28 August 2018 that one of its debtors, Sihlulekile (Pty) Ltd had begun a liquidation process. Sihlulekile (Pty) Ltd suddenly took a turn for the worse due to the flooding of the industry by imports. Hot Steel (Pty) Ltd was owed an amount of R100 000 that was included in accounts receivable at the end of the reporting period. The notice indicated that creditors may expect a liquidation dividend of 20 cents in a rand.

The financial statements were approved on 30 September 2018 for the reporting year end 30 June 2018.

REQUIRED:

1. Identify if the information above will be treated as an adjusting or non-adjusting event after the reporting period in terms of IAS 10.
2. Explain your answer in (1).
3. Discuss the recognition criteria applicable in terms of Generally Accepted Accounting Practice and IFRS.

EXAMPLE 15.1 Suggested solution – Hot Steel (Pty) Ltd

1. **Identification:**

   Adjusting event after reporting period (event that provides additional evidence of conditions that existed at year end).

2. **Motivation:**

   The liquidation of Sihlulekile (Pty) Ltd, a debtor, occurred after the reporting period. Loss exists at the end of the reporting period on the accounts receivable amount. The condition that caused the loss (flooding of imports) existed before year end.

3. **Recognition:**

   An entity will adjust the amounts recognised in the financial statements to reflect adjusting events after the reporting period. Hot Steel (Pty) Ltd needs to adjust the carrying amount of receivables to R20 000.

   The loss of R80 000 will be recognised as an expense (credit loss).

15.4 RECOGNITION AND MEASUREMENT

Non-adjusting events after reporting period: The entity does not need to adjust the amounts recognised in the financial statements. If the amount is material, the entity needs to disclose the details of the transaction in the notes to the financial statements.

EXAMPLE 15.2 Bad Picture (Pty) Ltd

Bad Picture (Pty) Ltd was notified by Mutrisolve Liquidators on 31 August 2018 that one of its debtors, Kumatima (Pty) Ltd, had begun the liquidation process. Kumatima (Pty) Ltd suddenly took a turn for the worse due to the floods that cut across KwaZulu-Natal during the week of 11 July 2018. Bad Picture (Pty) Ltd was owed an amount of R100 000 that was included in accounts receivable at the end of the reporting period. The notice indicated that creditors may expect a liquidation dividend of 20 cents in the rand.

The financial statements were approved on 30 September 2018 for the reporting year end 30 June 2018.

REQUIRED:

1. Identify if the information above will be treated as an adjusting or non-adjusting event after the reporting period in terms of IAS 10.
2. Explain your answer in (1).
3. Discuss the recognition criteria applicable in terms of Generally Accepted Accounting Practice and IFRS.

EXAMPLE 15.2 Suggested solution – Bad Picture (Pty) Ltd

1. **Identification:**

   Non-adjusting event after reporting period (event that is indicative of conditions arising after the reporting period).

2. **Motivation:**

   The liquidation of Kumatima (Pty) Ltd, a debtor, occurred after the reporting period. Loss did not exist at the end of the reporting period on the accounts receivable amount. The condition that caused the loss (floods) arose after year end.

3. **Recognition:**

   The entity will not adjust the amounts recognised in the financial statements. If the amount is material, it may need to be disclosed in the notes to the financial statements.

15.5 EXCEPTION

Going concern principle: If, after the assessment of the going concern status, management realises that it is no longer appropriate to assume that an entity will continue to exist and that it will have no realistic alternative but to liquidate, the events after reporting period will have to be adjusted for and disclosed no matter whether they are adjusting or non-adjusting.

15.6 SUMMARY

This chapter dealt with the underlying principles of IAS 10, the standard on the events after reporting period. The definitions, recognition criteria and the measurement of the adjusting and the non-adjusting events after reporting period were discussed, with examples to illustrate the underlying principles followed. The presentation and disclosure of the events after reporting period were also discussed.

EXERCISES

Exercise 15.1 Independent questions

1. Mr Viljoen, a debtor of Sizabantu (Pty) Ltd, was in sound financial position at the end of the reporting period, but on 22 January 2019, a natural disaster struck and it fell into liquidation. The financial year end is 31December 2018 and financial statements will be ready for publication on 31 March 2019.

    How should Sizabantu (Pty) Ltd treat this in their financial statements?

A	Non-adjusting event
B	Adjusting event.

2. The financial year of NAN-DOES LTD ends on 31 December 2018 and the financial statements will be ready for publication on 31 March 2019. On 20 February 2019, a fire damages some inventory that was being stored in the warehouse. The value of the damaged inventory is considered to be material.

    How should this be treated in the financial statements of NAN-DOES LTD for the year ended 31 December 2018?

A	An adjusting event
B	A non-adjusting event.

3. Events after reporting period are defined as:

A	those events that occur between the end of the reporting period and the date after the financial statements are authorised for issue
B	those events that occur between the end of the reporting period and the date exactly when the financial statements are authorised for issue
C	those events that occur before the end of the reporting period and the date when the financial statements are authorised for issue
D	those events that occur between the end of the reporting period and the date before the financial statements are authorised for issue.

4. The financial year of Hannah Ltd ended on 30 June 2019 and the financial statements were ready for publication on 30 September 2019. On 1 September 2019, the directors declared an additional dividend of R2,50 per share to the ordinary shareholders registered at year end.

    This should be treated as _____ in the financial statements of Hannah Ltd for the year ended 30 June 2019.

A	a provision
B	a contingent liability
C	an adjusting event after reporting period
D	a non-adjusting event after reporting period.

5. The financial year of DHS Ltd ended at 31 December 2018 and the financial statements were ready for publication on 31 March 2019. On January 2019, one of the debtors filed for bankruptcy. The cause of the bankruptcy was the signing of a deal that went wrong on 30 November 2018.

    How should this be treated in the financial statements of DHS Ltd for the year ended 31 December 2018?

A	a provision
B	a contingent liability
C	an adjusting event after reporting period
D	a non-adjusting event after reporting period.

Exercise 15.2 Masondo Ltd

Masondo Ltd presented its financial statements for the year ended 28 February 2019 to the board of directors on 31 May 2019 for approval.

The following events have taken place after the reporting period:

1. The accountant of Masondo Ltd received notification on 1 April 2019 that Rim Ltd, a customer, was in liquidation and that Masondo Ltd would be paid 40% of the outstanding debt. It was further determined that Rim Ltd was experiencing financial difficulties at year end. The amount owed by Rim Ltd was R60 000, which was included in trade receivables at reporting date.

2. During March 2019, a water pipe burst, causing damage to the warehouse and to stock, amounting to R350 000 and R140 000 respectively. The damage was not covered by the insurance policy. Shesha Repairs agreed to repair the damage to the building at a cost of R220 000.

3. A customer sued Masondo Ltd on 15 March 2019 for selling substandard products to them during 2018. Masondo Ltd appointed attorneys to defend the action. Legal costs amounted to R25 000. The attorneys advised Masondo Ltd that it was too early to determine the costs of the case or the outcome.

REQUIRED:

1. For each of the above-mentioned cases, state whether an adjusting event or a non-adjusting event after the reporting period should be recognised in the accounting records of Masondo Ltd. Provide reasons to substantiate your answers.

2. Explain the disclosure that is required in each case.

www.ingramcontent.com/pod-product-compliance
Lightning Source LLC
Chambersburg PA
CBHW080252200326
41519CB00024B/6968